ALSO BY PAUL COGGINS

The Lady Is the Tiger

OUT OF BOUNDS

*How the American Sports Establishment
Is Being Driven by Greed and Hypocrisy—
and What Needs to Be Done About It*

Tom McMillen

with Paul Coggins

Simon & Schuster

New York   London   Toronto   Sydney   Tokyo   Singapore

SIMON & SCHUSTER
Simon & Schuster Building
Rockefeller Center
1230 Avenue of the Americas
New York, New York 10020

Copyright © 1992 by Tom McMillen and Paul Coggins

Designed by Irving Perkins Associates
Manufactured in the United States of America

10 9 8 7 6 5 4 3 2

Library of Congress Cataloging in Publication Data

McMillen, Tom, date
   Out of bounds: how the American sports establishment is being driven by
greed and hypocrisy—and what needs to be done about it / Tom McMillen
with Paul Coggins.
      p.   cm.
   Includes bibliographical references (p.)
   1. Sports—United States. 2. Sports—Social aspects—United States. 3.
Sports and state—United States. 4. Sports—United States—Corrupt practices.
5. Basketball—United States. 6. McMillen, Tom, date. 7. Basketball players—
United States—Biography. 8. Legislators—United States—Biography. I.
Coggins. Paul, date.   II. Title.
GV583.M37   1992   92-8753
796'.0973—dc20   CIP

ISBN: 0-671-70776-0

Cartoon and photo credits

Cartoon of Tom McMillen from *The Capital Gazette* copyright Eric Smith/*The Capital
Gazette*. Used by permission.
Tank McNamara copyright 1991 Miller/Hinds. Distributed by Universal Press Syndicate.
Reprinted with permission. All rights reserved.
"Tough Bracket" copyright 1991 by John Branch/*San Antonio Express-News*. Used by
permission.
1. Copyright 1970 by Neil Leifer/*Sports Illustrated*. Used by permission.
2. Archive Photos. Used by permission.
3. Archive Photos. Used by permission.
4. Rich Clarkson, *Life* Magazine © 1972 by Time Warner Inc. Used by permission.
5. Copyright 1982 by Ronald Modra/*Sports Illustrated*. Used by permission.
6. Copyright 1982 by Ronald Modra/*Sports Illustrated*. Used by permission.
7. *People Weekly* © Stanley Tetrick. Used by permission.
8. Copyright 1987 by James Drake/*Sports Illustrated*. Used by permission.
9. © Marty LaVor. Used by permission.

To Mom and Dad for their love and inspiration.
                                    —Tom McMillen

To Gina, Jessica, Mom, and Dad for their love and support.
                                    —Paul Coggins

ACKNOWLEDGMENTS

In sports and politics, any successful project is the product of a good team. This book would not have been possible without many people on my team and I want to take this opportunity to thank:

My longtime friend, classmate at Oxford, and coauthor, Paul Coggins. His creativity and perseverance made this book a reality.

My family, especially my Mom, for saving all those old high school sports clippings in the attic and for all her love and support, and my father, whom I miss, but whose inspiration still remains. Thanks also to Jay, Paul, Sheila, and Liz for their help and guidance over the years.

Those who worked with Paul and me in bringing this book to print. My gratitude to Jan Miller, our agent, for her unbridled enthusiasm and support in keeping us focused on the book; to Bob Turner and Ginny Gannon, our researchers, for spending those long hours poring over reams of microfilm looking for sports trivia; to Bob Asahina and Sarah Pinckney at Simon & Schuster for their assistance and expertise; to Patty Spence for typing all the last-minute changes from Paul and me; and finally to Jeff Vawrinek for his suggestions and help.

I would also like to thank Chairman John Dingell of Michigan and Chairwoman Cardiss Collins of Illinois for holding hearings in Congress and my colleagues Senator Bill Bradley of New Jersey and Representatives Ben Nighthorse Campbell of Colorado and Ed Towns of New York for their support on sports-reform issues.

Finally, the membership and staff of the Knight Commission should be commended for their efforts in reforming intercollegiate athletics, and I benefited greatly from exchanging ideas and information with them.

CONTENTS

A sound mind in a sound body is a short but full description of a happy state in this world.

JOHN LOCKE, *SOME THOUGHTS CONCERNING EDUCATION*

FOREWORD

Senator Bill Bradley

Tom McMillen played collegiate sports at its highest level—on a nationally ranked basketball team at a major university. He then went on to a career in the National Basketball Association, and now is a United States congressman.

From those experiences Congressman McMillen attempts to place the American love affair with sports in its proper perspective, and elevates the level of the debate on the role of sports in our society and the role of government in striking a balance between academics and athletics in our schools. In *Out of Bounds*, he explores these issues from his perspective as an athlete and legislator concerned about abuses in our educational system, and our overall competitiveness in the world economy.

Tom McMillen has established a reputation for being tough and fair. This book takes on the tough questions about collegiate sports and treats them fairly. It raises provocative questions that surround the trade-offs necessary for "student-athletes," and ex-amines how our educational system often seems to be a pipeline for a handful of elite athletes to reach the professional leagues rather than a place for educating those athletes.

Tom's message is simple: We cannot shortchange our youth by sacrificing them at the altar of big-time sports. We must challenge our kids to excel in academics as a condition to participating in sports in order to prepare them for the greater challenges in their future. We must challenge ourselves to recognize that failure to educate our kids today is leaving them unprepared for the global competition of the next century.

I hope *Out of Bounds* will be read not just by basketball fans but by educators, administrators, politicians, parents, and, finally, students themselves. From his experience, Tom McMillen brings a perspective that is valuable to all of us.

Introduction

TRIPLE OVERTIME

It was SATURDAY, November 1, 1986, only two days before the voters would decide whether to send me to Washington to represent the Fourth District of Maryland or to the sidelines. Either way my campaign had made history. I was not, of course, the first pro athlete to enter politics; but by playing the entire 1985–1986 basketball season for the Washington Bullets, I became the first active athlete in U.S. history to run for Congress.

In a furious burst of eleventh-hour campaigning, I was crisscrossing the Fourth Congressional District, which stretches from the city limits of Baltimore to the District of Columbia boundary and south of Annapolis. The district encompasses everything from blue collar neighborhoods to yuppie pockets and had been held by a Republican since its creation in 1972, despite a three-to-one edge for Democrats among registered voters. The Fourth District had been targeted by the GOP as one of seventeen "must win" seats in 1986, and my Republican opponent had been boosted by massive campaign contributions from the party as well as by per-

sonal appearances by luminaries such as former President Gerald
Ford and James Baker, then the White House chief of staff.

Now I learned that I was eight points down in a Baltimore *Sun*
poll with two days to go. How could this have happened? How
could I have plummeted from being the front-runner with high
name identification, an ample war chest, and a double-digit lead
in the early polls? How had I fallen so far, so fast? What had I
done wrong? Had we allocated time and money foolishly? Had
I spent too much time in some communities? Too little in others?
Was my message incoherent? After all, the editorial boards of
the Baltimore *Sun* and *The Washington Post* had both endorsed
my opponent. What should I do now?

My mind kept returning to my opponent's last TV ad, which
was simple but hard-hitting. My image hovered at the top of the
screen in a basketball uniform while my Republican opponent
lurked at the bottom of the picture in a business suit. A serious
voice ticked off his accomplishments in the state legislature, and
with each he rose a notch on the screen. Then the grave voice-
over, suddenly accusatory, turned to me and my background in
sports. The message emerged clearly that I had wasted my life by
playing a child's game while my opponent had tended to the
serious business of government. Next to my opponent in a dig-
nified suit, I looked silly in a basketball jersey. With each verbal
jab I sank lower on the screen. By the end of the commercial,
my five-foot-seven-inch opponent was towering over my six feet
ten and a half inches. The classic "David versus Goliath" spot
worked.

With only two days left in the campaign, there had been no
time to respond to the ad. I felt helpless, like a benched player
watching his team fall farther and farther behind; and I was angry
because my opponent had successfully turned my accomplishments against me, my positives into negatives. Thirty-four years
old, I thought I had taken the right steps to prepare myself for
public service. High school all-American. Valedictorian. Three-
time college all-American. Youngest member ever to serve on the
President's Council on Physical Fitness and Sports. Phi Beta
Kappa. Olympian. Rhodes scholar. National Basketball Associ-

ation veteran. Budding businessman. Assistant to the finance chairman of the Democratic National Committee.

Yet my opponent had, in the space of a half-minute commercial, trivialized my accomplishments. Even more unsettling, for the first time I faced the prospect of losing and losing big.

During the campaign, which had received extensive national media exposure, the polls had consistently shown me ahead, with leads varying from six to fourteen points. Even my opponent's slanted polls had interpreted the race as a dead heat. Now suddenly I was tortured anew by the good-natured nicknames that had been pinned on me during my sports career. As early as college, when my hair began turning prematurely gray, my Maryland teammates had called me "Senator"—a nickname that was later picked up in the NBA. During my last season with the Washington Bullets, Manute Bol, the seven-foot-seven-inch rookie center from Sudan, began calling me "Congress" in his broken English after I announced my candidacy. Tonight the nicknames seemed to mock me.

By 1986 I had started feeling a little old for the NBA. It was not simply the gray hair and the nicknames, but more of my

teammates and competitors seemed to be from another generation. During my last NBA road trip to Dallas, as our team bus
passed Dealey Plaza on the way to Reunion Arena for a game
against the Mavericks, I explained to my Bullets teammate Kenny
Green that I always became emotional near the site of John Kennedy's assassination. JFK was an inspiration to me and had
planted the seed of public service in my mind, and I had been
traumatized when my teacher, John Heaps, broke down and cried
while telling his class of twelve-year-olds in Mansfield, Pennsylvania, that President Kennedy had been killed. Kenny brought
me back to earth by saying, "Gee, I wasn't even born back then."
I felt old.

I had thrived on the NBA treadmill for eleven years and even
managed to survive the dual treadmills of pro ball and hardball
politics for ten grueling months. For a decade I had devoted my
time, thought, and energy to basketball, politics, and business—
in that order. Suddenly I faced the prospect of losing two of my
three focuses.

The shock of the *Sun* poll slowly receded, and I began to face
the question that haunts almost all athletes—What do I do with
the rest of my life? Five months after my final game, I had still
not confronted the issue because for me, unlike most athletes,
the cheering had never stopped. Without missing a beat, I had
graduated from the cheering at the Capital Centre to the cheering
on the campaign trail. In two days, however, if the new poll were
accurate, the cheering would die. Suddenly. Finally.

Gradually, however, I began to assess my situation and to realize
that I had been blessed far beyond most former athletes. From
junior high school through college, I had played with and against
thousands of talented athletes. Only a handful of my contemporaries had reached the pro level, and most of those had washed
out after a year or two.

I had witnessed careers end with the bang of a serious injury
or with a whimper from the bench. Worst of all, I had known far
too many gifted athletes who had invested everything into their
fantasy of a lucrative pro career and sacrificed their shot at a good

education. Too many had bought into the myth that a good jump shot would grease their ride through life.

In contrast, I had been blessed with parents who had insisted on the primacy of academics over athletics. Until midway through college, I had planned to be a doctor. At every step in my basketball odyssey, I had a backup career if an injury sidelined me permanently. Even now, on the brink of a predicted defeat at the polls, I had a growing business in the wings. More important, I had received a solid education at the University of Maryland and Oxford.

The longer I reflected about my teammates, friends, and acquaintances who had ended their playing careers with little or no prospects for life after sports, the more ashamed I became at my self-pity and the greater my anger toward those who had short-sightedly sacrificed their futures for a game. How could their priorities have been so skewed? How could they have consigned themselves to living in the past at the age of thirty-five? Twenty-one? Sixteen?

I thought about my options if I lost the election. Should I throw myself fully into my business? Should I take another shot at politics? Perhaps at a local office? Maybe I could return to the NBA for a twelfth season. After all, a couple of teams had expressed interest in me if I lost the race. The longer I pondered my options, the more I realized how lucky I was. By the next morning I realized that I would survive, win or lose.

On Sunday morning I was eager to fight back. Black leaders in my district escorted me to their churches, and the enthusiasm of the congregations of true believers was contagious. Buoyed by their faith, I campaigned till late into the night like a boxer who, though wobbly, refuses to fall.

On Monday I was more like a boxer who throws a flurry of punches but lands very few. I was too unfocused and directionless, as I hit a string of shopping centers in a helter-skelter blitz of retail politics. Quick in, quick out.

On Election Day, I rose at dawn to work the polling places at the heavily Democratic precincts in Prince Georges County, which was the heart of my support according to the polls; but by late afternoon I had begun to venture into more Republican-leaning precincts in the county. In basketball, whenever we beat a team ahead of us in the standings, we called it a "twofer" because it was not only a victory for us but also a defeat for the front-runner. A victory in such circumstances guaranteed that we had gained ground. Likewise, every hand I pressed on Tuesday represented a potential twofer—a vote for me and a vote wrested from my opponent.

In politics as in basketball, I might be beaten, but I would not be outhustled. As darkness descended, a reporter asked me how long I intended to work the polls.

"How long do the polls stay open?" I asked.

"Till eight," he responded.

"Then that's how long I'll stay at the polls."

Intimating that I must be more worried about the results than my opponent, the reporter informed me that my opponent had not campaigned hard on Election Day but had retired to his hotel suite in the afternoon to luxuriate in a whirlpool and add the finishing touches to his victory speech. I do not know if the reporter's account was true; but the image of my nemesis relaxing in a whirlpool, a pen in one hand and a cool drink in the other, spurred me to work the polls to the last minute, despite the dark and the cold.

By the time the polls closed at 8 P.M., I had shaken approximately one thousand hands that were on the verge of pulling the lever. Then I hustled to my room at the Radisson Hotel in Annapolis to catch the early returns, which proved even worse than we had feared. CBS news anchor Dan Rather, in effect, pronounced the last rites by calling the race for my opponent, who had jumped ten thousand votes ahead by 10 P.M. I flipped the channel in time to hear another network correspondent project me as the loser in my maiden race. The supporters who had earlier swelled the ballroom for my victory celebration dwindled to about one hundred hardy souls in the wake of Rather's prediction; and Jerry Grant, my campaign manager, suggested that I prepare a concession speech.

While I was drafting the speech, however, a campaign worker in the field called with news that the tide was turning as a string of strong precincts in Prince Georges County prepared to report. Within a half hour, the ten-thousand-vote margin had been cut to fifteen hundred; and we had still not heard from Howard County, which was expected to be strong for me. By 11 P.M. we were two hundred votes ahead, and the overflow crowd of supporters, which had drifted to other election parties when the outcome looked bleak, began to flock back to the ballroom. We finished the long night into morning with a lead of twelve hundred votes. But thirty-five hundred absentee votes still remained to be counted. Because historically the GOP garners about 65 percent of the absentee vote nationwide, the race promised to be razor close.

The outcome was not certain for two weeks, during which my staff exiled me to Florida before I drove everyone crazy. The uncertainty added to the suspense as attorneys from both sides scrutinized the laborious process.

With all the ballots counted, I won the 1986 race by only 428 votes of approximately 150,000 cast, or by less than one-third of 1 percent of the vote. The newspapers described my election as a "triple overtime victory," and I was hailed as "Landslide" McMillen.

Again and again I thought of those thousand or so voters I had greeted immediately before they entered the voting booths. Of course, a number of them would have voted for me even without the last-second handshake, and a portion were doubtlessly unmoved by my presence. Nonetheless, if I succeeded in winning over only one in four of those voters, that was the margin of victory.

After the hoopla and celebration of a come-from-behind victory, I promised myself not to forget where I had come from, where I had been, what I had been through, and why I had charted my course toward politics in the first place. Although I had overcome the jock stereotype to emerge with a narrow victory, I still had to prove myself in Congress. I was a rookie all over again, and I was determined not to be outhustled.

Now, however, at least I would not have to wince when Manute Bol called me "Congress."

Sports have been very good to me. Through athletics I traveled the world, earned a good living, met scores of fascinating people, and learned important lessons about teamwork, discipline, and desire. Because sports have given so much to me, I am resolved to return something to the game.

Unfortunately, not everyone is learning the same beneficial lessons from sports that I did. At every level of competition, we have allowed sports to transgress their proper bounds, to cross the line between a game and an obsession. Several years after retiring from the NBA, I am convinced that the greatest threat to sports is the mind-set that views every contest—from grade school to the big leagues—as a win-at-all-costs war where rules are made to be broken. After several years in Congress, I am equally convinced that it will take a concerted effort by all interested parties—including athletes, parents, coaches, teachers, administrators, reporters, fans, and even politicians—to rescue sports from their corrupting influences and return the games to their proper perspective.

Although I am critical of the attitudes and practices that are corrupting athletics, this book is written in a spirit of optimism. With so much of value in sports and so many reform-minded individuals devoted to the task, sports can and must be saved. And this book is both a call to action and a blueprint for reform.

Chapter 1

SURVIVAL OF THE FITTEST

The Jungle of Youth Sports

RARELY DOES A week pass that I am not visited by a grade school class from my Maryland district, and I make every effort to welcome them personally to Washington, usually on the steps of the Capitol. I give the schoolchildren a brief talk about the workings of our government. I describe the separation of powers, the system of checks and balances, the role of a congressperson, the importance of committees, and the steps in the passage of a bill. Finally I ask a few questions. "How many of you want to be a professional athlete, like Michael Jordan or Chris Evert, when you grow up?"

Invariably a healthy majority of the kids raise their hands.

"How many of you want to be a movie star, like Tom Cruise or Julia Roberts?"

Again most of them raise their hands, dreaming of dual careers in sports and Hollywood.

Then I ask, "How many of you want to be a congressman, like me?"

At most one or two hands will be lifted timidly, often belatedly. Sometimes not a single student will respond to the last question. The results of my admittedly unscientific polls are remarkably consistent, whether the young students hail from an inner-city public school or an exclusive private academy. The poor pol will finish a distant third as a hero for the kids, far behind Michael Jordan and Tom Cruise. The message is clear—sports and entertainment are number one.

The myth of sports stardom develops early in our society and seduces too many of our youth. Sports have become the great national lottery to many of our youth, who envision a lucrative pro contract as their shot at the big time, often their only shot. But as in a lottery, the odds against hitting the jackpot are astronomical. According to research by the Center for the Study of Sport in Society at Northwestern University, only one in every one hundred high school athletes will play NCAA Division I college sports; and the odds against a high school player making the pros are ten thousand to one.[1] Stated differently, of the 30 million children participating in youth sports in this country in any year, fewer than two hundred will ultimately reach the pros, and many of these "winners" will wash out after only a year or two in the big leagues, often without savings or job skills.[2]

The National Federation of State High School Associations gives a slightly different but still sobering line: Of the 5.4 million high school athletes on a varsity or junior varsity team, only one of fifty will make a college team, and only one in one thousand ever reaches the pros.[3]

Thus, a youngster gambling his future on a pro contract is like a worker buying a single Irish Sweepstakes ticket and then quitting his job in anticipation of his winnings. Despite these staggering odds, many kids cling desperately and self-destructively to the myth, often failing to face the true odds against them. And the problem is especially acute in the black community.

A recent Lou Harris poll reported that 43 percent of black high school male athletes believe they will someday play pro ball.[4] Similarly, a 1989 study by the American Institute for Research revealed that 44 percent of the African-American football and basketball players at predominantly white colleges expected to turn pro, as compared with 20 percent of their non-African-American teammates.[5] This is dangerously delusional.

According to Arthur Ashe, African-American parents are eight times more likely than white parents to steer their child toward a sports career.[6] As Professor Henry Louis Gates, Jr., of Harvard points out, there are only twelve hundred black professional athletes in the United States, which means there are twelve times more black lawyers than black athletes and fifteen times more black doctors than black athletes.[7]

I do not enjoy stepping on anyone's dream, but sports in our society have crossed the line between a dream and a delusion for many. Because sports have been good to me, I do not want to destroy them. The greatest threat to sports is posed not by reformers but by those who expect too much of sports—whether participants who treat athletics as their only shot at the brass ring, spectators who elevate sports to a religion, or nations that tout their athletic conquests as barometers of their health.

It is impossible to tell when sports passed beyond a pleasant diversion and became a national obsession in our country. As late as 1970, James Michener opined that, in the United States, the emphasis on sports was about right.[8] Although I suspect Michener was being overly generous to our country even then, his reading is no longer valid. Today far too many of our citizens focus too much of their time and energy on games that have often long ceased being fun. In the twenty years between my high school career and the present, I have witnessed the sports sections of papers expand until the big sports stories burst onto the front pages—drug deaths, multimillion-dollar contracts, strikes, gambling scandals, holdouts, and the defection of franchises.

Sports are increasingly viewed as the superhighway to vast riches; and unfortunately the superhighway runs straight through our grade schools, junior highs, high schools, and colleges, with fewer and fewer exits to the classroom for a sports-obsessed student body. But the roads not taken, though perhaps not as fast and glamorous as the sports superhighway, are usually surer and safer routes to the destination of a good and useful life.

The obsession with the big payoff corrupts not only the athletes but also the programs through which they pass. Sports at all levels are no longer allowed to be merely games or recreation but are reshaped into the pro image. Just as kids idolize pro athletes, youth sports teams model themselves on pro programs.

American sports are infected with a creeping professionalism, which has already warped the values of our colleges and now threatens our high schools and junior highs. To an alarming degree, colleges have prostituted themselves into serving as pipelines to the pros, as a link in a sports feeder system, as a cog in the well-oiled machinery of the sports myth. The "college" scandals involving recruiting, redshirting, phony courses, bogus grades, and payola are surfacing in high schools and junior highs, as those schools are being seduced from their educational mission by the same temptations that have corrupted universities: mainly TV money.

This is not surprising since America is being bombarded by sports on TV. When I was growing up in the small town of Mansfield, Pennsylvania, I was lucky if one or two basketball games a week were televised. Today there are probably fifty professional and college basketball games a week on the networks and cable, and the coverage is proliferating as the insatiable cable stations add high school contests to broadcast schedules that are already crammed with pro and college games.

In 1989 a national cable network signed a five-year contract with the National Federation of State High School Associations, which is composed of fifty-one high school athletic associations in the United States, to televise a weekly package of high school sporting events, mainly football and basketball.[9] Gatorade has paid $600,000 to SportsChannel America, a cable company jointly owned by NBC and Cablevision that reaches seven million homes, to sponsor high school football and basketball games.[10] Mike Lardner of SportsChannel predicts that ". . . high school sports are going to be the TV sport of the 90's. Now the college fan is wanting to follow the kids, and teen-agers are part of a $10 billion market."[11] Can the televising of junior high games be far behind?

In light of the harrowing abuses in big-money intercollegiate athletics, it is frightening to consider the effect of pumping TV dollars into high school sports and intensifying the pressure on teenage athletes, many of whom are already overwhelmed by the expectations of their parents, coaches, and peers.

Is it healthy for a sixteen-year-old to approach the foul line in the fourth period of a tight game, knowing that he is being scrutinized by a television audience numbering in the millions? What happens to the seventeen-year-old field goal kicker who shanks a short attempt in the waning seconds of a close contest before a nationwide audience? Are we confident that the parties involved adequately weighed the interests of the kids and of society in general before signing the lucrative TV deals? Are we placing too much pressure on our kids on the fields and courts but not enough pressure on them in the classrooms? How soon will the media begin to dictate the schedules for high schools, as they often do for colleges?

The intrusion of TV into high school sports is a college scout's dream but sends the wrong message to our youth. Most high schools already devote too much time to varsity and junior varsity sports and not enough time to the classroom, and TV will skew the balance even more.

One of the leaders in the move to ban live national telecasts of high school football, basketball, and hockey is John E. Roberts, the executive director of the Michigan High School Athletic Association. Unfortunately, Roberts's proposed ban was voted down by a four-to-one margin at the 1990 convention of the National Federation of State High School Associations. Like the NCAA, the Kansas City–based National Federation espouses a laissez-faire attitude toward the creeping commercialization of athletics.

Despite Roberts's lopsided loss at the 1990 convention, he is not alone in his call for reform. Many major national educational groups, including the American Association of School Administrators and the National School Boards Association, have backed the ban on televising high school games.[12] I am now working with a group of secondary school principals to study the effects of televising high school games.

At a minimum, the televising of high school games should be barred until three major issues are resolved. First, can young athletes cope with the increased exposure and pressure? If not, sacrifice the broadcasts before the kids. Second, the schools (not the networks) must dictate the schedules so as to prevent the disruption of classroom time. The networks are notorious for arranging late games for colleges in order to beam their games to different time zones, even if this leaves the players too exhausted to attend classes the next day. Finally, and above all, high schools must avoid the "college trap" of tying big TV money to winning, which increases the incentive to cheat.

High school athletic programs are plagued by problems that are remarkably similar to those of college sports: (1) loss of class time to sports and other extracurricular activities; (2) controversy over the effectiveness and wisdom of no pass–no play; (3) poor sportsmanship by players, coaches, and fans; (4) proliferation of interstate competition sparked by national rankings; (5) commercialization of sports events; and (6) recruitment of elite athletes by schools with and without open enrollment policies.[13]

The costs of this creeping professionalism are reflected not only in the lost lives of the losers in the sports lottery but also in the widespread loss of faith in our academic institutions, which have compromised their ideals, flouted their own rules, and forfeited their positions of moral leadership in order to chase the gold ring.

The system that links our playgrounds to the pros is increasingly concentrating on the elite athlete to the exclusion of mediocre or unskilled participants. Parents, coaches, agents, recruiters, brokers, and a host of hangers-on race to identify future sports champions at ever earlier ages. A vast, unregulated, under-the-table futures market in young athletes is flourishing in this country. Technology permitting, these parasites would conduct an Olympics of the Maternity Ward or even an Olympics of the Womb.

Investigative reporters Alexander Wolff and Armen Keteyian

have exposed the seamy underbelly of college basketball recruiting, with legions of leeches loitering around eighth and ninth grade playgrounds and gyms trying to spot the next Magic Johnson, "buy" the budding star with trinkets, tennis shoes, and "chump change," and then broker the prize athlete, often with the complicity of his relatives, to a cash-hungry college and sometimes to the pros.[14]

Top athletes are increasingly being pushed to specialize in one sport, and the days of the two-sport or three-sport letterman are numbered as training turns into a year-round grind. For example, the actual basketball season may no longer be of paramount importance to a seventeen-year-old hungry for an athletic scholarship. His stats during the actual season might prove less important than his performance at a summer basketball camp or an all-star game before an audience of coaches, scouts, and agents.

"If a player has a good summer now, it means more than having a good senior year," Texas Christian University coach Moe Iba admitted. "I wouldn't be too crazy about that if I was a high school coach."[15]

There are hundreds of basketball camps across the country, which offer kids the chance to hone their skills, compete against talented players from other states, and catch the eye of a college scout. The Nike/ABCD All-American Basketball Camp, for example, annually attracts 123 of the nation's top players (who are provided transportation, food, hotel lodging, shirts, shorts, and, of course, Nike shoes). The elite camps try to assemble the top high school roundballers from across the country in order to provide "one stop shopping" for college coaches.[16] With time at a premium during the regular season, a college coach or scout can concentrate his recruiting efforts on the summer.

The Nike Camp does not even purport to be an instructional camp where players are drilled on the fundamentals; it is, instead, a showcase. But for younger players or those seeking a heavier dose of instruction, training camps have sprouted across the country, often under the auspices of a major college basketball program (and to the enrichment of a big-time college coach). In fact, my first business venture after graduating from college was a basketball camp in Delaware, in partnership with Rich Miller, my high school coach and chemistry teacher.

I had attended my first basketball camp (Virginia coach Bill Gibson's camp at Gettysburg, Pennsylvania) in the summer following the fourth grade. At twelve I was six feet; and at fourteen when I arrived at North Carolina coach Dean Smith's basketball camp, I was six-feet-four. Dean was shocked at my size; and after I had dominated my age group for a few days, Doug Moe, one of the counselors and later a pro player and coach, convinced Dean to pit me against the seventeen-year-olds for the rest of the program.

I was a repeat customer at many summer camps, including four visits to camps run by Bill Gibson and Bucky Waters, the head coach of West Virginia, and three apiece to Dean Smith's and a camp at the University at Maryland. In the summer before my junior year in high school, I hit five basketball camps.

I even returned to Dean's camp as a counselor, although I was not expected to do much counseling. Because of my height and skill, I was someone for the coaches to watch closely. I had become a prospect for Dean Smith by the time I hit the ninth grade, and he was the first famous college coach to pay attention to me. Years later my closeness to Dean would complicate my choice of a college and almost tear apart my family, which had been driven frantic by relentless recruiters.

Perhaps the most valuable aspect of the camps was my exposure to inspirational stars such as Jerry Lucas and Bill Bradley. When Bradley appeared at Bucky Waters's camp, I was fourteen, and the Princeton star and Rhodes scholar instantly became a role model for me. Here was someone who had succeeded in the academic and athletic worlds and who was aimed toward a life in public service after his basketball career.

In 1970 the Dapper Dan Classic confirmed my status as a "blue chip" recruit. Each year the Dapper Dan matches the best high school players in Pennsylvania against an all-star team of competitors from ten other states. Like the high-flying Las Vegas Invitational and other all-star contests, the legendary Dapper Dan is a magnet for the best talent in the nation. These events are even more time efficient for coaches and scouts than the summer camps, and a player's performance in a single all-star game may make or break his chances for a major scholarship.

Even though I had set a Pennsylvania high school scoring record by averaging twenty points as a freshman, thirty points as a sophomore, forty as a junior, and almost forty-eight as a senior, I had played for a small school, and there were still a few skeptics who wondered if I could compete against stronger talent.

I was nervous before the game, mainly because I was feverish and had not been cleared by the doctor to play until two hours before the start. Moreover, I was performing before a crowd of over thirteen thousand, by far the largest audience I had played before; and in that capacity crowd were coaches from 275 colleges. Agitated by the whirlwind of publicity surrounding me, including a cover shot on *Sports Illustrated,* which touted me as the best high school player in America, several of the opposing players had declared their intentions of knocking me down a few notches in the eyes of the coaches and scouts. I was only the second high school player in history to be featured on the *Sports Illustrated* cover.

Even though my Pennsylvania team lost, I scored a game-high total of thirty-seven points, tying a record set by Calvin Murphy in 1966, and was voted the team's most valuable player. Unfortunately, my performance exacerbated the recruiting frenzy surrounding me, which was already out of hand before the Dapper Dan.

Concerned that certain players were abusing the all-star circuit, the NCAA ruled several years ago that any student who played in more than two all-star games during high school would forfeit his collegiate eligibility.[17] The NCAA is also turning its attention now to the summer camps, which have also gotten out of control. Because the summer camps are presently unregulated, the National Association of Basketball Coaches, under the able chairmanship of Southern Cal's George Raveling, has proposed legislation to enable the NCAA to run its own regional camps. The NCAA-administered camps would be the only ones college coaches could attend.[18] Describing summer camps as a "festering problem," Raveling claims that many of the directors use their camps to become involved in the athlete's selection of a college.[19] The proposed legislation would have little impact on instructional camps but would help curb the worst abuses of the all-star camp circuit.

Camps and all-star tournaments are, of course, not limited to basketball. There are tennis "boot camps" where teenagers, at a cost of up to $50,000 a year, immerse themselves in a totalitarian regimen.[20]

Many of these tennis camps are patterned after the legendary Nick Bollettieri Tennis Academy near Sarasota, Florida—a tennis factory that has turned out Andre Agassi, Jimmy Arias, Carling Bassett, Jim Courier, and Monica Seles. The first order of business according to Bollettieri is to break the bond between the child and the parents in order to elevate the sport to the place of primacy in the child's life.[21] In such a hothouse environment, sports are no longer fun; and whenever youth sports cease to be fun, something is seriously wrong with the system.

One of the indelible television images in my memory is of Jimmy Connors's mother in the stands during one of his Wimbledon matches, early in his great career. She was shouting at the top of her lungs, a cross between the ugly American and the ultimate Little League mom. I could not make out her words, which was probably a blessing. To most of the TV viewers, the scene was probably comical, but I cringed at the sight of the overbearing parent in the stands, riding her son during a pressure-packed match.

The scene hit close to home.

My father, James Joseph McMillen, was born in 1904 and raised in a poor family of nine children. A devout Catholic, he suffered through periods of rabid anti-Catholicism during his youth, and he overcame childhood polio to become a star athlete. He turned down offers of basketball scholarships in the 1920s in order to attend the University of Pittsburgh; and as he struggled through college and dental school, holding down jobs as a gas station attendant and a mortician's assistant, he second-guessed himself for not accepting a sports scholarship. He could not waste much time daydreaming about sports, however, because he was saddled not only with his own tuition but also with the tuition of his brother Adrian during the depths of the Great Depression.

During the Depression, he moved to the rural community of Mansfield, Pennsylvania, with a population then of about fifteen hundred and a need for a dentist since the recent death of its only practitioner. Mansfield is geographically close to New York State but culturally more akin to the mountain region of West Virginia. It is so heavily Republican that a deceased Republican candidate once won an election.

Dad scratched hard for a decade at his dentistry practice before marrying at the age of forty. A year later Jay, the first of his three sons, was born. I was the youngest of his three sons, born in 1952, seven years after Jay, five years after Paul, and two years after Sheila. I was shaped like a pole at birth, twenty-two inches long but only six pounds, and Dad sensed that he had a basketball player on his hands.

Because of the seven-year gap in our ages, I witnessed Jay's sports odyssey from a relatively safe distance. Many years later, however, Jay was finally able to express to me the full extent of the frustration that led to his temporary alienation from sports and Dad. Dad loved and cared so much about his kids that he attended practically all of their games and many of their practices in all sports, but he demanded perfection and pushed everyone too hard, especially himself.

Jay had the mixed blessing of being the first son in the family. To push Jay athletically, Dad urged him to play baseball with kids who were two years older than he. Petrified and unseasoned, Jay became the "strikeout king" of Little League in Mansfield. But above the groans and boos of the fans at the ballpark rose my father's voice, as he both exhorted and berated my hapless brother. Instead of pulling Jay back with his age group, Dad rode him harder and harder, and naturally Jay grew increasingly frustrated. As difficult as it was for him to face his coach and teammates after a bad game, it was harder still for Jay to face Dad.

Sometimes he would pedal his bike for hours to avoid going home.

Basketball saved Jay, or at least reprieved him. While Jay developed into a fair baseball player, he shone at basketball. He became addicted to the sights, sounds, and smells of the gym, and he fed his addiction with hours of practice a day. He was starved for success at sports and, of course, for his father's approval. Dad was still perched in the bleachers, magnifying every missed shot or errant pass and chiding Jay if he was not the top scorer and rebounder in the game; but because Jay was usually the star of the contest, the criticism was muted.

As Jay's reputation as a basketball player blossomed, my father's sense of pride swelled. Trailing seven years behind Jay, I watched his every move and learned that athletic success meant the difference between being the toast of the dinner table and riding for hours down the lonely streets of a small town.

Fortunately my parents were not blind to the importance of academics. Indeed, I grew up in a house stocked with five thousand books, and our dinner conversation was often an intensely intellectual experience, like a round of *Jeopardy*. Both parents were widely read, and Dad was a self-educated expert on British history, English literature, and the Civil War. Our parents bombarded us with questions about the meaning of words, forced us to recite passages from Shakespeare, and grilled us on current events. We went through probing "report card" dinners during which every grade in every course was revealed and analyzed.

In reading about the Kennedy clan years later, I noted several similarities to my family—the iron-willed father who instilled a drive to succeed in his offspring; the gentler mother who was a community activist; and the competitive atmosphere among the children, who went on to successful careers in politics, academics, medicine, business, journalism, and the arts.

But sports were always my father's first love, and he was not alone in admiring Jay's basketball skills. College coaches came from Maryland, Duke, NYU, Virginia, Penn State, and about two hundred other schools. Our town was besieged, and our house was deluged by mail. The phone never stopped ringing.

I watched the heady horrors of a recruiting war from the front lines; and noticing the glances of the coaches in my direction, I could read their minds. How tall will this kid be in seven years? Will he be strong enough then to crash the boards? Will he inherit his brother's soft touch? Can he jump?

Dad beamed with pride at the attention heaped upon Jay, and the hoopla reinforced Dad's belief that sports was the way to get ahead in life. When Jay selected Maryland, Dad expected great things of his son and the team, but before long he became bitterly disappointed with both. Both Jay and Maryland had checkered basketball careers during this period, although at one point Jay was starting on a Maryland team that was ranked fifteenth in the nation.

During Jay's sophomore year, the Terps began to fade; and Jay, who had never really played for a losing team, lost his drive toward excellence. He settled for being a good college player on a mediocre team, which infuriated my father. Jay rebelled against Dad by partying through college and wasting his talents, both on the court and off. The louder Dad shouted from the sidelines and the harder he pushed his son toward medical school, the more Jay rebelled, until finally Dad in exasperation transferred his attention to me.

My father's attention was, of course, a two-edged sword. But as hard as my father drove me, I pushed myself even harder, especially after two early scares of my childhood. Between the ages of four and eight, I could not focus my eyes. The doctors initially prescribed special glasses, a special screen on our TV, and exercises but were ultimately forced to operate twice to improve my vision. I recall little about the operations, except that there were no beds in the pediatric ward long enough for me even then.

The second crisis spanned my grade school years. As a child, I could barely run because my knees banged together so hard that I often tripped myself. In fact, I knocked out my front teeth after tripping over my own bandy legs. When I was seven, Dad noticed that my legs bowed inward at the knees, which he attributed to my rapid growth. Nonetheless, he took me to an orthopedic surgeon, who delivered the staggering prognosis that, while I would grow very tall, I would probably not be able to run or jump, much less play basketball.

Although I was in danger of being horribly knock-kneed for life, my father went to elaborate lengths to meet my medical needs, as he did for his entire family. He paid great attention to Paul's multitude of ailments (including serious, recurrent problems with his pancreas), and he was not about to give up on me. My mother and father were willing to sacrifice everything for their kids.

Fortunately the doctor prescribed leg braces to be worn at night to correct the curvature of my knees. The braces were actually heavy shoes connected by metal bars. I wore those braces every night for five years as I lay awake worrying about the future and feeling guilty over a bone defect. In those braces I became a prisoner of the bed, unable to rise without removing them. I lived in fear that I would be hobbled for life, unable to compete in sports at all, much less excel.

Finally freed from the metal contraption, I became goal oriented in sports, but my childhood afflictions of the eyes and legs convinced me of the necessity of a backup career. My parents never needed to be convinced of this. While my father pushed me in sports, my mother hammered home the importance of a good education. Even in grade school, I adopted the habit of daily carrying a three-by-five-inch card with me on which I listed things to accomplish that day, such as shoot one hundred free throws and finish a particular book. Every night I prepared my card for the next day, and every day I worked my way down the card.

As with Jay, Dad initially pushed me in baseball as well as basketball; but unlike Jay, I never improved to the point of being even an average baseball player. My every appearance at the plate or chance in the field was excruciating, another chance to fail before my harshest but most loyal critic. Always tall for my age, I became the lightning rod for my father's unleashed energy and ambition.

Despite the pressure, I loved baseball, largely because of the steadying influence of John Heaps, my Little League coach and grade school teacher. Coach Heaps had a talent for creating opportunities for even the less skilled players. He bragged that he never worried about an overthrow when I played first base.

Because Dad died during my senior year at Maryland (and Jay's final year at Maryland's medical school), he never really saw me fail at basketball. A three-time all-American in high school, I was recruited by hundreds of colleges and became an all-American in college. Dad never hesitated to drive ten hours round trip to watch me play at Maryland, even as his health was failing.

It was a postgame ritual for him to dissect my performance, and he always wanted me to do more. He was a stickler on the importance of free throws and offensive rebounds, and those two topics dominated almost every critique.

Our freshman team at Maryland was undefeated going into the last game of the season. With Dad and Jay in the stands, I scored twenty points, and Maryland won, capping a perfect season. Yet, when Dad burst into the locker room, he was riding me for being outscored by two of my teammates. While Jay tried to restrain Dad or at least silence him, the embarrassing scene flooded me with memories of similar scenes from junior high and high school games. The time our high school team lost the state championship my senior year is one I vividly recall, not so much because of the defeat itself but because Dad was so distraught that he wrecked the car the following day. The postgame tirades were so disruptive that my freshman coach, George Raveling (now the head coach at USC), was forced to ban Dad from the locker room. Even in the glow of a perfect season at Maryland, I was not safe from my father's drive for perfection.

To this day I often wonder how Dad would have reacted to my pro career. In eleven years in the NBA, I carved out a steady career as a hard-nosed backup with a soft touch and a gritty determination on defense. I was not, however, the star.

The ultimate irony is that Jay, who rebelled against Dad and basketball for a few years, is closer to the sport now than I am. After turning his back on basketball for a time, Jay renewed his love for the game in the Italian League, where he played for a year. He also steeled himself against failure and dedicated himself to medical school, graduating in the top 10 percent of his class. Today he plays basketball two or three times a week with his peers and almost every night with his ten-year-old son, who loves to play all sports with his supportive father.

On the other hand, I have played and watched very little basketball since my retirement from the NBA in 1986. For me sports became too much business and too little recreation, and I am still fighting to recapture the sense of fun.

I have trouble getting "juiced" over a pickup contest or a TV game. I never attempted to dissociate myself from sports; but even as I was competing in the pros, I began to seek challenges outside the gym. From an early age, I was attracted to the challenges of public service, but I never dreamed that I would find a way to fuse the worlds of politics and sports.

While I recognize that my father's overbearing nature caused a great deal of pain at times, I credit him with instilling in all of us a drive toward excellence and a commitment to seeking and mastering new challenges.

But when adults—whether parents, coaches, scouts, agents, or boosters—feed their egos and wallets through the accomplishments of youngsters, or when a city, state, or nation uses them to boost its esteem, sports enter the dangerous territory of a religion or an obsession.

For decades prior to the reunification of Germany, the West enviously decried the sports factory in East Germany, a small country of 18 million which became a superpower in the Olympics and other international competitions. Judged on a per capita basis, the sports culture of East Germany was far and away the most successful in the world at accumulating gold, silver, and bronze medals.[22]

In the 1950s the German Democratic Republic established a network of special sports schools that trained athletically gifted children in Olympic events. A child was admitted into a sports training center at the age of ten for a ten-year period on a decision made jointly by the family, the head of the child's school, and a trained physical education teacher. Even within the regular schools, there were "special tracks" and "training groups" for promising athletes. Because of my height and determination, I would have been a likely candidate for the sports training center in the old East German system.

In its efforts to apply science and medicine to sports, the GDR pushed its search for champion athletes back to nursery school and began to maintain a "sports file" on all children.[23] Competition was institutionalized for young children according to age and ability in a nationwide effort to scout top athletes and encourage them to transfer to the special sports schools. School, district, and provincial competitions were held, culminating every two years in a "Spartaciad" in Berlin.[24]

Removed from their families, children became the experimental subjects of high-performance theories in state-sponsored sports research laboratories. The East German athlete was considered so valuable to the state that he or she was accorded a degree of medical attention comparable to a cosmonaut.[25]

After reunification, confidential government documents were released indicating that East Germany had fed steroids to practically all of its Olympic track and field stars throughout the 1980s, often beginning when the athletes were fourteen years old and in dosages far in excess of those admitted by athletes in the West.[26] Indeed, there was apparently even more extreme experimentation involving the harvesting of organs for transplants from living patients.[27]

International criticism of the East German model was, no doubt, motivated at least partly by jealousy over the staggering successes of the GDR in the Olympics; but a realistic appraisal of the strengths and weaknesses of the East German machinery is especially important today because a reunified Germany is now offering to export its expertise to medal-hungry nations, such as the United States.[28] There is a migration of sports experts (some of whom carry a dangerous message) from East Germany, which can now support only about fifteen hundred employees of the vast sports bureaucracy that once had twelve thousand workers.[29] It is likely that some of the also-ran nations that in the past belittled the GDR's achievements will now become its disciples.

Despite its many flaws, the East German model had at least one important advantage over the American way of grooming champions: The expressway toward sports stardom detoured through the special sports schools. Soviet athletes also trained in special sports schools, which were separate from the regular school system.

The superhighway in the United States, at least in football and basketball, tunnels straight through our public schools and has corrupted other components of our educational system. We are the only nation in the world that attempts a "coexistence" between academics and big-time sports.

Despite this apparent disadvantage, however, we should not rush to adopt the practices and technologies of the GDR. We need to wean ourselves away from the misguided notion that sports triumphs (and especially Olympic medals) measure the worth of a nation, a state, or a city. There are much more important measures, such as the care and attention we devote to our least-privileged members. We should be less concerned with lavishing medical attention upon pampered athletes than in delivering basic health care to the poorest children in our society, many of whom are homeless. We should worry less about the training tables of our champions than about the empty tables of our poor.

Moreover, the manufacture of robokids does not necessarily elevate the level of health of the general population. A noted authority on East Germany has pointed out that the great majority of East Germans did not regularly and actively participate in sports, and he suggested that the relentless search for champions might have adversely affected the interest in sports and morale of the general populace.[30] By focusing on the elite athlete, the GDR drove ordinary athletes away from the pools, gyms, and playgrounds. Thus, for both financial and ideological reasons, reunified Germany has destroyed East Germany's government sports program.[31]

Indeed, the harshest indictment of youth sports in the United

States is that, for far too many of our kids, sports have ceased to be fun, and there is no reason to believe that importing anything from the East German arsenal will remedy this flaw.

Youth sports are big business in the United States. An estimated 30 million of our kids participate in some form of organized sports competition every year.[32] There are now more than forty thousand Little League baseball teams, and Little League Baseball, Inc., is the world's largest sports organization.[33] Each fall thousands of junior football teams sprout in leagues such as Pop Warner.

Nonetheless, while youth teams are proliferating in football, basketball, and baseball—the "big money" sports—youth participation in lifelong sports such as swimming, tennis, archery, and the like is actually declining.[34] Kids are participating less in the types of activities that can be continued into their adulthood.

Even more distressing is the authoritarian control by adults over every facet of the youth sports enterprise. Adults control the franchises; draft the players; promulgate reams of rules; establish the times and places for the games; and to a shocking degree litigate in adult courts every issue from player eligibility to tournament appearances.

Professor Edward Devereux of Cornell persuasively argues that the spread of "Little Leagueism" threatens to wipe out the spontaneous culture of free play and games among American children, robbing them of not only fun but also a valuable learning experience.[35] With Little League and its imitators, the structure of the game is rigidly fixed by adults and imposed upon the children.

By contrast, in spontaneous self-organized and self-governed children's games, the kids must learn to choose the game, select the sides, set the rules, enforce the rules, perhaps change the rules in midcontest to restore competitive balance, and decide when to end the game—all of which give children a greater stake in the whole activity.

Devereux contrasted the impoverishment of the game culture in the United States—where kids were either under strict adult supervision or alternatively "hanging around"—with the rich, spontaneous game culture of other countries, particularly Japan. He was impressed with the ability of Japanese youngsters to play a wide repertory of complex, evolving games wholly without adult instigation or supervision.[36]

In a similar vein, Joe Paterno, the great teacher and football coach at Penn State, described the problem succinctly as follows:

> Whatever happened to the good old days when if you felt like playing baseball you would round up your buddies, get a bat and ball and would go out and play? What do we do now? We dress up our kids in uniforms, give them professional equipment, tell them where to play, when to play, organize their games for them, give them officials and put them in the hands of a coach who doesn't know the first thing about the sport or what's good for an 8-year old.[37]

We can no longer assume that highly competitive, adult-supervised sports for kids automatically build character or teach them the right lessons. Adults—whether parents, coaches, or parent-coaches—bring a whole complex of frustrations and expectations to the Little League parks. What lessons does a child learn from a win-at-all-costs coach who orders his pitcher to "brush back" the best hitter on the opposing team? What feelings does an ex-pitcher take away from the game when he belatedly realizes that he "threw out" his arm by throwing curves on the orders of his untrained coach? What emotions are churning inside the less skilled players who are buried on the bench or run off the team?

And what lessons do the parents instill when they ride the umpire over a bad call? Berate the players for an error or a strikeout? Bribe them for a victory or a home run? Spend more time with their kids at the ballpark than the library? Attend every sporting event but pass on parent-teacher conferences?

How many kids are afraid to leave the locker room after a bad game to face their parents? How many quit a sport permanently or are chased away? How many suffer career-ending injuries or use a real or imagined injury to escape from an overstressful activity? With kids being thrown into competitive leagues at the age of eight or sometimes even earlier, how many burn out before high school? Before junior high?

After ten months of following twenty-eight teams in baseball leagues, a sociologist came to doubt that Little League baseball was a positive experience for most of the participants, concluding that the fun it provided was outweighed by the tension it produced.[38] For this reason about 70 percent of the children participating in organized sports in the United States drop out by the age of thirteen. "Most said they simply got tired of being yelled at," reports Fred Engh, president and chief executive officer of the National Youth Sports Coaches Association (NYSCA).[39]

To help remedy this situation, the NYSCA has launched a program to train and certify Little League coaches, which requires them to sign a pledge to "place the emotional and physical well-being of my players ahead of any personal desire to win" and "lead, by example, in demonstrating fair play and sportsmanship to all my players."[40] The training reinforces the differences in goals between a professional coach (winning games, earning money, and providing entertainment) and a youth coach (teaching effectively, caring for a child's well-being, developing each child, and making the experience fun).[41]

I am not arguing for the abolition of Little League baseball or Pop Warner football but for a realistic appraisal of their roles in shaping kids. Organized sports teach kids lessons, both good and bad; but more important, they fail to teach them some of the beneficial lessons of spontaneous play and games.

The most important issue in youth sports is whether the child is having fun and learning values, not whether his team is winning or whether he has the talent to rise to the next level of competition. Fun and stress are inversely related for the losing as well as the winning players.[42] Accentuating the fun side of a sport reduces the stress on all players. Forcing a child into a highly stressful situation in which he is not having fun threatens to extinguish his general interest in sports and physical activities.

One of the great talents of my Little League coach and teacher, John Heaps, was his ability to make baseball fun and, by doing so, to encourage kids to participate who would not otherwise have done so. This was a more important measure of his coaching ability than the team's win-loss record.

Our society suffers from a misplaced sense of priorities, investing more resources in organized competitive sports than in

physical activity and general health. This consigns the vast majority of children to the sidelines at an early age. Creeping professionalism forces kids to become either stars or spectators, with
no middle ground.

Because of the massive sums of TV money at the top of the
sports heap, systemic abuses are seeping downward, sometimes
as far down as grade school. The greater the money at the top of
the sports world, the greater the pressures at the bottom of the
pile. Because the abuses are systemic and pervasive, it is not
feasible to attempt to reform sports at only one level, such as
intercollegiate competition. Failure to address the abuses at all
levels will exact greater damage upon individuals, institutions,
and society as a whole.

Chapter 2

TICKET TO RIDE

The Recruiting Merry-Go-Round

ALTHOUGH IT HAS been more than twenty years since I was re-cruited by colleges, many of my memories of the experience are still vivid, and a few are painfully so. I emerged on the verge of a nervous breakdown and with an abiding belief that there had to be a better way to recruit athletes.

"It was a miserable, miserable time in my life," my mother recalls painfully. "We were a peaceful, close family till your re-cruiting. It caused members of our family to take sides, and we had never done that before." Even after two decades, she refuses to discuss the topic further.

In a long, emotional letter written after my final decision, Dean Smith, the highly regarded coach of the North Carolina Tar Heels, admitted:

Tom, I have never been through anything like these past five months. I know you have not either. All of this in college athletics is not worth it. I am talking about hate letters, phony letters, lies, insin-uations, threats of investigations, etc. In fact, Tom, I would get out of coaching, but it is too great a challenge right now, and I never want to be accused of quitting.[1]

In many ways my experiences are typical of the two or three dozen "blue chip" high school seniors who are flooded with scholarship offers from several hundred colleges. The names and faces change every year, but the hype, hysteria, and overkill are constant. The recruiting of basketball players is particularly cutthroat because a single star can transform a mediocre basketball team into a contender. With football or baseball teams, the effect of any single individual is somewhat diluted.

But my experiences are atypical of the basketball prospects who are hardened by inner-city street life and who view basketball as their only shot at a better life. I was fortunate to have been raised in a small town and guided by caring, middle-class parents who were committed to my goals of a first-class education. And I had already been exposed to the heavy-duty recruiting of my older brother, Jay.

Today there are kids who, before they reach seventeen, have been through the grind of recruiting at three different levels—junior high, high school, and summer league. As Lefty Driesell, my college coach and now the head coach at James Madison, recently told me, "Coaches know who the good players are by the eighth and ninth grades because of the scouting reports and summer camps; and if you're good, 150 schools are recruiting you." The information age has reshaped recruiting, and it is no longer possible for a college coach to "hide" a hot prospect in a small high school and land him without competition from dozens or hundreds of other schools.

An athlete who has been hustled this hard and long is probably saddled with an inflated ego and is vastly overconfident of his odds of a pro career. He has been told too many times by too many people that he is the next Michael Jordan or Joe Montana, and he desperately wants to believe the hype. Many such victims of the myth view their schools as names on a uniform and the classroom as merely a breather between practices.

My mother summed it up best when she said, "Recruiting

gives athletes an elevated opinion of their importance and disrupts family life.''

My parents and I were fully prepared for the deluge of letters, calls, and visits from the three hundred colleges that sought my services. (I still have dozens of boxes of correspondence.) Because the letters began to trickle in while I was in junior high, I cannot say exactly when I became a target for the recruiters; but Dean Smith began to keep tabs on me at his summer basketball camps, which I attended for the first time at the age of fourteen.

Dean was not the only coach to show an early interest. I became accustomed to flocks of coaches and scouts jamming the stands of my tiny high school gym. Indeed, when I played against legendary Power Memorial of New York, where Kareem Abdul-Jabbar had starred in high school, there were approximately one hundred coaches and scouts in the stands.

Near the end of Adolph Rupp's remarkable career at Kentucky, which included four national championships, he flew through a snowstorm to a small town near Mansfield to watch me play a high school game and pronounced me a "can't miss" college prospect. It was the first high school contest he had seen outside Kentucky in over two years. His failing health had forced him to curtail almost all scouting trips, and I was touched that he made an exception for me.

Primarily because of Rupp's interest, I made a trip to Kentucky. The Wildcats arranged for a private jet to bring Rich Miller, my high school coach, and me to Lexington, where I was greeted at the airport by about three thousand fans. A bachelor at the time, Coach Miller was accompanied on the rounds by a *Playboy* Playmate, and I was escorted by identical twin cheerleaders at Kentucky, who went on to become the "Doublemint Twins" on television commercials.

The weekend in Kentucky was a whirlwind of dinners and tours. On Saturday afternoon, a group of boosters introduced me to John Y. Brown, then the owner of Kentucky Fried Chicken, at a

Lexington racetrack. As we chatted in the clubhouse, a booster asked Coach Miller and me for a couple of dollars each to place bets for us. Minutes later the booster returned with our winnings. Again we trusted the booster to lay down our bets, and again we won. Coach Miller and I continued our winning streak until we had each accumulated several hundred dollars. Unfortunately, Coach Miller decided to wager one final bet for both of us as we were leaving for our flight, and he managed to blow our combined winnings on the last race.

I turned down far more offers of campus visits than I accepted. For example, an alumnus of Southern Cal offered Coach Miller and me an all-expense-paid week's vacation in California on the condition that I visit USC one afternoon and UCLA the next. Coach Miller was excited about the trip, but I told the alumnus to save his money for someone who was seriously considering his schools. On another occasion I passed up a trip and tickets to the Super Bowl that were being dangled by a Louisiana businessman. (In 1970, unlike today, boosters were allowed to recruit on behalf of colleges.)

One of the most imaginative stunts (also now prohibited by NCAA regulations) was arranged by Coach Bill Gibson of Virginia during my trip to his campus. After a tour of the impressive facilities, Coach Gibson and I talked about the school for an hour or so. Then he led me from his office to the entrance of the basketball arena, where I was confronted by a life-size blowup of me in my high school uniform, with arms outstretched and palming a basketball in each hand.

My parents and I made it abundantly clear to the recruiters that I was interested primarily in a good education and that even a hint of impropriety on their part would backfire. For that reason I was never offered any illegal inducements to sign with any college, but I am certain that I would have been deluged with promises of under-the-table remuneration if I had sent the signals.

The more prescient coaches attempted to capitalize on my keen interests in academics (particularly medicine) and politics. For example, among the hundreds of letters and telegrams I received from coaches and boosters was a telegram from more than seventy-five doctors and dentists extolling the premed preparation at their alma mater, Davidson.

Because of my family's devotion to medicine (Dad was a dentist, and Jay eventually transferred from dental to medical school) and my bone defect as a child, I was leaning toward a career as an orthopedic surgeon. On campus visits, I insisted on touring the medical school. The University of Virginia scored points by inviting me to watch an operation by Dr. Frank McCue, its famed orthopedic surgeon. After the successful operation, Dr. McCue answered my long string of questions about his procedures, medicine as a career, and the premed facilities at Virginia.

Not to be outdone, Coach Bucky Waters of West Virginia suddenly turned to me during a grand tour of his campus and asked, "Tom, would you like to meet the president?"

After regaining my composure, I replied, "Sure, there are a lot of questions about the university I would like to ask him."

"No, Tom, you don't understand," Bucky explained. "I don't mean the president of the university. I mean the president of the United States."

I was dumbfounded as Bucky whisked me to the airport to stand in a receiving line between Congressman Harley Staggers and Senator William Jennings Randolph. President Johnson deplaned and swaggered rapidly down the reception line. LBJ was a large, imposing man; but when he reached me in the line, he looked up and said, "You've gotta be the basketball player."

Weighing in for Penn State were Governor Raymond Shafer and Coach Joe Paterno, and Maryland countered by rolling out its big guns—U.S. Senator Joseph Tydings and Governor Marvin Mandel. Senator Tydings, whose high-powered family tree included a father who had been a U.S. senator and a grandfather who had been ambassador to Russia and the first chairman of the Federal Trade Commission, treated me to lunch in the U.S. Senate dining room and years later arranged a summer job for me as an operator in the Senate cloakroom. In our first meeting, he encouraged my growing interest in a career in public service. It was also Senator Tydings who first piqued my interest in a Rhodes scholarship.

Because of my academic and political aspirations, I occasionally exasperated the coaches with questions that were unusual for a recruit. For example, I pointed out to Lefty Driesell that the library at Maryland was not as large as its counterparts in North Carolina or Virginia. Without blinking, the fast-thinking, resourceful Lefty pledged on the spot that, as soon as I finished reading every book in Maryland's library, he would personally secure for me any book I wanted but could not find there.

It was obviously a heady experience for a seventeen-year-old to meet the leaders in politics, industry, sports, academia, and medicine; but there were many dark sides to the process. Though initially exhilarating, it soon became oppressive. During my senior year in high school, I was overloaded with the demands of serving as student council president, fighting to maintain an A average, playing trombone in the school band, and devoting four hours a day to basketball.

On top of my tight schedule, I was receiving about fifty letters a day from coaches, alumni, and fans, and the phone rang nonstop from 6 P.M. to midnight. If Dad had not been worried about emergency dental calls, we would have disconnected the phone. "We had to take the phone off the hook to dine in our own home," Mom recalls. Coaches and recruiters dropped by our house unannounced, claiming to have been "just passing through" my isolated hometown of twenty-five hundred. Deep in the backwoods of Pennsylvania, Mansfield is not a place that anyone just happens to pass through.

After one high school game, coaches from North Carolina, Maryland, Virginia, and West Virginia showed up at our house for coffee at the same time. Worse still, none of the four coaches wanted to break the stalemate by leaving first, so we were finally forced to turn out everyone at midnight.

The family was being driven to the edge of its sanity. My family was wined and dined so often that once my nine-year-old sister Liz asked if we could stay home one night and eat hot dogs. With Jay, the recruiters had not really begun visiting our house until his junior year; but in my case they became semipermanent fixtures at our place during my freshman year. By the end of my freshman year, I had been contacted by sixty colleges. After my sophomore year, I had heard from one hundred fifty institutions; and after my junior year, three hundred colleges. In retrospect, the family was probably overconfident of its ability to handle the pressures because of our experience with Jay's recruiting. We were all to pay for this hubris.

To escape the pressure, I was being pushed to reach an early decision or, at least, narrow my choices. As with everything else in my life, I was methodical—perhaps too much so—in winnowing out institutions. I had gathered reams of data on dozens of colleges, covering everything from the size of their libraries to their teacher-pupil ratios. Unfortunately I was compiling more data than I could process.

The first cut proved to be the easiest. I was interested only in schools on the Eastern Seaboard with excellent academic standards and top-rate athletic programs.

At the outset of my senior year, my family and Rich Miller collaborated on three form letters. Even at the height of the frenzy, I answered every initial inquiry. The first form letter was a polite "thanks but no thanks." The second affirmed my interest in the school but requested that the coaches and recruiters wait until the end of my final season in high school before contacting me again. The first letter generally achieved its desired effect; the second rarely did. The third form letter, which was sent to about ten schools, indicated that the recipient was one of my top choices.

By the end of my senior season, I had eliminated all but eight schools: Kentucky, Duke, Virginia, West Virginia, Princeton, Pennsylvania, Maryland, and North Carolina. All boasted excellent academic and athletic programs and were close enough for my father to drive to most of the games. I visited all eight campuses and, in addition, received scouting reports from my brother Jay, who was then attending dental school at Maryland; my brother Paul, a banker in Chapel Hill, North Carolina; and my sister Sheila, an undergraduate at Penn.

When the recruiting battle heated up, Paul could not make a move in Chapel Hill without its being reported by the local paper; and after I made my final decision, Paul was grilled for three hours by NCAA investigators about his job at the bank. They pored over Paul's tax returns and phone records to investigate insinuations that Paul's job at Chapel Hill was linked to the Tar Heels' efforts to recruit me. Although the accusations were never substantiated, our family (and especially Paul) suffered from their wide circulation.

By early April I had shaved the list to three finalists: Maryland, North Carolina, and Virginia. The Ivy League schools, Princeton and Pennsylvania, were eliminated because they did not provide athletic scholarships, and I wanted to spare my parents the expense of my college education. After imposing upon myself a deadline of April 15, I offered each of the three coaches a final chance to pitch me in person in Mansfield. I arranged to meet Coach Gibson on April 10, Dean Smith on April 11, and Lefty Driesell on April 12.

My decision was complicated by knowing all three of the head coaches personally. I had known Bill Gibson the longest because he had been the coach at Mansfield State College from 1956 to 1962. During his tenure there, he had watched me grow and had become close friends with the entire family. That friendship survived Bill's departure for Virginia in 1962. Among my family Mom was his strongest advocate. Lenny Snyder, a local businessman, was Gibson's best friend, as well as a close friend of our family. He was also the brother of Paul Snyder, who would in 1975 sign me to my first pro contract with the Buffalo Braves.

I had grown close to Dean Smith during his summer basketball camps, and he was the first college coach to pay close attention to me. I was impressed not only with his obvious coaching and recruiting abilities but also with his scholarly, almost bookish demeanor. A true intellectual, Dean is to college basketball what Joe Paterno is to college football; and the Tar Heel basketball program has been the most consistently successful powerhouse in the country for the past two decades, attracting stars such as Michael Jordan, James Worthy, Sam Perkins, Charlie Scott, Mitch Kupchak, and Larry Miller. There was a religious dimension to Dean's character that immediately won me over. While my parents came to resent Dean, Coach Miller and I were influenced by the

Tar Heel mystique and by the great respect of his former and current players for him.

If Dean was the master of the "soft sell," Lefty Driesell was the king of the "hard sell." I was the first prospect Lefty scouted after being named head coach at Maryland, and he repeatedly stressed that I would fit perfectly into his team's system, which had already produced two all-American centers.[2]

While I did not know Lefty at this point nearly as well as I knew Bill and Dean, the firebrand coach at Maryland held two aces in his hand. First, my brother Jay, who was then in Maryland's dental school, had forged a successful basketball career at the school and was convinced that Lefty would deliver on his immoderate pledge to make Maryland "the UCLA of the East"—a phrase coined by Jay.

Just as insinuations were spread about Paul's banking position in Chapel Hill, which had been offered during my recruitment, a few eyebrows were raised when Jay was accepted into Maryland's medical school. Before I committed to Maryland, Jay was placed on a waiting list for the class entering Maryland's medical school in 1970 but was accepted for the following year. Jay told my parents that he had been accepted but neglected to tell them that his admission had been deferred a year, afraid this would turn my parents against the school.

While I was being recruited, Governor Mandel, Lefty, and others pressured the medical school to accept Jay immediately, but this probably backfired as the school resisted outside interference. After I decided to matriculate at Maryland, someone dropped out of the medical school, and Jay was admitted in 1970. The circumstances of Jay's admission and Paul's employment raised eyebrows but never became the major story that would be written today.

As a second ace in his hand, Lefty had hired as an assistant coach Joe Harrington, who is now the head basketball coach at Colorado. Joe had been Jay's teammate at Maryland (I had watched many of Jay's games at Maryland, some of them from the team bench) and had spent a summer during his college career with our family in Mansfield. He was practically a member of the family. It was no secret that Joe had been hired by Lefty partly to assist in recruiting me; and to Joe's credit, he never tried to hide this fact from our family. And Joe resisted putting the hard sell on me. I always respected his advice and friendship and knew that he would become a successful coach, as he has proved at Colorado University.

I was to discover later that hiring someone close to a blue chipper was and is a common recruiting technique. In my case Coach Miller was offered a head coaching job in Louisiana if he delivered me to the school. Sensitive to the dangers of a conflict of interest, Coach Miller disqualified any school that dangled a "package deal" involving both of us.

In mid-April I thought that all three "final" interviews went well, but I realized later that a series of incidents had irrevocably alienated my parents from the Tar Heel coach. Before Dean's visit on April 11, 1970, both of my parents were openly hostile to him. Dean had sent me a package of Tar Heel basketball equipment, and my parents were convinced that he was trying to make me feel obligated to select North Carolina. Worse, to my parents, was Dean's encouraging me to call Tom Burleson, a seven-foot-four-inch high school all-American, to discuss the advantages of our playing together for the Tar Heels. My mother absolutely forbade me from making that call because I would be acting as a recruiter for North Carolina—a serious breach of ethics in her eyes. Despite my mother's misgivings, I called Burleson. Unfortunately, Mom barged into the living room and caught me on the line. Confronted by my angry parents, Dean tried to downplay the situation, but my parents were adamant. Worst of all, Mom firmly believed that Dean attempted to exclude her from my meeting with him; and he probably preferred to talk to me alone because he sensed my parents' antipathy toward him.

On April 13 I played hooky with my principal's permission at his secluded house, armed with boxloads of information and game films of the three schools. I was on a collision course with my strong-willed parents, and my parents would argue for hours with each other over the merits and demerits of North Carolina, Virginia, and Maryland. Once I even slept in the backyard to escape an especially heated argument over my college choice.

Around 11 P.M. the following day, I called Dean in Chapel Hill. I meandered for a few minutes before finally asking, "Coach Smith, how will I look in Carolina blue?"

Dean was ecstatic. At his request I called the sports publicist at North Carolina to arrange an immediate press release, and we agreed to hold the signing ceremony at a restaurant in Elmira, New York, about twenty miles from Mansfield, where we had met many times.

I was at peace with my decision . . . for about eight hours. The next morning I realized that I had greatly underestimated my parents' opposition to Dean and North Carolina. Their feelings were so strong that neither would accompany me to the signing ceremony. Without the signature of at least one parent, even if I signed a letter of intent to matriculate at North Carolina, it would not be legally binding.

On April 15, 1970, my self-imposed deadline for a final decision, Rich Miller called Dean at my request to cancel the press conference and inform him of the depth and intensity of my parents' opposition to my choice. I was in a quandary, and so was Dean. On the other hand, Bill Gibson and Lefty Driesell felt as if they had been reprieved. The next morning Coach Miller arrived at work early to find that he had already received seventeen calls from coaches and reporters, asking about my college plans.

Over the next several months, not a waking hour passed that I did not worry about where I would be studying and playing next year. Poor Dean had fallen from grace in my parents' eyes; and the harder he tried to extricate himself, the deeper he dug his hole. My parents did not want me to play in the Dapper Dan Classic that spring, but Dean encouraged me to compete. I decided to play, and my parents unfairly blamed Dean.

On June 23, I called Dean with the news that I was ready to sign the letter of intent despite my parents' veto; and the next day we went through the signing ceremony, although both of us realized that a letter would be invalid without a parent's signature.

Our thinking was that a signing ceremony might diminish the zeal of recruiters from other schools and the hostility of my family. On June 23, 1970, the cameras captured me in the act of signing my name in Dean's presence. The cameras failed to reveal that I was signing not a letter of intent but a napkin.

The next day my parents blasted Coach Smith in an AP story that was carried in newspapers across the country, and suddenly the rift between my parents and me was public.[3] My parents accused Dean of trying to undermine their parental authority and alluded to "valid reasons" for not wanting me to attend North Carolina. Dad described recruiting as a "nasty, dirty business." The same stories carried Mom's vow that I would never attend North Carolina with my parents' blessing. "I do not blame my son," she told the reporters, "he's been brainwashed. I do blame the coach."[4]

Dean was alarmed that the phrase "valid reasons" implied that he had committed recruiting violations; and I was concerned that the situation between Dean and my parents was deteriorating further. Rumors mushroomed that I had visited North Carolina eight times and that a credit card had been furnished to me on these visits. Of course, none of these rumors was true.

Coaches began to snipe at Dean, most behind his back but a few on the record. For example, Jack Kraft, the Villanova coach, leveled the following charge at the press:

> I'm disgusted to be associated with a group—I'm talking about college basketball coaches—who are splitting up families. I'm 100% in agreement that something has to be done in a strict and serious way. This is the worst case of all, when you are splitting people up.[5]

I was still determined to attend North Carolina. At my request Dean traveled to Mansfield on June 27 for a last chance to make peace with my parents, but my parents remained adamantly opposed to Dean and North Carolina.

In July, while I was at the Air Force Academy in Colorado with the Olympic development team, Mom opened a letter purportedly from the president of the "Tar Heel Club," which "confirmed" an alleged arrangement with Dean whereby I would receive cash and credit cards to attend North Carolina. Of course, Dean had never offered me any illegal inducements. Indeed, I would have immediately severed ties with any coach or school that tendered such a proposal. Although the letter was an obvious fraud, I am not certain that Dean totally convinced my parents of this. At about the same time, we received an anonymous letter that accused the radio broadcaster of the North Carolina basketball games of writing pornographic novels under a pseudonym.

In mid-August I toured Europe and the Soviet Union with the Olympic development team, playing exhibition games in Poland, Finland, Estonia, and Russia. Among my teammates were Julius Erving and Dennis Wuycik, a North Carolina player who took every opportunity to extol the virtues of his school. Outside the country and away from the press, a sense of calm settled over me for the first time in months. I belatedly realized I would probably be happy at any of the three schools.

Returning to the United States more committed than ever to the Tar Heels, I was met at the plane by Mom with the sobering news that my father was very sick. Then sixty-five, Dad was misdiagnosed as suffering from chronic bronchitis when he actually was in the early stages of pulmonary fibrosis, an occupational hazard of dentistry in the days before the present filtering and suction devices removed the dangers of inhaling tooth filings. Suddenly I felt enormously guilty over the stress under which we had all been living for the past year.

As a result, I began to weigh more heavily my parents' wishes in the process. I thought then and still believe that my folks were way too hard on Dean Smith, but I knew that they truly wanted what was best for me. My father had never missed a single one of my games, and I realized that the distance to North Carolina was weighing on his mind. Months ago I had ruled out any West Coast schools solely because of their distance from Mansfield. (With the present proliferation of games on TV, including the televising of all North Carolina games, my decision might have been different today. Even from as far away as Mansfield, a devoted parent with a satellite dish could follow his Tar Heel son on cable now.)

Moreover, because I had delayed my decision so long, I was able to judge by late August the success of the three schools in recruiting that year. In high school games, opposing teams frequently had collapsed two and sometimes three players on me, and I wanted to play on a college team with enough strong players and scoring threats to prevent the defense from keying on me. Although North Carolina had signed Bobby Jones, the Tar Heels had not garnered any other blue chip recruits that season (losing Tom Burleson to North Carolina State), and Virginia was even thinner in freshman talent.

In contrast, Lefty had hit the jackpot at Maryland. In his first full year of recruiting, Lefty had landed three high school all-Americans, including a six-foot-nine-inch superprospect from Power Memorial in New York, Len Elmore. I preferred to play forward, but there was a danger at either North Carolina or Virginia that I would be moved to center. With a rebounder like Elmore on my team, I was practically guaranteed of playing forward at Maryland.

Another ingredient in my decision was the proximity of Maryland to Washington, D.C. In my senior year of high school, President Nixon had appointed me as the youngest member ever of the President's Council on Physical Fitness and Sports, and I had been bitten by the political bug early. In his recruiting pitches, Senator Tydings repeatedly stressed the excitement of attending a school only a half hour from the nation's capital; and Lefty shrewdly reminded me that, if I played for the Terps, the president of the United States would be reading of my exploits in *The Washington Post*.

All these factors and more were whirling in my mind in the early morning of September 10, which was registration day at all three schools. An ACC rule required a student to matriculate by September 10 in order to be eligible for basketball that year. Despite my vow to reach a final decision five months before the actual deadline, I was still undecided with only hours to go.

The final day of my recruiting was loaded with intrigue. Coach

Gibson lobbied me till 1 A.M. on the 10th while playing bridge with my parents, and Virginia had stationed a pilot next door to Coach Miller, presumably as a lookout. Dean Smith was in Europe on a basketball tour, but he repeatedly called the house for updates; and an assistant coach from North Carolina was reportedly holed up in a motel a mile from my house. All the while I was packing to leave for school, not knowing where I was going.

By this point the tide had shifted in Maryland's favor because of Dad's illness and Lefty's last-minute appeals. I sensed an unpleasant climax and called Jay in Maryland for help. Coach Gibson blanched when Jay entered the house around midnight, essentially to close the deal for Maryland. I was up the rest of the morning with Dad and Jay, rehashing every shred of information about the three institutions. With Jay ready to drive me to College Park, Maryland, Coach Gibson at hand with a private plane to zip me to Virginia, and reportedly another plane fueled for a ride to North Carolina, I made my decision at the last minute.

On the way out of town, I stopped by Coach Miller's house and knocked on the door. I could tell by the expression on his face that I looked ragged. "Where are you going?" he asked.

"Well, Jay's got my bags locked in his trunk, so I guess I'm off to Maryland," I replied.

At approximately 9 A.M. on September 10, Mom called Coach Gibson with the disappointing news that Jay and I had left for Maryland. Because Dean Smith was still in Europe, I wired a telegram to Chapel Hill that read:

VERY VERY SORRY HOPE YOU UNDERSTAND GOING TO MARYLAND FOR REASONS YOU KNOW.

About a week later, Dean sent me a touching letter that I have kept to this day in which he said that ". . . not being your coach in college after having counted on it has been the greatest disappointment in my career."[6] He also offered the sage advice not to second-guess the decision I had made. Throughout my basketball career and to this day, Dean has always been a perfect gentleman, a good friend to me, and a coach I greatly admire.

For weeks following my enrollment at Maryland, the papers were filled with stories of my recruiting "flip-flop," and my parents and I received lots of negative mail, mostly from North Carolina. A few of the letters contained threats, and some accused me of being a "Momma's boy," which was ironic in light of Mom's preference for Virginia.

Because of the media coverage of my recruiting, a Virginia reporter wrote that I was "one of America's best-known sports figures" even though I had not played a varsity game for the Terrapins.[7] Even *Playboy* ran an exposé of this sad, painful episode in my life.[8]

But I have never regretted my decision and was blessed to accomplish at Maryland all my college dreams (except a national title)—a Rhodes scholarship, all-American honors, a strong premed background, the experience of the Olympics, a job on Capitol Hill, and great contacts across the country.

And it was exhilarating to be courted by the headliners in sports, politics, business, and medicine. I was exposed to figures that most seventeen-year-olds only read about. Still, the negative aspects of my recruiting experience outweighed the positive. There were periods when I was estranged from my parents (and they, from each other), and often I wished I had been left alone to reach a decision. In retrospect I realize how lucky I was to have a family that cared about my decision and how many young athletes truly are cast adrift on their own in a shark-filled sea.

I was also blessed by growing up in a small, isolated community with only one junior high school and one high school. In larger cities, just as college coaches recruit high school players, high school coaches hustle junior high stars to transfer into their districts. In this win-at-all-costs atmosphere, where the mercenary values of professional sports are seeping deeper into the system, recruiters from colleges, high schools, and junior highs have begun to "bird dog" grade schoolers.

For example, when Rashard Griffith was a six-foot-ten-inch eighth grader, he became the object of an intense recruiting war among Chicago high school coaches.[9] He was exposed at the tender age of fourteen to the same high-pressure tactics of recruiters that I experienced at seventeen. With all my advantages of family and community, I was barely able at seventeen to cope with the pressures of recruiting. How can a fourteen-year-old be expected to handle the madness?

With increasing frequency one reads of a high school, such as Evansville Catholic High School in Indiana, being placed on probation for improperly inducing players to transfer.[10] Moreover, the incidence of high school recruiting will likely increase with the passage of "open enrollment" or "choice" legislation that permits students to select their schools. Although I agree with the concept of "choice" for public schools, it is sobering to speculate on the number of students whose choice will turn on the schools' athletic programs.

A recruiter for a major university pointed out: "Everyone looks at college athletics and says, 'Boy, that's a big problem.' But there's at least as big a problem at high schools, especially with the brokering of players. There's a lot of coaches or boosters giving $1,000, even $10,000."[11]

Despite the gravity of the problem, there is little or no regulation of high school recruiting in most jurisdictions. The NCAA has no jurisdiction below the college level, and no other authority enforces high school sports regulation nationwide.[12] Thus, high school recruiting may be even dirtier than its collegiate counterpart.

In 1991 the Washington Metropolitan Athletic Conference became the first area private school league to promulgate recruiting guidelines.[13] In other words, the conference recognized the legitimacy (or perhaps the inevitability) of recruiting athletes for high schools and is attempting to regulate the practice. It is questionable whether a ban on high school recruiting of athletes, even if desirable, is feasible. Nevertheless, Anne Arundel County, which is in my congressional district, took the healthy step in 1988 of including a clause in every high school coach's contract that recruiting an athlete will jeopardize the coach's position.[14]

But overall the message being drilled into our kids is clear and

TANK McNAMARA®   by Jeff Millar & Bill Hinds

dangerous. Athletes are valuable commodities who are hotly re-cruited, flown here and there, greased through their classes, prom-ised everything under the moon, and beamed into our homes by television. Academics are invisible. Superstars sign five-year con-tracts for $20 million. Teachers sign one-year contracts for $20,000. In these circumstances to whom will you listen, your teacher or your coach? Where will you spend your time, in the library or the gym?

Even more destructive are the lessons gleaned by our youth, whether athletes or not, who witness schools at every level and in every region bend or break the rules to produce a winning team. The father of a high school star is offered a cushy job at an auto dealership to lure his son into a new school district. To save the eligibility of the starting center, a test score is altered. An illegal payment is tendered to land a blue chip college pros-pect. In Texas, a former governor lied outright to the NCAA to cover up illegal payments to SMU football players, which were part of a wide-ranging conspiracy to propel SMU out of football obscurity and into the national rankings.[15] The corruption of the present system runs the gamut from the ghetto to the governor's mansion.

As a teenager inside the fishbowl, I naturally focused on the pressures bearing down on the beleaguered recruit. Now, as I approach middle age, I can better appreciate the pressures on coaches, scouts, and recruiters whose jobs hang upon the whims of a seventeen-year-old superstar. It is degrading for a flock of fortysomething headhunters to follow, flatter, and cajole a kid, and it is destructive for the prey to have his ego inflated to a point where it will inevitably be shattered in the coming years.

Bobby Bowden, the successful football coach at Florida State, said that recruiting probably drives more coaches out of football than anything else because of its demands and pressures:

> Coaches spend weeks competing with anywhere from five to 20 universities for the services of 75 top athletes. Each player is a separate contest that a coach must win. When he doesn't sign a great player that he has been trying to recruit over seven months, it gnaws at him as if he'd lost a ball game. Instead of an 11-game season, he is experiencing a 30-game season.[16]

Bowden described his recruiting machine at FSU, which revolves around a recruiting coordinator, a full-time secretary, ten assistant coaches, and five graduate assistants. The cadre of recruiters will screen over seven hundred high school seniors a year, from which seventy-five will be invited for an official visit to the campus in the hope that twenty-five will sign with Florida State.[17]

To remain competitive, other colleges with big-time aspirations must match Florida State's commitment to recruiting blue chip prospects, even if the process costs hundreds of thousands of dollars a year. To indicate the warped values of the system, most Division I schools spend more to recruit athletes than they do to attract top scholars or teachers. There is an "arms race" mentality that compels a school to match or beat its opponents' efforts, even though the expense is guaranteed to exceed the payoff.

The average big-time college sports program spends between $400,000 and $1 million on recruiting, with travel expenses swallowing roughly half of the budget and phone bills of $100,000 for the year.[18]

The temptation to cheat for a hot prospect is overwhelming, as exposés of dirty recruiting have recounted.[19] The Report of the Carnegie Foundation on American College Athletics (often called the "Savage Report") documented the pervasive abuses in inter-collegiate sports in 1929, and its findings are depressingly timely today, more than a half century later.[20]

The NCAA regularly tinkers with the rules of recruitment in myriad ways, such as restricting the number of campus visits or telephone contacts allowed recruiters; but we have fundamental problems with our sports programs that cannot be fixed by tinkering or by focusing only on the college level.

In 1991 the NCAA reduced the number of times a coach can contact a recruit. Before the 1991 measures went into effect, a coach was allowed to contact an athlete off campus fourteen times a year in football and six times in other sports and to visit a high school an unlimited number of times for evaluation during certain periods. At the 1991 convention, however, the number of personal contacts by a school to a recruit was cut to three a year and evaluations to four a year.

But such rules are really cost-cutting measures; and while they were long overdue, they do not meaningfully reform recruiting. Other cost-cutting rules enacted in 1991 restricted the timing and number of telephone calls to recruits; limited the mailing of re-cruiting materials, such as videotapes; reduced the number of official visits to campus a college can offer its class of recruits from eighty-five to seventy in football and from eighteen to fifteen in basketball; and directed the coaches' association to study ways to shorten the recruiting season from four months to three.

These piecemeal changes were welcome but will do little to restore the proper balance between academics and athletics. They will, however, add pages to the already imposing and complicated rule manual of the NCAA. For example, the rules on contacting recruits have changed six times in the last eight years, making it difficult for coaches and recruiters to stay abreast of the amend-ments.[21]

Furthermore, it is unclear how long the 1991 changes will re-main on the books. The ink was barely dry when efforts within the NCAA were at work to increase the number of contacts with a recruit, the number of visits to a recruit's high school, and the duration of spring football practice.[22] And at the 1992 NCAA convention, coaches reversed a cost-cutting measure passed the previous year to reduce the size of full-time football coaching staffs from nine to eight.

Like the IRS, the NCAA has a deep and abiding faith in the proliferation of rules and a fetish for tinkering with peripheral issues. Yet Lefty Driesell insists that "recruiting is more cutthroat now than it was twenty years ago." This is true because the incentives for winning and cheating are even greater now than they were two decades ago and have been largely untouched by the NCAA. The present rules presuppose a healthy balance between athletics and academics in our schools, which simply does not exist. As long as the stakes from athletic success are astronomical, the system will naturally be skewed in favor of athletics at the expense of academics.

There are two general issues in recruiting—how a school can recruit and whom it can recruit. This chapter deals with the former issue; the next chapter, with the latter.

An immediate goal is to bring the recruiting of athletes more in line with the recruiting of scholars. If colleges are truly first and foremost places of learning, there is no justification for allowing extreme and costly measures in sports that are not used in academics.

The circus atmosphere of my recruiting was destructive not only to my family but also to the youngsters who followed in the media the absurd efforts of colleges to land me. No valedictorian was so hotly recruited nor received 1 percent of the press coverage devoted to me, not in 1970 and not today. It is impossible for me to calculate how much Maryland and other colleges spent to recruit me, but several hundred thousand dollars is a conservative estimate—far more, I imagine, than was normally spent back then to recruit a college president or a top professor. That estimate includes the ten trips I took to campuses (and I did not inflate the amount by visiting schools that had no chance with me), the hundreds of trips to Mansfield by coaches and recruiters, the reams of printed materials that deluged me, and the nonstop telephone calls that nearly drove us from our home.

And the topsy-turvy process repeats itself every year. A simple reform would be to forbid off-campus visits to prospective athletes by coaches, recruiters, or anyone connected with the colleges. There is little need today for off-campus recruiting of athletes. With scouting reports, magazines like *SuperPrep,* and now TV coverage, college coaches can evaluate high school players without leaving their offices.

Besides, college recruiting is often a matter of keeping up with the Joneses. "I didn't really need to see Tom McMillen play in high school to know that he was a player," Lefty Driesell admitted, "but I had to be there in case Dean [Smith] and Bill [Gibson] were there."

Worse still, the hoopla over hotshot high school athletes contributes to the myth that sports will bail out a lousy student. It is no wonder that a 1990 survey found that more high school students think their best chance for a college scholarship lies in athletics rather than academics, music, art, or ten other fields.[23] Yet colleges award far more academic scholarships than athletic grants, so this is a serious and dangerous misperception of reality.

The fact that the term *student-athlete* is frequently and loosely aired in our country is telling, because this term is not widely used in Europe. We coined the phrase, which reflects the uneasy coexistence of academics and athletics in our school, a distinctly American phenomenon. We do not hear equivalent terms such as *student-artist* or *student-musician* because art and music do not rival athletics for control of our institutions of learning.

Restoring the proper balance to our institutions calls for fundamental reforms in the incentive structure of college sports, and the NCAA has not demonstrated the heart or stomach for such reforms. Indeed, my first brush with the NCAA suggests that it must be dragged toward real reform.

As a freshman congressman, I was shocked to discover that many of our Division I-A public institutions were graduating fewer than one in three football players and one in four basketball players within five years of their entry into the school.[24] Those raw figures were made available by the NCAA. The NCAA did not, however, release the graduation figures of athletes on an institution-by-institution basis—in order to prevent the embarrassment of schools with shockingly low graduation rates.

I believed that such institutions should be embarrassed publicly, and Senator Bill Bradley and Representative Ed Towns concurred. We believed that a high school recruit needs to know about an institution's commitment to educating its athletes before signing with the school. Recruits are peppered with so many false representations about their likelihood of starting, starring, and catching the eyes of pro scouts. At a minimum, they should be told the truth about the school's record of educating its athletes.

Bradley, Towns, and I joined forces behind the Student Right-to-Know and Campus Security Act (Student Right-to-Know), which requires a school in recruiting an athlete to provide him or her with data on the graduation rates of athletes at the institution. The measure was essentially a consumer information bill, and we expected it to be noncontroversial. We reasoned that if Congress forced airlines to make public their records in achieving on-time arrivals, surely colleges should be required to make available their success at graduating their students in general and their athletes in particular. Our bill was like a surgeon general's warning to schools with poor graduation rates for athletes—WARNING: PLAYING BASKETBALL AT SHOWTIME UNIVERSITY IS HAZARDOUS TO YOUR EDUCATION.

But the NCAA initially fought the bill on the ground that the matter should be handled by the schools without interference from the government. Under the threat of our bill, the NCAA rushed to adopt a watered-down version. Nonetheless, our bill passed in 1990, partly because of Congress's justified skepticism of the NCAA's commitment to publicizing the black sheep in college athletics but also to cover institutions outside the NCAA, such as junior colleges and NAIA members.

We must look anew at the six-foot-eight-inch teenager and see him as more than a ticket to a winning season and short-term job security for a swarm of scouts, recruiters, and coaches, as more than this season's number 14 on our TV screens. Even more important, it is necessary for the teen to look inward and see himself as more than some coach's meal ticket, a transitory image on a TV screen, and a nameless, faceless number who will soon become obsolete.

Athletic fame is as fleeting as a recruiter's puffery (or a politician's campaign promises). Nowhere is the ephemeral nature of sports stardom more poignantly presented than in a poem entitled "To an Athlete Dying Young" by A. E. Housman, which should be required reading for all budding athletes as an antidote to the recruiters' exaggerated claims:

> The time you won your town the race
> We chaired you through the market-place;
> Man and boy stood cheering by,
> And home we brought you shoulder-high.
>
> Today, the road all runners come,
> Shoulder-high we bring you home,
> And set you at your threshold down,
> Townsman of a stiller town.
>
> Smart lad, to slip betimes away
> From fields where glory does not stay,
> And early though the laurel grows
> It withers quicker than the rose.
>
> Eyes the shady night has shut
> Cannot see the record cut,
> And silence sounds no worse than cheers
> After earth has stopped the ears:
>
> Now you will not swell the rout
> Of lads that wore their honors out,
> Runners whom renown outran
> And the name died before the man.
>
> So set, before its echoes fade,
> The fleet foot on the sill of shade,
> And hold to the low lintel up
> The still-defended challenge-cup.
>
> And round that early-laureled head
> Will flock to gaze the strengthless dead,
> And find unwithered on its curls
> The garland briefer than a girl's.[25]

Tragically there are athletes who are unable to read that poem, even after four years of college. Until we can remedy their plight, Bruce Springsteen's "Glory Days" should be required listening for them.[26] It is a poignant ballad of the faded glory of, among others, a star baseball pitcher. In the song Springsteen captures the lament of those who are trapped by past glory, who have suspended their lives in an endless replay of their yesterdays, who have outlived their fame and purpose in life.

Our country cannot afford to surrender the lives, dreams, and futures of the kids who are lured onto the expressway to sports stardom. During their youth their ears will be filled with promises of fame and riches, but the vast majority of them will wind up, like the characters in Springsteen's song, repeating "boring stories of glory days" on the sidelines of life.

Against the slick patter of the recruiters, we must raise our voices to remind the young athletes that the cheering for them will stop soon . . . when they are twenty-five . . . twenty-one . . . eighteen . . . even thirteen. But we must reassure them that life does not end when the cheering dies.

Chapter 3

SOUND MIND

The Primacy of Academic Integrity

SENATOR BILL BRADLEY, Congressman Ed Towns, and I were waiting for Dick Schultz, the executive director of the NCAA. It was
1988, the year after we introduced the Student Right-to-Know
Act, which was fast gaining support in both houses. We wanted
to question Schultz about the NCAA's objections to our measure
and perhaps win him over.

While I waited in Bill's commodious office in the Hart Building,
my mind returned to numerous meetings with him in the distant
and not-so-distant past. Years after meeting him at Bucky Waters's
basketball camp in West Virginia, I had sought his advice about
deferring my entry into the pro draft in order to accept a Rhodes
scholarship. Like Bill, I risked millions by putting my pro career
on hold to attend Oxford; and like him, I never regretted my
decision.

Despite the gravity of our upcoming meeting with Schultz, I
caught myself reminiscing. I joined the Knicks during my second
year in the NBA when Bill was in the final season of a fabled
career that earned him two championship rings and a place in the

Hall of Fame. I also recalled a crucial meeting with Bill in 1985, after I had decided to run for Congress in 1986. Despite my decision, the Washington Bullets were tempting me with a contract for the 1985–1986 season, and I was torn by their offer. I still enjoyed basketball, and the Bullets' proposal was very generous, but I feared that a full season of basketball would hamstring my first campaign. Bill urged me to play the 1985–1986 season in order to maximize my TV exposure and improve my fund-raising opportunities.

I heeded his advice, which again proved correct. My last year in the NBA, which was capped by my being named the NBA Player of the Week in February 1986, proved one of my most successful seasons; and I managed to squeeze out a victory in my maiden campaign for Congress. Fortunately none of my opponents demanded equal time when the game announcers conveniently mentioned my run for Congress.

So I was comfortable to be in Bill's camp on the issue of balancing academics and athletics in our colleges. I was equally comfortable with Ed Towns, a genial, hardworking congressman from New York who had originally conceived the bill. The three of us were convinced that serious problems plagued intercollegiate athletics, and we wanted Schultz's input on the scope of the problems and the NCAA's responses to them.

Finally Schultz arrived with Michael Scott, his lawyer-lobbyist from the high-powered D.C. firm of Squire, Sanders and Dempsey. As charming and smooth as Scott was, I was somewhat troubled by his presence and by Schultz's belief that he needed an attorney at this meeting. Big-name lobbyists do not come cheap in D.C. Later I would learn that Scott's influential firm was paid more than $600,000—almost double its fees from the NCAA in the previous year—in 1987, which not coincidentally was the year the Student Right-to-Know Act was introduced.[1]

Even before the meeting, however, I had been disturbed by the time, effort, and money the NCAA was expending to defeat or alter our bill. After all, weren't we all on the same side? Why shouldn't colleges be forced to publicize the graduation rates of their athletes? Why hadn't the NCAA required them to do so long before we launched our crusade? Why was the NCAA, which enjoys a tax-exempt status to promote education and amateur athletics, fighting our modest bill?

At the outset Bill reminded the NCAA director that, before resorting to legislation, he had tried unsuccessfully to convince the NCAA to release a college-by-college breakdown of graduation rates voluntarily in order to identify the schools with lousy records. "This is a no-brainer," Bill insisted, exhorting the NCAA to show leadership in this area.

Adept at public relations and private negotiations, Schultz replied that, while he personally had no objection to the bill, some of the members of his organization were troubled by congressional interference with intercollegiate athletics. "This will be a big paperwork burden," he complained before raising the "red herring" that the release of graduation rates might violate the Buckley Amendment, which was designed to protect the privacy of individuals, not to cover up the dereliction of institutions. But he quickly dropped this specious defense and moved to another.

Playing to Bill's Princeton roots, Schultz pointed out that the Ivy League schools, because of their tougher academic standards, might be disadvantaged in comparison with schools with lower standards. Bill was unmoved.

During the meeting I became increasingly alarmed by Schultz's consistent attempts to downplay the problems. Several times he defended the status quo with the dubious claim that the graduation rates of athletes among NCAA institutions meet or exceed those of the general student populations at the schools.

The meeting ended in an impasse. There was, however, much more at stake here than our bill. I left the meeting fully convinced that our colleges were compromising their educational missions and that the NCAA was not prepared either to lead the crusade to reform college sports or to follow our lead.

The following year my fears about the NCAA intensified during Schultz's testimony before Congress's Subcommittee on Postsecondary Education. Echoing his defensive attitude during our meeting, the NCAA executive director repeatedly downplayed the problems:

> I take flat issue with those who would characterize the conduct of intercollegiate athletics today as disgraceful, out of control, or worse. In my judgment, intercollegiate athletics in 1989 is under greater "hands on" control by the chief executives of our member institutions and provides greater benefits for more young people— men and women, of whatever ethnic origin or economic circumstance, professional prospect or not—than at any time in this century.[2]

He characterized the NCAA as a "very proactive organization" which was "dealing directly" with the problems of intercollegiate athletics and which had "never been in a better position to control major rules violations."[3]

He resorted three times in his testimony to the claim that the graduation rates of student-athletes were equal to or greater than the rates for the student body as a whole.[4] He capped his speech with the incredible claim that "almost everything occurring in intercollegiate athletics today is exceptionally positive."[5]

But are the pitiful graduation rates of Division I-A football and basketball players exceptionally positive? Is it exceptionally positive that athletes are spending more time on their sports than on attending and preparing for classes? Is it exceptionally positive that a college star can complete four years at an institution of "higher learning" without being able to read at a seventh grade level? Without being able to read at all?

Schultz dismissed the epidemic of rules violations as the misdeeds of a few "rotten apples," claiming that serious problems have usually been the result of one of the following two situations:

> Either a coach has become so powerful that they can circumvent the normal chain of command with the athletic director and the chief executive officer and get involved directly with the governing boards or alumni to create situations that are to their advantage, or the reverse has happened—governing boards or alumni have become so involved that they, in turn, have circumvented that chain

of command and have involved themselves directly with coaches and athletic programs. In either case it has usually been a disaster.[6]

But the claim of parity in graduation rates between student-athletes and the general student population has been thoroughly discredited, and the idea that the serious problems are caused by a few bad apples is a dangerous denial of the systemic nature of the crisis in education and athletics.

Prior to the threat of the Student Right-to-Know Act, the NCAA refused to publish the graduation rates of athletes on an institution-by-institution basis. This would seem to be a surprising stand by the NCAA if, as Schultz claims, the graduation rates of athletes equal or exceed the rates for the student bodies as a whole.

Besides, it is patently unfair to compare, as the NCAA repeatedly does, the graduation rates of athletes on full scholarships with the rates for students who receive little or no financial aid, many of whom are forced to drop out of college for economic reasons.[7] Indeed, one of the tragedies of the present system is that we subsidize too many athletes to masquerade as students while a growing number of real students cannot afford to matriculate at college or to remain there.

The alleged parity in graduation rates between athletes and nonathletes disappears when the former are compared to students who attend colleges full-time for four consecutive years, about 74 percent of whom graduate.[8] "Athletes aren't really graduating at about the same rate as other students," states William Friday, president emeritus of the University of North Carolina and a cochairman of the Knight Commission. "Athletic departments would like you to believe they are, but they aren't."[9]

The General Accounting Office (GAO), which gathers data and performs analyses for the government, prepared a report in 1989 on the academic performance of student-athletes at the request of the House Subcommittee on Postsecondary Education.[10] The GAO confirmed that the graduation rates for student-athletes at the NCAA's 287 Division I schools were higher than the average for all students at the schools; but this finding was reversed when the GAO examined the major revenue-producing sports at Division I-A universities.[11]

Significantly, the graduation rates of men's basketball and football players at Division I-A schools fell below those for all students at these institutions. While 55 percent of all students graduated within five years at Division I-A schools, only 38 percent of the men's basketball players and 45 percent of the football players did.[12]

The GAO's findings were buttressed by an important survey of 262 Division I colleges that was compiled by *The Chronicle of Higher Education* and published in 1991, a year before the Student Right-to-Know Act will require such disclosures on an annual basis.[13] The survey revealed for each reporting institution the percentage of freshmen in 1984, both athletes and nonathletes, who had received their degrees within five years. Ironically the report was released only days before the semifinal match in the 1991 basketball tourney in which Duke, which graduated over 96 percent of its male athletes, upset UNLV, which graduated about 20 percent of its male athletes.[14]

While *The Chronicle* concluded that overall the graduation rates of recruited athletes in Division I colleges exceeded those of nonathletes, male basketball and football players at Division I-A schools graduated at lower rates than nonathletes or even than other athletes in Division I-A. Indeed, the graduation rates of male basketball players trailed all other groups of students in every category of institution.[15] Thus, the major problem in balancing academics and athletics surfaces, not surprisingly, in the big money sports at the most competitive colleges.

But the NCAA and many of its member institutions often manipulate (and thereby inflate) the graduation rates of athletes by adjusting the figures to, for example, subtract athletes who left the school in good academic standing and those who completed their athletic eligibility but were still enrolled in the school. Such adjustments, which are made only for athletes, are misleading and generally inflate their graduation rates.[16] And the overall graduation rates of Division I athletes are skewed upward by more than a dozen private schools, including the Ivy League universities, with large athletic programs and very high graduation rates for athletes.[17]

One of the most depressing aspects of the GAO report and the *Chronicle* survey was the large number of Division I schools with graduation rates falling below 50 percent or even 25 percent.[18] Athletes at more than one hundred Division I schools graduated at a lower rate than the nonathletes at their schools, and more than fifty of the reporting institutions graduated less than a third of their athletes within five years.[19] It is true that the problems are greatest in Division I-A football and basketball, which represent only a minority of college athletes; but the gladiators of Division I football and basketball are the most visible sports figures in college athletics. Their exploits are beamed into millions of living rooms, heralded in headlines, and embellished in countless conversations at work and school. To tens of millions of sports-addicted fans, young and old, Division I football and basketball are the essence of college athletics.

It is important to determine when and under what circumstances athletes and nonathletes drop out of college. There is evidence that white student-athletes who leave school tend to do so in the first or second year whereas black student-athletes are as likely to drop out in the third or fourth year as the first and second.[20] According to Richard Lapchick, the director of Northeastern University's Center for the Study of Sport in Society, black athletes may be so far from a diploma upon the exhaustion of their athletic eligibility that they do not bother to go on.[21]

Finally, any defense based upon graduation rates underestimates the ingenuity of athletic departments in fashioning "gimme" courses and degrees for their coddled athletes, the sole purpose of which is to ensure their eligibility for four or five years. And the so-called academic assistance programs are often tailored and run by the athletic department to maintain eligibility, not ensure a sound education.

At the federal criminal trial of sports agents Norby Walters and Lloyd Bloom, two former University of Iowa football players testified that they had been directed by their coaches into such bogus courses as billiards, watercolor painting, and recreational leisure.[22] At Creighton University, Kevin Ross was enrolled in Theory of Basketball, Theory of Track and Field, Theory of Football, Ceramics, and Marksmanship.[23]

Late night talk show host David Letterman brought down the house one night when he aired one of his trademark "top ten" lists. This one revealed the following top ten courses for athletes at SMU, which had recently drawn the NCAA's "death penalty":

10. Subtraction: Addition's Tricky Pal
 9. The First 30 Pages of *A Tale of Two Cities:* Foundation of a Classic
 8. Sandwich-making (final project required)
 7. Alumni-owned Hotels, Restaurants and Car Dealerships: The Interlocking Economy
 6. Pre-Law Seminar: Age of Consent in the 50 States
 5. The Denny's Menu: Recent Discoveries
 4. The Bunny and the Wolf: Hand Shadow Workshops
 3. Draw Winky
 2. From *First Love* to *Looker:* The Films in Which Susan Dey Appears Naked
 1. The Poetry of Hank Stram[24]

Many college presidents are engaged in a game of cat-and-mouse with their athletic departments. The cagey coaches invent "hideaway" courses for their stars; and by the time the president has flushed out those courses, the coaches have fashioned new hiding places. The NCAA has no rule proscribing the creation of phony courses and degrees for athletes, which is far more destructive of the institution than the selling of a few complimentary tickets or the other minutiae that dominate the NCAA's enforcement program.

A 1990 report by the United States Department of Education highlights the issue:

[C]ollege varsity athletes, particularly football and basketball players, may complete bachelor's degrees at a respectable rate, but it takes them longer to do so than other groups, their grades are lower, and their curricula are, to put it mildly, less demanding along the way.[25]

Sadly, a college degree may merely reflect the ability of the athletic department to outwit the college president and the public. A recent study of former varsity athletes found that, a decade after they had left school, they were the least likely of any group to believe that their higher education was relevant to their work. They were also the only group to claim to work less with ideas than with people and paper.[26] Because the global economy is increasingly dominated by ideas and information, ex-athletes may be positioned to slip farther behind their peers, with or without a degree.

In any event, the issue is too complex to be reduced solely to graduation rates, which are not conclusive either way. A high graduation rate does not by itself prove that athletes are receiving a sound education; and conversely, a low graduation rate does not automatically condemn a school, because different institutions have different missions.

When Duke upset UNLV in the basketball semifinals in 1991, much was made by the press of the victory of the scholar-athletes over the semipros.[27] But a flat comparison between the two schools is unfair because Duke is a private, residential school for the privileged and well prepared, with a graduation rate for all students of about 92 percent, while UNLV is a commuter college with a graduation rate for all students of about 20 percent.[28]

In assessing the graduation rates of schools, taking a snapshot of a single year (as *The Chronicle* did) is less valuable than calculating a rolling average over several years (as the Student Right-to-Know Act will require); and with more part-time students forced to work while in school, it may be more meaningful to examine graduation rates six or even seven years after matriculation.[29] The key issues are the comparison of athletes and non-athletes at a school in academic performance and the trend in graduation rates for both groups over time.

Raising graduation rates will be no panacea, especially if this is accomplished by cheapening degrees until they are practically meaningless. We need workers with real skills, not phony degrees. The crux of our national educational crisis is that we have been too undemanding in the classroom not only of our athletes but of all students throughout the system, and sports has been used as an excuse to drop the standards even lower for an athletically gifted few. This is a systemic problem that demands a systemic cure. It will not be solved by focusing only on colleges, and it certainly will not be tackled by the NCAA.

The gravity of the crisis surfaced in the testimony of another witness before a Senate subcommittee in the same year that Schultz testified—football great Dexter Manley. On and off the football field, Manley is hard hitting, brash, colorful, and controversial. Formerly a star defensive end for the Washington Redskins, Manley played football for Oklahoma State University from 1977 to 1981. He was ostensibly a student for four years as well.

Manley somberly testified that, despite sixteen years of formal schooling, he was functionally illiterate. He could not follow the general practice of submitting a written statement to the subcommittee because he could neither read nor write.

Manley took a courageous step in testifying publicly that he was illiterate. Unfortunately his courage was not matched by the administration of his alma mater. In the wake of Manley's dramatic revelation, John Campbell, the president of OSU, pledged to reform the athletic program to prevent the recurrence of such a tragedy, appointing a blue ribbon panel to tackle the problem. Less than a year later, however, Campbell began to backtrack by seeking the reinstatement of seven football players who had flunked out of his college.

And Campbell's defense of OSU during the Manley affair reeks of cynicism:

> There would be those who would argue that Dexter Manley got exactly what he wanted out of OSU. He was able to develop his athletic skills and ability, he was noticed by the pros, he got a pro contract. So maybe we did him a favor by letting him go through the program.[30]

This is a bulletin for John Campbell—you did not do Dexter Manley a favor by accepting him when he was not prepared for college, by allowing him to coast through four years at your school without learning to read or write, by paying him little more than room and board while he filled your stadium and coffers, and by allowing him to masquerade as a student-athlete. You certainly did no favors for Manley's many teammates who never made the pros and, thus, learned sooner than Manley (but still perhaps too late) that the real world is a tough place for the undereducated.

The word for what you did to Dexter Manley, President Campbell, is not *favor* but *exploitation*.

Just as the college president and faculty performed no favors for Dexter Manley, neither did his high school principal and teachers, nor the faculty and administration of his junior high school. Finally, the NCAA certainly does no service to Manley and his colleagues by attempting to cover up the crisis beneath a mountain of meaningless and misleading statistics on graduation rates.

There are no statistics on the number of athletes who enter and leave high school or college unable to read or write, but Manley is not alone. The U.S. Department of Education reports that 25 to 30 percent of high school senior football and basketball players leave high school functionally illiterate.[31]

Andre Hayes, a football player for the University of Washington in the late 1980s, recalled that one of his teammates could not complete an application to rent a house. "I was wondering how this guy was getting through his classes," Hayes remarked.[32]

At some institutions struggling athletes receive the special dispensation of having their exams read aloud to them and of responding orally because they are too deficient in reading and writing skills to digest the questions on their own and prepare written answers, as their classmates are required to do.

I can recall a telling comment by one of my teammates on the Atlanta Hawks who, like Dexter Manley, had spent four years in a highly regarded college. On a flight from Atlanta to Seattle for a game, the puzzled athlete turned to me to ask, "You mean that Washington is a state as well as a city?" Evidently, geography was not a required course at his college, high school, junior high, or grade school—at least not for star athletes.

In 1991 I flew on a commercial flight with boxer Mike Tyson and his entourage several months before his rape indictment. While I waded through reams of reading material compiled by my staff, Tyson and his buddies wasted the hours on the plane playing cards and making calls. The scene took me back to the hundreds of basketball trips I had taken in the pros and in college, during which many of my teammates had wasted thousands of hours playing cards instead of reading or studying.

Schultz's Pollyannaish statements on intercollegiate athletics go a long way toward explaining the NCAA's abandonment of its charge in article two of its own constitution "[t]o promote and develop educational leadership and to encourage our members to adopt eligibility rules to comply with satisfactory standards of scholarship."

After serving with Schultz on the Knight Commission, I can attest that he is an honorable man of good intentions, but good intentions and well-turned phrases will not effect true reform. As much as Schultz might want to prod the NCAA, he is constrained to incremental improvements because the NCAA is essentially a trade association, and a large component of the job of the executive director is to wring the most revenue for his trade members.

The NCAA was not originally established to deal with the academic integrity of our colleges. Instead, it was created to make college football safer for the players, following a wave of sports-related deaths and injuries around the turn of the century, which peaked in 1905 with eighteen football-related deaths. President Teddy Roosevelt, who was a robust sportsman and avid competitor, was outraged by the carnage and threatened to abolish the sport unless college presidents addressed the safety crisis.

Today our universities face a crisis just as devastating as those deaths and injuries. Too many of our athletes are leaving college handicapped like Dexter Manley. Too many of our students, whether athletes or not, limp away from college without the proper training and education to compete in the world marketplace. Without a sound education, a person is crippled for life, as surely as the athlete who has been paralyzed by a blow.

The myths of the student-athlete and of sports stardom are mutually reinforcing. Only by deluding themselves that college athletes are receiving a valuable education in return for their sweat equity can the administration, the boosters, and the fans deny that the athletes are being exploited by the system, trading away their futures for a few seasons in the sun. Likewise, the athlete must lie to himself about his prospects of making the pros in order to quell his uneasiness about facing the future without a true education.

The crisis in American education did not begin in the athletic departments, and it will not end there. Nonetheless, the sports machinery in our schools has contributed greatly to the problem. The Carnegie Report recognized this sad fact when it reported in 1929:

> [A]t no point in the educational process has commercialism in college athletics wrought more mischief than in its effect upon the American undergraduate. And the distressing fact is that the college, the Fostering Mother, has permitted and even encouraged it to do these things in the name of education.[33]

Even if the NCAA persists in wearing Rose Bowl–colored glasses, most college presidents are painfully aware of the extent to which the obsession with sports has undermined the educational aims of their institutions; and so is the public. In a 1989 survey of college presidents, academic deans, and admissions directors, more than 85 percent of the respondents said that the "pressure for success and for financial rewards in intercollegiate sports today has reached a level where it is interfering with the prime educational mission of America's colleges and universities." Only 10 percent of the college administrators disagreed, with a few ostriches expressing no opinion.[34]

In the same year, a Harris poll of public opinion revealed that the vast majority of Americans and even self-described sports fans believed that college athletics had "gotten out of control." Indeed, 77 percent of those surveyed agreed that sports scandals and the colleges' pursuit of money through sports "have undermined the traditional role of universities as places where young people learn ethics and integrity."[35]

The enterprise of big-time, big-buck college sports is not, as the NCAA preaches, a tiny wart on an otherwise healthy organism; it is a malignant growth on a diseased body. Under the right circumstances, sports and other extracurricular activities can round out a person's education and better prepare him for life; but sports are a luxury not a right, whether for the student or the school. Before indulging in any extracurricular activities, a student should be required to demonstrate his proficiency in the classroom. He must not be allowed to punt in the classroom while punting on the football field. It is vastly more important for a young person to learn to compete in the world marketplace for a lifetime than to be drilled to compete on the court for four years.

The zeal of our schools for sports is unmatched by any other country in the world. No other nation has erected a national, tiered network of semiprofessional sporting franchises on its college campuses that approaches the American model in scope and sophistication. But we are falling behind our competitors on the scorecards that truly matter, despite massive expenditures on higher education. Each year the United States invests $160 billion on higher education, more per student than any country in the world except Denmark; and almost half of this money comes from the federal, state, and local governments.[36]

Yet, of Americans between the ages of twenty-one and twenty-five with only a high school degree, less than 60 percent read at an eleventh-grade level; and of those with a college degree, only four-fifths read at an eleventh-grade level.[37] Perhaps because of the dubious value of many diplomas, most of our students do not bother to pocket one. The attrition rate among college students is staggering. Of entering freshmen at four-year colleges, only 41 percent will collect a bachelor's degree after six years.[38]

Low standards in high schools and colleges feed off each other.

Too many high school students will do only the minimum to get into one of the thirty-six hundred colleges and universities in this country, most of which are so desperate to survive that they willingly compromise their academic standards to enroll more bodies. The colleges are being forced to recruit from among high school students who average an hour of homework a day, far less time than they spend before the television.[39] This spells disaster for the present and future needs of our country for an educated work force.

Much of our reform effort is concentrated on the top tier—the colleges. But our colleges are often teaching what students should have learned in high school; our high schools are dwelling on lessons that should have been mastered in junior high; our junior highs are focusing on grade school material; and grade schools are sometimes little more than day care drop-offs. About two-thirds of college faculty members believe that their schools are increasingly teaching what students should have learned in high school.[40]

If our standards are too low at one level, standards inevitably suffer at all levels. Likewise, if colleges persist in compromising their educational function in order to attain sports superiority, the secondary schools will follow their lead. If college athletics sells itself as a stepping-stone to the pros, high school athletics becomes merely a stepping-stone to college athletics.

Recognizing the need for systemic reform, the Knight Commission devoted several paragraphs of its 1991 report to the secondary schools. Even though the mandate of the Knight Commission was intercollegiate athletics, we knew that we could not ignore the related problems in our high schools.

The admission by a university of a youngster solely to play ball without any hope, chance, or prayer that the athlete can perform college-level work represents a failure on the part of the college, the recruit, his family, his high school, junior high, and grade school. Every time a college accepts an athlete with a seventh grade level of reading and comprehension, a message is hammered into the impressionable minds of scores of youngsters who are debating whether to spend an hour in the library or on the courts.

The message is that the rules of academia do not apply to sports stars. Nor do the rules of admission. Nor the rules of class attendance and course requirements. Not even the rules governing test scores and grades.

Far too many recruited athletes, whether prepared for college or not, are not committed to their roles as students. Iowa State football coach Jim Walden candidly admitted that "Not more than 20 percent of the football players go to college for an education. And that may be a high figure. That leaves at least 80 percent who I believe are there because 'they said I could play football.' "[41]

Not too many years ago my alma mater outdueled hundreds of other colleges for Moses Malone's signature on a letter of intent. Ultimately Moses decided not to attend Maryland, going straight to the pros from high school. But the point is that Maryland and hundreds of other colleges were salivating at the prospect of landing him despite the consensus that he was not ready for college-level classes. He was ready for the pros, as his great career has demonstrated, but he had not been prepared for college. Moses wisely rejected the charade that he was a student-athlete, but I shudder to think of the message that was conveyed to our youth.

The standards in our schools are so low already that we cannot afford to relax them to coddle athletes. Instead, we must raise the standards of our schools at every level. It is not enough for Harvard grads to compete successfully against Yalies or for Maryland alums to square off against Virginia grads. Our graduates are competing against the Japanese, Germans, and Koreans in trade battles that will become fiercer over time. Just as competition in sports is now worldwide, competition in every other field is global as well.

We cannot afford to compromise the integrity and mission of our institutions of higher learning by converting them into "profit centers" in the sports-entertainment field. Our schools are failing miserably in their primary tasks and have forfeited much of their credibility and good will by chasing after sports dollars. By doing so, they jeopardize the public support of higher education, which is already wavering.

With the collaboration of the NCAA, colleges are exploiting their athletes in at least three ways. First, universities are knowingly and willfully accepting athletes who are not ready for college. Second, the institutions are "baiting" the athletes with grants that are subject to review and withdrawal every year. Finally, even those athletes who are capable of performing college-level work are often prevented from doing so by the unreasonable demands placed upon them by the athletic departments.

Colleges are courting disaster unless they change the image of the scholarship athlete as a gladiator who is trotted out to entertain the masses for four years and then thrown to the lions. Colleges ought not admit any student who does not have a reasonable chance of performing college-level work; and once a student is admitted, whether he is an athlete or not, the school should provide the necessary support services, such as tutors and counselors. Such services are especially important to minority students at predominantly white institutions, who feel isolated.

As an important step in demonstrating that universities treat scholarship athletes as more than entertainment fodder, more than seventy colleges have joined the National Consortium for Academics and Sports, which requires the schools to pick up the tab for any former scholarship athlete in a revenue sport who did not obtain a degree. Under this program former college athletes have ten years to return to their campuses, tuition-free, to work toward a degree; and in return the ex-athletes agree to participate in outreach programs, lecturing at local schools on the importance of education. More than two thousand former college athletes have returned to campuses under this program since 1985.[42]

Tragically, the NCAA has failed for decades to protect the athletes from pressures that have relegated them to the status of second-class or even third-class students. Consider the justification of the president of Oklahoma State University for his efforts to reinstate the seven football players who had flunked out of his college. "These students are viewing films, lifting weights, running and practicing for 30 to 40 hours a week during the fall semester,"

President Campbell rationalized. "We're asking a lot of them, and I think we owe them something."[43]

Campbell's reasoning is a telling, if unwitting, indictment of big-time college sports. Because the sport is exacting thirty to forty hours a week of the collegian's time, the college president encourages the school to lower its academic standards to accommodate the beleaguered athlete. Did it ever cross Campbell's mind that the problem was not with the academic standards but with the unreasonable demands placed upon the athletes?

In fairness to Campbell, in this respect OSU is apparently the norm. A recent study by the American Institute for Research (AIR) found that college football and basketball players devoted about thirty hours a week to their sports during the season, which was more time than they spent preparing for and attending classes. In the same study the athletes reported missing about two classes a week during their seasons.[44]

The AIR study was a shocking and revealing confirmation that college players are semipro athletes first and students only as an afterthought. Thirty to forty hours a week is a full-time job. Even the best students could barely struggle through college if forced to hold down a full-time job, and athletes have not historically been the strongest students. Moreover, after devoting thirty plus hours a week to their sports, athletes are often so exhausted that they can barely pry open their eyes, much less cram for tomorrow's classes.

Equally revealing was the NCAA's reaction to the AIR study. At its 1991 convention the NCAA passed a measure that limited the time an athlete was required to spend on his sport to twenty hours a week, with at least one day off each week. The limit was packaged, pushed, and passed by the college presidents at the convention in a good faith effort to assist the athletes. Unfortunately, I fear that the measure will be more honored in the breach than the observance, especially in light of its large loophole—the rule allows athletes to spend as much "voluntary" time on their sports as they want, including some activities under their coaches' supervision. The line between "voluntary" and "involuntary" will inevitably be blurred.[45]

When I played for Maryland, I usually trained by myself during the off-season and largely controlled my own schedule, much to Lefty Driesell's chagrin. He often chided me for not training more often with my teammates. Yet, regardless of when and where I was training, Lefty was aware of every second that I (and each of my teammates) was practicing. Through some mysterious sixth sense, he just knew this.

Would the twenty-hour rule have protected me from the grind of the season? Would it have spared me the countless all-nighters, the weekend cram sessions, and the long nights during which I nodded off with an open book for a pillow?

I doubt it, just as I doubt the twenty-hour rule, however well intentioned, will materially improve the college athlete's academic performance. The time limit reflects the NCAA's fetish with rules. Rather than address the fundamental issue of the incentive structure underlying college sports, the 1991 convention adopted a series of "fringe" rules, such as the twenty-hour limit, which exacerbate the complexity of the NCAA manual and will be difficult (if not impossible) to enforce. How does the NCAA police the twenty-hour rule, and how does the NCAA treat the college athlete who practices on his own? Is the rule fair to the outstanding swimmer with good grades who wants to practice more than twenty hours a week? If there is widespread cheating on the time rule, as is likely, the NCAA will encounter in the future even thornier enforcement problems and greater disrespect for its byzantine rules. As the rule book thickens, the already awesome powers of the organization grow. If every school is cheating on the time constraints, the NCAA will have the power of life and death over every program.

Rather than achieving its intended goal of relieving the pressures on college athletes, the desperate, draconian twenty-hour rule is likely to become a cosmetic contrivance for schools that continue to recruit athletes who cannot perform academically.

There are a number of other reforms that should be enacted. The NCAA should shorten the basketball season (which currently runs from October to April) by a month and eliminate spring football practice entirely. Most important, freshmen should be ineligible for both football and basketball.

When I entered college in 1970, freshmen were ineligible for varsity sports, and I benefited greatly from having a year to establish myself as a student at Maryland, earning almost a 4.0 grade-point average. Our freshman team played sixteen games, mostly with schools close to our campus. In contrast, the varsity played more than thirty games, many involving long travel.

Throughout my college career, I put academics first. Because I was a chemistry major with mandatory laboratories in the afternoon, I consistently arrived late for basketball practice. I am sure that Lefty Driesell, my fiery coach, would have preferred for me to arrive on time, but he never belittled or punished me for my priorities. To the contrary, he was proud of my academic accomplishments.

If Lefty had pressured me to miss my chemistry labs in order to make practices or meetings, I hope that I would have had the courage and wisdom of Robert Smith, who quit the Ohio State football team in 1991, claiming his coaches elevated athletics over academics. A sophomore premed student, Smith had enjoyed a tremendous freshman year at Ohio State, averaging 6.4 yards a carry and shattering Heisman Trophy winner Archie Griffin's eighteen-year-old freshman rushing record.[46] "I questioned the importance of what I was doing relative to my larger goals in life," Smith explained in hanging up his cleats.[47]

In 1972 the NCAA changed its rules to allow freshmen to play varsity ball; and during my junior year, I played with an outstanding freshman guard, John Lucas. Although he was without question athletically ready for varsity ball, Lucas was probably not prepared educationally or emotionally for the pressures and stresses; and I often wonder if he was harmed by being dropped into the pressure cooker of big-time college sports too young. What difference might that extra year have made not only to his adjustment to college but also to his NBA career, which was handicapped by drugs?

Turning back the clock to make freshmen ineligible for varsity sports is no cure-all. For one thing, it will not prevent outlaw colleges from stockpiling athletes who fall short of the academic standards and using their freshmen years to make them eligible, by hook or crook. Because outlaw schools will invariably twist the rules to their advantage, a vigilant press is necessary to shed light on the newest tricks and evasions of the trade.

But any serious move to raise the academic standards of our colleges, and especially those of athletes, threatens the sweetheart deals between the universities and the pros and between the NCAA and the TV networks. Because of the NCAA's overriding fear of diminishing its "product" if star players are ruled ineligible, it will be a drag on any true reform. Preoccupied with generating fat TV contracts, the NCAA is more interested in PR victories than in improving the plight of overburdened, exploited athletes. To the NCAA, Nielsen ratings are more important than GPAs.

The time is past for piecemeal, reactive measures. Children should not be taught that success at sports is a substitute for success in the classroom. Instead, they should learn that success in the classroom is a precondition for participating in sports or other extracurricular activities.

If we have the confidence to challenge our children academically, they will meet the test, as has been demonstrated by the success of "no pass–no play" on the high school level and Proposition 48 on the college level.

In 1985, under the leadership of former Governor Mark White and billionaire Ross Perot, Texas became the first state to pass a comprehensive no pass–no play rule, which required a high school student to pass every class to be eligible for extracurricular activities. In the "football crazy" Lone Star state, the measure was highly controversial.

There were dire predictions that entire squads would be decimated; and at the end of Texas's first grading period under no pass–no play, almost 20 percent of football and basketball players were deemed ineligible. By the next grading period, however, most of the affected student-athletes had regained their eligibility. Furthermore, the opponents of no pass–no play had predicted that flunking players would drop out in droves, but this prediction also proved unfounded. Instead, student-athletes worked harder in the classroom and received fewer failing grades.[48] Thus, higher standards in Texas resulted in improved grades as students, teachers, and coaches rallied to meet the challenge.[49]

Unfortunately, only about fourteen states enacted extracurricular eligibility standards in the last decade, and almost 80 percent of the nation's sixteen thousand school districts were without such standards in 1990.[50] Thus, many high school students are still receiving the message that brawn is more important than brains. And both Mark White, the Democratic governor who spearheaded the Texas legislation in 1985, and Tom Luce, the Republican attorney for Ross Perot, who labored tirelessly for the measure, paid a heavy political price for their support of school reform. A year after the enactment of no pass–no play, White was defeated in his reelection bid by Bill Clements, who ironically was revealed after the election to have participated in the cover-up of illicit payments to SMU football players, which led to the NCAA's imposition of the "death penalty" on the football program at that institution. Four years later Luce lost in the GOP gubernatorial primary to Clayton Williams, a self-described "Bubba."

In high school I was fortunate to have been challenged academically by my parents and my coach, Rich Miller, who was also my chemistry teacher. Rich was a tough taskmaster on the court and in the lab; and he inspired me to major in chemistry, which is not an easy curriculum for a basketball player or anyone else.

By and large, we are not challenging our kids, and especially our athletes, today. A recent survey revealed that, in most high school districts, a student is eligible to play sports if he manages a grade point average of between 1.3 and 1.7, and makes a passing grade of D minus or higher in four courses during the grading period. Significantly, the illiteracy rate for high school football and basketball players is estimated at 25 to 30 percent, which is twice the national average for seniors.[51]

Impressed with Texas's initiative and the beneficial results of no pass–no play in other states, Ed Towns and I have again teamed up to introduce a reform bill—the Student Incentive (or STUDI) Act, which encourages school districts to adopt no pass–no play by dangling a carrot before them. If they insist that student-athletes maintain a C average (2.0 on a 4.0 scale) in core courses, school districts will receive a 10 percent increase in federal Chapter 1 aid to be targeted toward academically deficient students, including disadvantaged athletes, and distributed according to the number of students from low-income families in a district.

Unfortunately, in 1991 Anne Arundel County (which is in my congressional district) defeated the 2.0 requirement for participation in extracurricular activities, retaining its 1.6 standard. If the STUDI bill were passed and if Anne Arundel accepted the 2.0 standard, it would receive approximately $420,000 a year in additional Chapter 1 funds.

The theory behind the STUDI bill is simple—raise the hurdle for high school students and help those who have trouble with the hurdle (with special provisions and exceptions made for the learning-disabled child). Surely if Congress can strong-arm states to change their drinking ages by withholding highway funds, it can encourage states to strengthen their academic requirements by dangling funds before them.

While new academic standards should allow for an adjustment period by the student, we cannot afford to wait until athletes reach college or even high school. The surest way to improve the academic success of college athletes is to upgrade the academic performance of high school athletes.

A recent study by the Department of Education confirmed that varsity college athletes, particularly in football and basketball, entered college with weak academic backgrounds; they had taken more trade and business courses than their high school peers and were ranked lower in their classes.[52]

Through the STUDI Act, we can integrate the standards in high schools with those in colleges, such as Proposition 48. If the STUDI bill is enacted and followed, Proposition 48 will not be such a high hurdle for so many athletes. Ed and I are not deluding ourselves into believing that the battle over our STUDI bill will be quick or easy. The history of attempts to raise academic standards in high school and college shatters any such delusion. Since Proposition 48 was passed at the NCAA convention in 1983, it has been assailed as elitist and racist—the same charges that are being leveled against the STUDI Act.

Under Proposition 48, an athlete who fails (1) to score either a 700 (out of a possible 1,600) on the Scholastic Aptitude Test (SAT), or a 15 (out of 36) on the American College Test (ACT); and (2) to earn a 2.0 grade point average in a core curriculum is ineligible as a freshman and has only three years of eligibility remaining. A "partial qualifier"—an athlete who satisfies one of the two requirements—can receive an athletic scholarship as a freshman but not play or practice with the team that year.

Opponents of Proposition 48 were outraged by the use of standardized tests, which probably do contain cultural and racial biases. Although I share their concern about the fairness of these tests (and never tested particularly well myself), it is important to realize that the cut-off scores are very low. A student starts the SAT with a score of 400 simply for signing his name two times and really needs to earn only 300 points to meet Proposition 48. And a combined score of 700 would typically place the aspirant in the bottom 10 percent in the verbal portion of the SAT and the bottom 33 percent in math.[53]

Proposition 48 is neither antiblack nor antipoor. Athletes and their secondary schools have to be shaken from the cynical belief that a scholarship is really an athleticship. While the opponents of Proposition 48 concentrate on the plight of a handful of college athletes, many of whom are viciously exploited by the institutions, its proponents focus on the vast majority of poor youths who are the natural victims of the myth of sports stardom. Most black eighteen-year-olds are not receiving athletic scholarships, and most blacks on athletic grants are leaving college without a diploma or a pro contract. Although 12 percent of the U.S. population is black, black students represent only 4 percent of undergraduates in Division I schools; nonetheless, 37 percent of Division I football players and 56 percent of Division I basketball players are black.[54] Moreover, only about 26 percent of black student-athletes at Division I schools graduate within five years, about half the graduation rate of white student-athletes.[55] Justifiably outraged by this cynical system, Ed Towns declared that "it is simply no longer acceptable for athletes—and particularly black athletes—to be used up as sports commodities and then discarded when their eligibility is over."[56]

With the fate of Proposition 48 in the balance, Coach Joe Paterno of Penn State delivered an eloquent defense at the 1983 convention:

> I am really surprised that so many black educators have gotten up here and kind of sold their young people down the river. You have sold them short. I think you have underestimated what great competitors the young black people are today in all areas, football, basketball, athletics and other areas. If it takes 700 in the SAT to compete, and we give them time to be prepared, they will be prepared.
>
> . . . .
>
> We have raped a generation-and-a-half of young black athletes. We have taken kids and sold them on bouncing a ball and running with the football and that being able to do certain things athletically was going to be an end in itself. We cannot afford to do that to another generation. We cannot afford to have kids come into our institutions and not be prepared to take advantage of what the great education institutions in this country can do for them.
>
> . . . .
>
> I, for one, feel that unless we start to create some challenges for our young people, to give them some idea of what can be available to them as human beings and what kind of contribution they could make to themselves and to their families and to their race in this country, they are going to be people that when the athletic activity is over are not going to be ready to make a contribution in another world.[57]

The debate over Proposition 48 was still simmering when Proposition 42, which passed by a narrow margin at the 1989 convention, fanned the flames. Proposition 42 eliminated the partial qualifiers by requiring that a person pass both requirements of Proposition 48 to be eligible for financial aid.

The battle lines were drawn again, with Temple basketball coach

John Chaney branding the measure as "racist" and arguing that the NCAA had no role to play in academic matters.[58] Even more earthshaking was the boycott by Georgetown's John Thompson of two of his team's regular season games to protest Proposition 42. Amid massive media coverage and to the applause of his players and hometown fans, Thompson stormed from the Capital Centre in Landover, Maryland, where I had played so many games for the Bullets. In doing so, he delivered a dangerous message to the youth of this country that even the minimal standards of Propositions 42 and 48 were too high for them.

Although I am a proponent of Propositions 42 and 48, I can appreciate the frustrations of Chaney and Thompson with a system that fails to challenge kids until they are seventeen and then hits them with a seemingly insurmountable roadblock to college. There is a racist overtone to our failure to challenge kids, especially minorities, much earlier in their schooling.

Still, it is important to clarify what Propositions 42 and 48 do not do. The two regulations merely recognize, as Bobby Knight and others have pointed out, that college is not right for everyone.[59] The rules do not prevent an athletically gifted but educationally impaired youth from bettering himself at a community college or a junior college. Nor do they discourage schools from establishing affirmative action programs unconnected with their sports teams. Indeed, it is absurd for schools to lavish money on athletes who are not ready for college when the same funds could be channeled to scholarships for minority applicants who have demonstrated their capability of handling college work.

Most important, the propositions have not driven minorities from college sports, as the detractors feared. During the debate over Proposition 48, there were grave predictions that it would banish great numbers of blacks from college sports and erect a kind of "apartheid."[60] But athletes of all colors have risen to the challenge of the academic requirements, as Coach Paterno predicted they would.

Indeed, the percentage of blacks among athletes at Division I schools is virtually unchanged since the enactment of Proposition 48 (24 percent in 1985 and 23 percent in 1990).[61] About six hundred Proposition 48 students (approximately 6 percent of all scholarship athletes) have entered Division I schools every year since the passage of Proposition 48.[62]

The NCAA is currently conducting a five-year study of Proposition 48, which went into effect in 1986, to gain a better reading of its impact. While the long-range effects of the rule are still uncertain, the preliminary results are promising and indicate that higher standards are improving the academic performance of athletes of all colors.[63]

There is nothing sacrosanct about the precise language of Propositions 42 and 48, and both may need to be fine-tuned and perhaps toughened.[64] For example, at the 1992 NCAA convention, the Presidents Commission pushed through tighter academic standards for scholarship athletes, in terms of both initial and continuing eligibility, by raising the required grade point average to 2.5 in thirteen core courses (instead of the prior requirement of 2.0 in eleven core courses).

Perhaps even more important was the tightening of the "satisfactory progress" rule for continuing eligibility by requiring an athlete to complete 25 percent of the courses in his major by the start of his third year, 50 percent by the beginning of his fourth year, and 75 percent by the start of his fifth year. The purpose is to ensure that athletes are working toward a degree and not simply jumping from major to major until their athletic eligibility is exhausted (in effect, majoring in "eligibility").

As predicted by Dick Schultz, the Presidents Commission's commendable package at the 1992 convention met with little opposition.[65] Clearly there is room for much more experimentation with the rules of academic eligibility in order to weed out those with no chance to graduate while at the same time allowing schools to take a shot on a promising student-athlete. The key issues are whether the recruited athlete is capable of performing academically at the school; whether he meets the standards of the student body; and whether his admission is consistent with the practice of special admissions in nonathletic pursuits.[66]

We should explore the wisdom of linking the graduation rate of athletes with the number of athletic scholarships available to a school. Thus, for every athlete who failed to graduate within six years, the university would lose an athletic scholarship for a year or two. This would discourage a school from recruiting athletes with little or no chance to graduate, shuttling them from one hideaway course to the next with no real progress toward graduation, and then discarding them when their eligibility was exhausted.

An even more drastic reform (and one that I do not support at this time) is the abolition of athletic scholarships, as the Ivy League has done. The Ivy League universities treat athletic skill as a factor in the admissions process but not as the sole or overriding factor.

If we fail to clean up college sports, others will advocate a more radical approach. For example, at the 1990 convention of the Black Coaches Association in Atlanta, delegates decried the institutional racism that emphasizes athletic success and not education for black youths. Thomas Hill, an assistant athletic director and chief academic adviser at Oklahoma University, cited studies suggesting that by the year 2000, 70 percent of black males between the ages of eighteen and thirty-six "won't be a factor in our society" and predicted that "[w]e may soon see a black boycott of a major university because its graduate rate of black athletes is not acceptable."[67]

These black leaders realize, as do the four black cosponsors in Congress of the STUDI bill, that the front-line casualties of the present system are the youths who swallow the myths and mortgage their futures for a long shot at the pros. For every Dexter Manley with the good fortune to squeeze into the pros for a long career, a thousand Dexter Manleys finish their not-so-bright college years without a diploma, a real education, the tools to compete in the worldwide economy, or any prospects for a good job.

In his farewell address to the American people, President Eisenhower presciently warned of the emergence of the military-industrial complex, with its potential for misplaced power and priorities. With the same urgency, I am warning of the grave implications for our youth of the sports-entertainment complex mushrooming within our schools.

Sports Illustrated

FEBRUARY 16, 1970   50 CENTS

THE BEST HIGH SCHOOL
PLAYER IN AMERICA

Mansfield's Tom McMillen

In 1969, I was only the second high school student-athlete ever to appear on the cover of *Sports Illustrated*. The headline read: "The Best High School Player in America." While many athletes fear the dreaded "cover curse" of *Sports Illustrated*, it never jinxed my career.

2

After graduating from Maryland, I passed up several lucrative offers from the Virginia Squires and Buffalo Braves to pursue my Rhodes scholarship at Oxford. I relished the opportunity to study politics, economics, and philosophy, laying the groundwork for my later career in public service.

While studying at Oxford, I made the sometimes twice-weekly commute to Bologna to play in the Italian professional basketball league. The Italians' fanaticism for basketball matched their zest for wine and pasta.

3

The Olympic basketball final in Munich in 1972 provided me with the single most exciting and depressing moments, all within the span of minutes. When this picture was taken, we thought we had won the gold medal, only to have it taken away by an official.

4

5

For more than half of my NBA career, I toiled for the Atlanta Hawks and their enterprising owner, Ted Turner.

When I joined the Knicks in 1977, Bill Bradley was in the last year of his outstanding basketball career. Bill showed me the ropes in my rookie season in the NBA as he would do later during my campaign for Congress and in my first years there.

In my campaign for Congress, the four-foot-eleven-inch Maryland Senator Barbara Mikulski was an active point guard on my campaign, taking me on the rounds and introducing me to the Democratic faithful.

In 1986, Jim Bunning, the outstanding baseball pitcher, and I were elected to Congress. *Sports Illustrated* ran a story about the Jock Caucus—Jack Kemp, Jim Bunning, Mo Udall, Bill Bradley, and me.

Every year, Congress takes a break from its legislative duties to play the annual Republicans-versus-Democrats charity basketball game. With a six-inch height advantage and eleven years of NBA experience, I was a serious ringer to help the Democrats regain the title. Underneath the basket, a spry Senator Sam Nunn, always strong on defense, prepares to grab any loose balls.

There will always be those who warn that any move to raise academic standards at the expense of sports will drive marginal students away from schools. Such cynics are apologists for failure, and I am not ready to surrender to the mediocrity of our present system. The danger is not that we will set the hurdles too high for our youngsters but that we have set them too low for too long. We must have the courage to change the incentives, not only for our students, who are vulnerable to the myth of sports stardom, but also for our schools, which have abandoned their educational missions to chase the sports jackpot.

Chapter 4

JACKPOT

Colleges Chase the Sports Dollar

WHEN I MATRICULATED at the University of Maryland in 1970, freshmen were ineligible for varsity sports, and Spencer Haywood was challenging the "four year" rule banning professional basketball teams from drafting a player who had not completed his college commitment. The basketball world was structured like a classic cartel. An athlete debuted with a freshman team, exhausted his college eligibility (with or without earning a degree), and then entered the pro draft. As an eighteen-year-old, I never questioned this progression, which was a profitable and convenient arrangement for the powers.

My freshman year was a storybook season. Our team went undefeated, and we were widely touted by media and coaches as a Top Ten squad for the coming year. More important, I had weathered the transition from my small school in Mansfield, Pennsylvania, to the bustling campus at College Park, Maryland, managing nearly a 4.0 grade point average and becoming more confident that chemistry was the right major for me.

Then a face from the past almost turned my world topsy-turvy.

Paul Snyder had been raised in my hometown of Mansfield, where he had been a longtime dental patient of my dad's. After making a fortune in the frozen food business, Snyder bought the Buffalo Braves of the American Basketball Association. Although he was not a close family friend, he had kept in touch with my father over the years.

After seeing me play at a Buffalo Braves basketball camp following my freshman year in college, Snyder hit Dad and me with an offer we almost could not refuse—$1 million ($50,000 over twenty years) to play seven years for his pro team, starting immediately at the tender age of nineteen. At first we were too stunned to react to the offer, which seemed like a staggering sum for a freshman who had never played a minute of varsity ball. The team owner was tendering more for my signature on a long-term, no-cut contract than Dad had earned in a lifetime of hard work.

"It can't be done," I finally objected after recovering from the initial shock. "There are rules blocking college players from going pro early."

Snyder had anticipated this objection. By this point Haywood had won his landmark court decision, and the NBA had retreated to the fallback position that its draft restriction could be waived in "hardship" cases. Snyder had retained a prestigious New York law firm to squeeze me into the "hardship" category and was willing to foot the legal costs of stretching the exception to the breaking point. It seemed absurd to classify me—with my supportive, middle-class family—as suffering from a "hardship" of any kind. If I qualified for the NBA's elastic exception, it was difficult to imagine anyone who would not.

A panic-stricken Lefty pleaded with my father to convince me to remain at Maryland, but I was tempted by Snyder's offer. What if I had a career-ending injury playing college ball? While on a pro salary, why not finish my degree at Harvard a few years down the line?

After numerous conferences with the high-powered attorneys, I walked away from the money. Not right away and not without second thoughts. But my father and I ultimately rejected it without bargaining. We agreed that I must honor my commitment to Maryland.

I understood the importance of staying in school. After all, I still dreamed of becoming a surgeon. Although the Buffalo Braves were already interested in me, I knew that the odds were high against a pro career of more than two or three years, and I was determined not to hang all my hopes and dreams on the thin reed of a pro contract. Besides, I was still young and skinny and not sure that I was ready for the pounding of the pros.

I eventually delayed my entry into the draft a year after college graduation in order to attend Oxford. When I finally placed my name in the draft in 1975, I signed with Snyder's Buffalo Braves for $1.25 million over five years.

With the escalation of pro salaries in the 1970s and 1980s, Snyder's original proposal would have been disadvantageous for me, but I do not begrudge him for making the offer. After all, he was willing to sign an untested underclassman to a long-term contract and pay the hefty costs of challenging the league policy in court. He was giving me an option that my contemporaries did not enjoy and college football players were effectively denied until 1990.

In retrospect I made the right decision for me, but it was not necessarily the right decision for every college athlete. If I had been admitted into college despite an obvious inability to do college work (or perhaps even read), guided into Eligibility 101, driven thirty or forty hours a week by the coaches to fill the stands for State U. without date money and with as little chance of receiving a degree or a real education as of being crowned the heir to the English throne, Snyder's offer would have been even more attractive.

"I never told a kid not to leave school early for the big dollars after I looked into his refrigerator," said former Marquette coach Al McGuire. "I recruited those kids. I knew the environment they had to escape. I would have been a total hypocrite to tell them to stay in school. For what? They only came to play basketball and get noticed."[1]

But if a college willingly and regularly sacrifices its academic goals for economic gain, at some point it forfeits the right to call itself a college. If a university exists only to grub for money while hiding behind its tax exemption, the charade will soon be discovered by its students and the public, just as the charade of the student-athlete has been exposed.

The college sports empire preaches amateurism but practices professionalism, and the only way to end this hypocrisy is to face the following six truths about college sports:

1. Amateurism is dead.
2. Big-time athletics is undermining the educational mission of colleges.
3. The NCAA is a jealous bureaucracy designed to benefit itself and its member institutions. Any trifling benefit to the student-athletes is coincidental.
4. College athletics are losing money, and the taxpayer is footing the bill.
5. Tradition and loyalty mean nothing in the mercenary world of college sports.
6. Universities cannot control the monsters they have created by breeding their athletic departments with the TV networks.

Big-time college sports, as marketed by the Division I powers, are the not-so-poor stepchildren of professional sports and shamelessly exploit the student-athletes.

TRUTH #1: THE LONG, LINGERING DEATH OF AMATEURISM

In the world according to the NCAA, college athletics are amateur as long as all revenues from the production and marketing of the games, regardless of the immense sums involved, are retained by the schools and the NCAA, with no "trickle down" to the athletes, except for scholarships of dubious value and nominal incidentals.

In other words, the NCAA, the schools, the TV networks, and the coaches are allowed to cash in on the popularity of college sports, but the athletes are forbidden from doing so upon pain of ineligibility.

The NCAA's concept of amateurism is anachronistic, much as was Avery Brundage's obsession with Olympic amateurism. While the Olympics has largely jettisoned Brundage's outmoded definition, the NCAA still clings to its outdated view.

With huge sums being raked in by all parties except the athletes, the present system reeks of exploitation. In 1989 the NCAA and CBS entered into a historic pact in which the network shelled out $1 billion for exclusive coverage of the college basketball tournament for seven years, beginning in 1991. As a result of this lucrative, long-term contract, the NCAA's television revenues from the tournament will jump from $55 million in 1990 to an average of $143 million a year for the next seven years.[2]

The nineteen college football bowl games played between December 8, 1990, and January 1, 1991, distributed about $65 million to their thirty-eight participants, with the teams in the Rose Bowl taking home $6.5 million each.[3]

In a move that left the rest of the field far behind, in February 1990 Notre Dame sold to NBC the rights to televise its home football games from 1991 to 1995 for $38 million, becoming the first university in history to negotiate its own national television package outside the aegis of the NCAA, the College Football Association (CFA), or a conference. To counter Notre Dame's unilateral move, the other sixty-three schools in the CFA negotiated a five-year, $210 million package with ABC.[4]

As UNLV Athletic Director Brad Rothermel candidly admitted, "College athletics is amateur in one sense, but when you go to the Final Four, each team gets paid about 1.5 million dollars. Is this amateur athletics? Our athletic department is a 10 million dollar corporation that will generate about six million in basketball this year. It's a big business."[5]

While the players are denied their cut of the billions of dollars of bowl money, gate receipts, and TV contracts, college coaches are reaping the windfall profits of endorsement contracts from shoe companies. The top college coaches earn as much or more than their pro counterparts. Significantly, while the NCAA bird-dogs athletes to guard against their receiving discounts on clothes, free rides to school, or extra pizza money, the NCAA sets no limits on the compensation of college coaches, who benefit immensely from the NCAA-imposed mandate of poverty for the players.

For example, the embattled Jerry Tarkanian, whose Runnin' Rebels copped the basketball championship in 1990, received a bonus of 10 percent of UNLV's net proceeds from the tournament (worth about $100,000 to the coach) atop his annual salary of $186,000, as well as perks including product endorsements, basketball camps, newspaper columns, radio and TV shows, the free use of a Cadillac, part ownership of a shopping mall restaurant, and commissions from an airport shop that hawks merchandise with the Runnin' Rebel logo.[6]

Thus, while UNLV pocketed about $1.5 million and its controversial coach collected a six-figure bonus for the team's virtuoso performance, the NCAA limited the athletes to a pittance of $10 a day in spending money during the tournament.

Tarkanian is not alone in flexing his entrepreneurial clout, unencumbered by competition from his players. High-profile college coaches, such as Indiana's Bobby Knight and Georgetown's John Thompson, enjoy six-figure endorsement contracts from shoe companies. Despite his growing misgivings about such lucrative contracts, LSU's Dale Brown planned to accept more than $250,000 a year from Converse for endorsing their sneakers.[7]

Indeed, Nike alone has under contract about eighty major college basketball coaches (at least ten of whom are paid $100,000 or more a year by the shoe company), who influence their varsity players to wear Nikes on the court and before the cameras.[8] Any college player who entered such a shoe contract would be deemed ineligible by the NCAA.

Bobby Knight defends the endorsement deals by arguing that a "coach's shoe contract is really no different than a faculty member's being able to contract with outside corporations as a consultant or adviser."[9]

But there are at least two important differences. First, a college coach is leveraging the name of his school and the skill of his players. "I've long felt that the sneaker company is buying the school (not the coach)," admitted LSU Athletic Director Joe Dean, formerly a promotions executive for Converse. "I mean, they're buying UCLA, they're buying Georgetown. Because they want the team to wear the shoes to create the exposure. Coaches should get something. . . . But I have to admit: Even when I was at Converse, I questioned whether a coach deserved to make all that money."[10]

Second, the athletes are pressured to model the sneakers for the cameras without receiving a cent for their efforts. IBM is free to hire a college student to act as a consultant, a gofer, or whatever, but Nike is not free to negotiate with a college basketball player. While a professor is forced to compete with his students for a consulting job, the NCAA protects college coaches from competition with their players for endorsement deals.

When the shoe contract of a coach approaches or exceeds his base salary from a college, the question naturally arises as to whether he is working for Nike or State U. Moreover, like other unsavory practices, shoe contracts have filtered down to the high school level, where the top coaches now benefit from endorsement deals in the restricted market.

The shoe contracts of college coaches were studied by the Knight Commission on Intercollegiate Athletics, on which I served along with the Rev. Theodore Hesburgh, president emeritus of Notre Dame; Dr. William Friday, president emeritus of North Carolina; Secretary of Education Lamar Alexander; seven other current or former college presidents; and others. In 1991 we recommended the banning of shoe contracts with college coaches in order to force the manufacturers to deal directly with the universities if they want college players to showcase their brands on the court.

In general, the rule should be to funnel all such outside income to coaches through the university. Then if the school chooses to pay its head football coach $700,000 a year, at least this practice will be open and aboveboard. Although the NCAA has not adopted this rule, it took a step in this direction at the 1992 convention by adopting a requirement for a coach to receive prior written approval from the school's president for all athletically related income from outside sources, such as shoe companies.

Almost all of the top college coaches also sponsor profitable basketball camps in the summer. In many cases the college subsidizes much of the expense, thereby maximizing the coach's profit from the enterprise. Even after stepping down as the head basketball coach at Maryland, Lefty Driesell continued to conduct basketball camps on the campus, which grossed $231,000 in 1986; and the Michigan basketball coach grossed over $350,000 from such camps in the same year.[11]

The result is that "[t]here are a lot of college coaches out there making upwards of 500,000 dollars a year," reports LSU Athletic Director Joe Dean.[12] They outearn their university's president (sometimes by a factor of three or four) and occasionally the entire philosophy department. And the mere rumor that a successful coach is being eyed by another school often prompts a college or its boosters to sweeten the pot for the wavering coach.[13] In 1991, the University of Illinois and its boosters moved to increase the salary of football coach John Mackovic (whose $350,350 package included summer camps and radio and TV shows) but could not match a successful bid for Mackovic's services by the University of Texas and its boosters of $5 million over five years.[14] All this sends a chilling message to students and the public about the priorities of our educational system and our society.

When former Chancellor Thomas Everhart left the University of Illinois to become the president of the California Institute of Technology in 1987, he explained his decision to the faculty in a farewell letter that quipped, "And frankly, an institution that pays its president more than its football coach can't be all bad."[15]

Even more revealing of the underside of college sports are the payoffs to coaches under fire. By now most college coaches have contracts that allow the schools to fire them without paying a penny in severance if their programs have been involved in major NCAA violations. Despite such provisions, however, most colleges prefer to negotiate their way out of a messy situation. After all, if pushed into a courtroom, an embattled coach can probably prove that higher-ups either condoned or closed their eyes to the misdeeds of the athletic programs. So it has become a time-dis-honored tradition for a coach whose program has been targeted by the NCAA to cut a sweet severance deal with the school and clear out before the NCAA surrounds the gym and opens fire on the innocent bystanders. The list of coaches who have bailed out with "golden parachutes" while their programs were burning includes North Carolina's Dick Crum, Clemson's Danny Ford, Oklahoma's Barry Switzer, Texas A&M's Jackie Sherrill, and SMU's Bobby Collins.[16]

Some coaches are literally paid to win and to make money for their schools. For example, Colorado's head football coach, Bill McCartney, and head basketball coach, Joe Harrington, receive generous financial incentives based on their teams' performance, as pegged to rankings, bowl appearances, and success in tournaments.[17]

On the flip side of the equation, Mike Steele was fired in 1991 as the head basketball coach at East Carolina because of his losing record. It was no defense that Steele's program had never been cited for an NCAA violation and had graduated an impressive thirty of thirty-one recruits.[18] Another blow was the firing by Tulsa of basketball coach J. D. Barnett the same year. Despite his winning record in six seasons, his basketball program was not making enough money for the school. "It doesn't make sense," said Barnett. "It destroys all the values I've believed in all my life."[19]

Wrong, J. D. It makes perfect sense if you view college sports as a cold, hard business with little to do with education and amateurism and everything to do with money and professionalism.

Like the high-flying coaches, the NCAA is not tied to a shoe-string budget. According to the NCAA's financial statements, it grossed more than $98 million in the fiscal year of 1989–1990.[20] The NCAA, which is widely viewed as the KGB of college athletics, skims a healthy cut of the action. With a staff of two hundred, the NCAA operates on about 13 percent of the revenues it generates from the sweat of athletes.[21]

To the public the NCAA is the bare-knuckle enforcer of the rules governing college sports, but the NCAA budget tells a different story. The NCAA annually spends less on enforcement than it does on public relations and promotions, which are mainly designed to protect its turf and take.[22] For 1991–1992, the NCAA has budgeted $2.5 million for legal expenses and governmental affairs and another $2.5 million for public relations and promotions.[23]

In 1989 the NCAA wasted hundreds of thousands of dollars in an intense (but unsuccessful) lobbying effort to derail the Student Right-to-Know Act. Somewhat naively I had entered the fray with the idea that the NCAA existed to fight for the student-athletes, but I came to realize that the NCAA had transmogrified into a bloated bureaucracy that is adept at turf battles, PR campaigns, and self-aggrandizement.

There was nothing amateurish or small time about the NCAA's negotiation of a $1 billion contract with CBS to televise the basketball tournament, and there is nothing second class about the legal and lobbying talents who are unleashed by the NCAA at the slightest challenge to its authority.

During the final three fiscal years of the 1980s, the NCAA spent almost as much money flying its committee members around the country first class and treating them to first-rate hotels as it invested in its enforcement program. In 1990 the organization lavished $1.4 million on committee entertainment, compared to a total expenditure of only $1.9 million on enforcement.[24]

The organization that polices athletes to make sure they do not enjoy a free meal at a coach's home or hitch a ride to school on a rainy day from an assistant coach is flush with cash, ending 1989 with $21 million in the bank. Because occasionally even first-class travel is not quite good enough, the NCAA leases a jet for its executive director, who is coincidentally a pilot. In addition, the top executives of the NCAA receive perks such as the free use of cars, low-interest mortgage loans, and free legal advice.[25]

In this climate of greed and hypocrisy, an underground economy flourishes to reward college athletes. This should surprise no one. Not even the NCAA, with its amazing powers of self-delusion, can deny that some college players are paid. How can this be denied when $1,000 in bills pops out of a package being shipped from a Kentucky assistant coach to Chris Mills, a highly sought-after recruit?[26] Or when Luther Darville, a former academic adviser to athletes at Minnesota, defends himself in court against charges of swindling the university of $180,000 by claiming that he administered a slush fund for athletes? And when several former football players corroborate Darville, one testifying to the receipt of $10,000 from him and another swearing he got $8,500 in cash and gifts?[27] When Jeff Ruland, a former NBA teammate of mine, admits to taking money from Jim Valvano, then the Iona coach, during both Ruland's recruiting and his college career?[28] When Charles Shackleford, an NBA forward, claims to have received $65,000 from sports agents while playing under Valvano at North Carolina State?[29]

In 1991 the staff of the House Subcommittee on Commerce, Consumer Protection, and Competitiveness, during our ongoing investigation of intercollegiate athletics, listened spellbound to several tapes containing secretly recorded conversations between Eric Ramsey, a former Auburn football player, and Auburn coaches. The tapes refer to cash gifts to Ramsey from coaches and boosters, in clear violation of NCAA rules. Ramsey's attorney revealed that both he and his client received death threats following their allegations against the Tiger program. Near the Auburn campus, a mock headstone was erected with the inscription RIP: ERIC RAMSEY AND THE *MONTGOMERY ADVERTISER* (the paper that broke the story), and RAMSEY MUST DIE was emblazoned on a car near the football stadium.[30]

While I was a pro, a number of my teammates, including Ruland, admitted to taking money in college from boosters and assistant coaches. Despite tons of anecdotal evidence, the NCAA buries its head in the sand and treats such incidents as isolated or the product of renegade programs.

According to a 1989 study by Professor Allen Sack of the University of New Haven, nearly one-third of current and former NFL players who responded admitted to accepting improper payments during college, and 53 percent said they saw nothing wrong with breaking NCAA rules to pocket extra cash. Most of the "guilty" players had received small amounts, in the range of $1,000 over four years, but one respondent collected $80,000 during his college career. Based upon his findings, Sack concluded that "[t]here's a substantial underground economy that's likely to be unstopped."[31]

This underground economy will continue to flourish and besmirch the already tainted image of college sports as long as the NCAA clings to the myth that top college athletes are amateurs and not semipros. Abandoning the myth, however, will prejudice the NCAA and its member institutions in their imminent battles with the IRS and could cost the money-hungry programs huge sums in tax payments. In short, the NCAA and the colleges face a dilemma between sticking to their hypocritical posturing, which forces athletes to reach under the table for their paltry cut of the riches, or facing reality by funneling money to college stars above the table and in full view of the IRS.

The NCAA is already devoting a portion of its $1 billion contract with CBS to establish catastrophic-injury insurance for all NCAA athletes and an emergency loan program. These measures, while laudable, do not address the real issue and do not go far enough. The emergency fund is a stopgap to avoid or postpone real reform and will have little effect on the widespread covert payments by coaches, boosters, and unscrupulous agents. The revenue-producing athletes will still ask themselves why they should settle for chump change when everyone else is milking the system. Isn't the athlete's sweat equity worth real money?

A growing number of influential coaches, including LSU's Dale Brown, Indiana's Bobby Knight, and Nebraska's Tom Osborne advocate paying college players a stipend based upon need or some other formula. The proposed stipends generally range from $200 to $1,000 a month and reflect estimates of the athlete's lost opportunity in forgoing a part-time job in favor of participating in athletics. In a recent poll college players said their greatest need was additional spending money, generally in the range of $200 a month, to cover living expenses at colleges.[32]

Unfortunately, a stipend may be too much reality for the NCAA to swallow. Dick Schultz, the executive director of the NCAA, stated, "I have a lot of problems with a straight stipend, because then you establish an employer-employee relationship with all types of problems."[33]

Wait a minute, Dick. An employer-employee relationship is exactly what exists in many of the top programs now, except that the employers have all the bargaining power and the employees none. While the employers (the colleges) are acting like pure capitalists in grabbing for TV dough, the employees (the athletes) are denied the rights to a fair salary or stipend, workers compensation, collective bargaining, and a whole panoply of labor rights.[34]

An alternative proposal is to recognize the college athlete as a semipro and pay him a salary, roughly the cost of a college education. In other words, if the institution values its tuition at $10,000 a year, pay the athlete that sum. If he then wants to invest his stipend in an education, fine. If not, he can pocket the money or spend it as he chooses, play till his eligibility expires, and then try to turn pro.

A more radical variant of the semipro model is to allow an athlete to cut his best deal vis-à-vis the college, perhaps employing attorneys and agents to assist him. Today's underground economy would be exposed, and athletic programs would be treated as taxable businesses with little or no relationship to the educational mission of their affiliated colleges.

The advantage of the semipro model is its honest recognition of the inherent conflict between big-time college sports programs and the educational missions of their schools. Honesty is important and sorely lacking in the treatment of sports by the NCAA and its members today, but honesty is not enough. We want our schools to be both honest and educational; and for that reason, the semipro model should be rejected. True reform demands that we reduce the financial incentives of winning for both the schools and the students.

TRUTH #2: THE ABUSE BY COLLEGES OF THEIR TAX-EXEMPT STATUS

The spectacle of a showdown between the IRS and the NCAA— two mammoth bureaucracies with a taste for blood and a distaste for due process—makes a football match between Notre Dame and Miami seem like a bridge game between beginners. It is like watching a war between Iran and Iraq and praying for both to lose.

The issue between these two leviathans is simple but portends doom for the NCAA. Universities and the NCAA enjoy tax-exempt status under the Internal Revenue Code. The Code, however, provides that an otherwise exempt organization, such as a college or a church, loses its privileged status, in whole or in part, by engaging in a trade or business unrelated to the purpose justifying its tax exemption. The IRS has ruled that the exemption for an educational institution does not extend to its ancillary business unless the school is merely a passive investor with no related indebtedness.

Like the athletes, the public, and practically everyone except the NCAA, the IRS realizes that the multimillion-dollar sports-entertainment fiefdoms within colleges do not further the educational goals of the schools and in many cases undermine those goals. The Los Angeles Lakers are taxed, as would be a farm team for the NBA. Why not tax the de facto farm teams for the NBA and NFL? Why should colleges be treated as tax shelters for semipro teams?

The NCAA's problem will be to keep a straight face while arguing that the big-time football and basketball programs of Division I powers fall within the nonprofit umbrella of higher education, that college athletes are not employees paid to perform, and that the institutions are merely passive participants in their athletic enterprises. At stake is what the NCAA values most—money.

Fear of the IRS partly explains the NCAA's desperate clinging to the myth of amateurism. The NCAA fears that paying college athletes, even if only a fair stipend to reflect their lost opportunity to work, will strengthen the IRS's position that the sports-entertainment centers are taxable businesses.

In the late 1980s the IRS began to disallow tax deductions by individuals who paid colleges for priority seating at athletic contests. The IRS correctly reasoned that such payments were not truly charitable but were akin to payments for good seats at other entertainment events, such as professional games or the theatre. But NCAA member institutions unleashed lobbyists on Congress, which in 1988 passed a bill to allow the purchasers to deduct 80 percent of their payments for priority seating.[35]

Ohio State University is now being billed $300,000 a year by the IRS to cover the taxes on the $1 million in annual revenues generated by selling ads on its scoreboard.[36] But Ohio State may fight the IRS in court, as the NCAA successfully did in blocking the IRS from taxing the income from ads in basketball tournament programs.[37]

The IRS has also determined that the thirteen college bowls that have garnered corporate sponsorship should be taxed on the income received from the sponsors.[38] After this IRS ruling, lobbyists for the bowl associations stormed the Hill; and in 1991 a bill by the late Silvio Conte was introduced in Congress to extend the tax exemption of universities more broadly to cover all such income. Conte's bill is now being sponsored by Ed Jenkins of Georgia.

I question the wisdom of Conte's bill because it seems ludicrous to view the bloated bowls, with their payouts of $70 million, as part of the educational mission of the schools. The bowls are big businesses, and too little of the largesse trickles down to academics.

A counterbill was introduced by Representative Paul Henry of Michigan in 1991. Under Henry's bill, the following items would be taxable income to the universities: (1) radio and television broadcast revenues, (2) contributions from booster clubs or similar groups to the athletic department, and (3) amounts contributed to an institution in connection with a preferred-seating program.

In Henry's floor statement to introduce his bill, he almost took the words from my mouth:

[I]ntercollegiate athletics have little to do with the educational mission of the universities which sponsor them. . . . [T]hese programs are large-scale businesses, operating under the golden dome of

higher education. I propose that tax policy simply reflect the reality
that has become more and more obvious.[39]

Big-time college sports programs justify their tax breaks by
invoking the very educational goals that they are undermining.
Just as semipro athletes masquerade as student-athletes, athletic
departments masquerade as educational centers.

It is also ironic that the NCAA and its affiliates and members,
which complained loudly about federal interference when we introduced the Student Right-to-Know Act, scurry to Congress for
help whenever the privileged status of college sports is threatened
by the IRS or others. Unfortunately, Congress has generally
played into the NCAA's hands on these occasions.

For the sake of the taxpayers and the future of our institutions
of learning, Congress must take a stronger stand when the NCAA
and its members flex their massive lobbying muscle. Tax deductions for the unrelated business of sports-entertainment are really
"tax expenditures," which are hidden costs to the taxpayers.
Whenever Congress intervenes to prevent the IRS from collecting
the income generated by the sports-entertainment empires within
our colleges, tax revenues will be collected from other sources to
compensate for the unwarranted and illogical tax breaks given to
big-time college sports.

The NCAA will probably argue that, with so many college
sports programs in the red, there will be little tax revenue generated by the IRS's aggressive stance. Why bother to tax our sports
empires, the organization will ask, for so little return? The
NCAA's "poor boy" argument is not persuasive for at least three
reasons. First, the fact that many businesses run deficits or even
fail has never been accepted as an excuse for not taxing the lucrative ones. Second, the IRS may increase its haul by disallowing
deductions that athletic programs are abusing. Finally, treating
(taxwise and otherwise) the sports fiefdoms within colleges as the
big businesses they have become removes the sham of the present
system.

One of the primary goals of college sports reform is to sever
the connection between winning games and making big money

from bowls and tournaments. Unfortunately, the NCAA has been timid in pursuing this goal. Congress should examine the feasibility of taxing the income generated by big-time college sports unless that income is distributed more evenly among the schools and the NCAA agrees to play more fairly with the schools and the student-athletes.

TRUTH #3: THE SELF-AGGRANDIZING BUREAUCRACY OF THE NCAA

The history of the exploitation of college athletes shatters the myth that the NCAA is a voluntary association of schools acting for the benefit of student-athletes. NCAA membership is not truly voluntary, for either the colleges or their athletes. Rather, the NCAA is the head of a rapacious cartel with the overweening goal of maximizing the profitability of the farm teams to the pros.

The NCAA's fear of genuine reform is especially evident in its refusal to accord due process protections to schools and students facing significant penalties. The NCAA's facile response to complaints of this nature is to invite the disgruntled party to withdraw from the "voluntary" association. But because the NCAA has been phenomenally successful at generating tremendous revenues for college sports, it would be fiscal suicide for a successful sports program to drop out of the NCAA. In light of these tremendous economic disincentives, it is absurd to describe membership in the organization as voluntary in any meaningful sense.

Because the power of the NCAA ultimately turns on its control of TV revenues, its grip on the cartel is strong but not absolute. As a result of a series of court decisions, the NCAA's position is currently stronger in basketball (where the NCAA still cuts the deals) than football (where the teams and conferences are rushing into the act). The power of the NCAA is diminished every time the networks bypass the NCAA to bargain directly with a team, a conference, or a superconference. Thus, fear of losing its place at the bargaining table with the TV moguls drives the NCAA to maximize revenues for its member institutions, even to the detriment of the educational needs of the athletes and the schools.

If NCAA membership is involuntary for the colleges, it is even

more so for the athletes. Alfred Dennis Mathewson, a law professor at the University of New Mexico, points out that student-
athletes have no real opportunity to influence the terms upon
which their colleges join the NCAA or to require accountability
by their universities toward them and others similarly situated
through bargaining.[40]

Stripped of bargaining power, athletes are treated as little more
than chattels by the NCAA. The athletes' money problems are
exacerbated because they, unlike the general student body, are
prohibited from earning outside income. Recently a constituent
called my congressional office concerning his son, who had received a small scholarship to play college baseball. During high
school the boy had worked in a local firm at a computer job,
gaining valuable experience for future employment. After he accepted the baseball scholarship, however, the college informed
him that NCAA rules required him to quit his computer job.
Thus, he faced the dilemma of playing baseball with no realistic
shot at the pros or preparing for a long-term career. The student
quit his job.

The NCAA has acted against the interests of student-athletes
in countless other ways. The enforcement apparatus of the NCAA
falls heaviest upon innocent student-athletes. By the time the
NCAA has levied penalties against a transgressing athletic program, the guilty parties (coaches and players) have moved on,
leaving behind innocent student-athletes to suffer from a ban on
postseason play or TV coverage.[41]

In some cases the delay between the alleged violations and the
punishment is absurdly long. Before backing down at the threat
of a legal challenge, the NCAA had banned the Runnin' Rebels
of UNLV from defending their national championship in the 1991
tourney, based upon alleged violations that dated back thirteen
years. In other words, the NCAA was prepared to punish college
athletes for alleged transgressions that occurred when they were
barely starting grade school.

Likewise, in 1990 when the NCAA slapped my alma mater,
Maryland, with a slew of penalties, including a three-year pro-
bationary period, a two-year ban on NCAA tournament play,

and a one-year TV blackout, the offending coach and players had skipped, and a new coach and innocent players are now paying for the sins of their predecessors.

The restrictions governing the transfer of a student-athlete further demonstrate the injustice of the present system. A college student who transfers to a new institution is barred by the NCAA from participating in intercollegiate athletics at his new school for a full academic year regardless of the reason for his transfer. The rule is designed to prevent raiding and preserve the facade of amateurism.[42]

Of course, there are many justifiable reasons for a student to transfer that have nothing to do with raiding or improper inducements. He may not like his coach or the locale of his school. His academic interests may change, and he may feel that another school is more suited to a new major. For personal reasons he may need to move closer to home.

Rather than enact sensible rules against raiding, the NCAA forces a player to sit tight at a school where he may be miserable or to sit out a year. But a coach under fire can bolt from a beleaguered institution and immediately jump into another college program.

The NCAA is preoccupied with keeping the contests competitive for the TV audiences, even at the expense of the best interests of the students. But the NCAA should err on the side of greater freedom for the students to transfer rather than protecting its package for the networks.

The NCAA's dereliction of duty toward student-athletes is evident in the provision limiting athletic scholarships to a maximum period of one year, renewable at the option of the school. This rule gives the athletic department tremendous leverage over its players. The decision by a coach not to renew a scholarship reflects an earlier miscalculation by the coach and the player. Why should the player bear the greater risk? If the NCAA were truly concerned with the students, athletic scholarships would be for a minimum period of five years, cancellable on athletic grounds only if the recruit does not participate in the sport, as the Knight Commission has recommended.

Finally, the shocking degree to which the NCAA has sold out the student-athletes (its revenue producers) surfaced in the recent flap over the rights of college players to enter the pro draft before the expiration of their college eligibility. For years the NCAA and the pro leagues enjoyed a cozy relationship in which college players faced roadblocks in trying to turn pro early. These roadblocks were designed to benefit the colleges and the pros but not the athletes, who lost their freedom of choice. The NCAA favored the pros' "hands off" policy because it allowed the colleges to hold on to their stars for four or five years. Between the ages of eighteen and twenty-one, an athlete discovered that college was the only game in town. Colleges were allowed to retain their meal tickets for little more than the cost of meals.

The NBA and NFL followed the "hands off" policy because they were saving billions by having a free farm system run by the accommodating universities. After football and basketball players were seasoned for four or five years in the most competitive colleges, the pros then became the only game in town. The colleges and pros divided the turf for their mutual benefit and to the detriment of those athletes who were ready, willing, and eager to turn pro early; and both the colleges and the pros hypocritically justified the impediments as being in the "best interests" of the students.

Balderdash.

Why not let the student-athlete decide his own best interest? Why not give an eighteen-year-old a chance to weigh the advantages and disadvantages of attending college or turning pro? And in making that choice, why not allow him to test his present worth in a pro draft, negotiate a contract with a pro team (with the assistance of attorneys and agents if he desires), and then decide, based upon the fullest information available to him on the free market, whether to sign with the pros or return to college? Why not allow him to play in the pros and then return to a college team if he has not exhausted his eligibility?

For some athletes the choice will be easy, because of either their strong desire for a college education or their total disinterest in school. The graduation statistics of college athletes and the time demands placed upon them belie the bleating of pro and college coaches that they are thinking only of the athletes and their futures. As late as 1989, NFL Commissioner Pete Rozelle was sticking to the "party line" that "full exposure to the educational opportunities and the social atmosphere on a college campus will benefit the athlete throughout his life, whether or not he obtains a degree."[43] But college is not for everyone, and both the individuals and the institutions suffer from the pretense that athletes benefit just from hanging out on a campus. The hypocrisy of the present system is never clearer than when the pros and the colleges seek to justify their mutually beneficial pact on the educational needs of the athlete.

Time has run out on the unholy alliance between the NCAA and the pros, not because of any self-enlightenment on their parts but because of litigation and the threat of litigation. Someday a Curt Flood of college sports will challenge the most odious restrictions on college players.

The alliance between colleges and the pros began to crumble in 1971, with Spencer Haywood's historic court decision; and the alliance almost completely collapsed in 1989, when the NFL created a new loophole for 1988 Heisman Trophy winner Barry Sanders, who was threatening to sue if not allowed to turn pro early.

Even today, however, the NCAA and the NFL continue to erect roadblocks to self-determination by athletes. The NCAA clings to its outmoded definition of amateurism by stripping a college athlete of his remaining eligibility if he hires an agent, authorizes an attorney or agent to contact a sports team on his behalf, or declares his intention to apply early for a pro draft.

With the "four year" rule sidelined, the NFL allowed juniors to declare themselves eligible for the 1990 draft. But if a junior can enter the pro draft, why not a sophomore? A freshman? A high school senior? Although thirty-eight juniors accepted the invitation, only eighteen were actually selected. But the remaining twenty juniors became ineligible to return to their college teams. The NFL to its shame requires an underclassman who enters the draft to sign a permanent renunciation of his college eligibility.

In defending the NFL's position before our Knight Commission in 1990, NFL Commissioner Paul Tagliabue said the league was "of an open mind" about letting those not drafted return to their college teams.[44] Tagliabue was adamant, however, against allowing any player who was drafted by an NFL club to regain his college eligibility.

Why?

While the commissioner bemoaned the deleterious effects on college programs of allowing players to "test the waters," the NFL's concern is selfish. The league is seeking to make sure that its draft remains the only game in town. The team owners do not want a player to have the option of tossing an offer back in their faces and returning to college ball.

Unfortunately, the NCAA jumped when the NFL snapped its fingers. In 1991 the NCAA Council was poised to place before the 1992 convention a proposal to allow undergraduates to test their worth in the pro draft without forfeiting their eligibility. When the College Football Association (CFA) and the pro leagues blasted the proposal, however, the council lost its nerve and tabled the proposal for a year. "[T]here have been so many concerns raised, not only by coaches but by the professional organizations themselves," said Ted Tow, associate executive director of the NCAA. "There needs to be more discussion with the NBA and the NFL."[45] At the 1992 convention, the NCAA voted to allow a college player to assess his value on the pro market but reaffirmed its position that he loses his eligibility by entering a pro draft, negotiating a pro contract, or hiring an agent.

The NCAA must abandon its "farm team" mentality and change its rules to allow players freely to test the water. And colleges must abandon the "plantation mentality" behind the threats of some college coaches to "lock out" pro scouts if too many underclassmen enter the NFL draft early. An athlete should be free to choose between staying in college and turning pro based upon all the available factors, including whether any pro team wants him and how badly. It is long past time for the NCAA to begin placing the interests of student-athletes ahead of the sanctity of the pro draft.

If the NFL wants a farm league, it can fund one, as baseball does. Addressing the 1992 NCAA convention, Dick Schultz recognized that it might be time for the NFL and NBA to establish farm systems and to stop relying on colleges to develop their players.[46]

Notre Dame's Lou Holtz has proposed a model similar to the defunct Soviet/East German academies.[47] The professional sports leagues would establish and fund a national system of academies for those whose main goal is turning pro. The academies could offer instruction in football, basketball, hockey, and baseball, along with a minimal load of courses, and they would compete against each other. The faculty at an academy would be free to dismiss an athlete who did not show promise of playing at the professional level, and the youth could then get on with his life. Such academies would alleviate some of the pressure, self-imposed or not, on colleges to prepare athletes for the pros.

The pressure on colleges could also be reduced if the NFL and NBA invested in developmental teams or taxi squads. The biggest hurdle to establishing such reserve teams is the opposition of the professional players' associations, which view these squads as repositories for "scabs" to break a strike. Perhaps the players' fears could be defused by a rule prohibiting management from drawing upon players on the developmental squad during the current year.

If colleges return to their true missions and bow out of the business of preparing athletes for the pros, the NFL and the NBA will assume their rightful responsibilities of training their future players. The leagues will not allow talented nineteen-year-olds to fall through the cracks, as the NBA has proven by investing in the Continental Basketball Association.

Presenting a young, gifted athlete with an array of choices—college, sports academy, farm team, minor leagues, foreign leagues, or pro—would make his decision to matriculate at and remain in college more of a voluntary one.

TRUTH #4: THE FOOL'S GOLD OF COLLEGE ATHLETICS

Of the scores of colleges mining sports for money and recognition, only a lucky few strike gold. The vast majority, intoxicated by the glitter, sacrifice everything dear to them and break their own rules but end up with nothing but fool's gold.

Whenever a college football or basketball program comes under fire, one of the traditional defenses is that, whatever the sins of the program, its surplus underwrites a host of less popular sports and nonathletic endeavors. To penalize or scale back big-time football or basketball, the defense goes, threatens the existence of golf, tennis, all women's teams, and jeopardizes the general fund-raising drive of the university. As goes the football team, the apologists argue, so go the contributions to the school.

Based on past history, however, schools would be foolish to bank on athletics to solve their financial problems. During the 1980s, football expenses increased at a higher rate than football revenues, and the percentage of Division I football programs reporting a deficit grew steadily.[48]

In 1990 the CFA, which includes the top football programs in Division I, compiled a financial report from data furnished by fifty-three of its members—forty-three state schools and ten private institutions. Of the respondents, seven reported an income from sports that equaled expenses; twenty-three indicated a surplus; and twenty-three had a deficit, ranging from $14,000 to over $5 million.[49]

For the first time since the CFA started its annual financial survey, the average expense of operating an intercollegiate athletic program in 1988–1989 exceeded the average income. Indeed, the NCAA estimates that 70 percent of the organization's 298 Division I programs currently operate at deficits.[50] And far more athletic programs would be in the red if not for the controversial tax exemption for college sports and the schools' taxation without representation in the form of student fees, which inflate sports revenues by an average of $861,000 for public institutions and $478,000 for private universities.[51]

After reviewing financial reports prepared by the NCAA for the last decade, a respected research team concluded that "as a whole, American intercollegiate athletics programs are unable to support themselves and that most programs run a deficit."[52] Robert Atwell, the president of the American Council on Education, estimates that the nation's colleges spend about $1 billion a year on all sports and collect less than that in revenue from TV, the gate, and other sources.[53]

The precarious position of Maryland, my alma mater, is illustrative. In 1991 Maryland's athletic department was mired in $4.75 million in red ink.[54] Furthermore, Maryland's deficit would have been even more staggering if not for the millions of dollars in fees levied upon its students. The revenue from student fees alone at Maryland has in the past covered the expenditures of all sports except football and basketball.[55]

Such student fees are unfair and mask the deficits of sports programs at Maryland and scores of other institutions. If levied at all, student fees should be dedicated to the maintenance of facilities open to the entire university. If a sports program in a state school is running a deficit, why not ask the taxpayers if they are willing to fund the shortfall rather than increase the costs of college through student fees?

Universities have been so successful in disguising the true revenues and expenditures of their sports programs that one of my colleagues, Congressman Paul Henry of Michigan, attempted to add a rider to the Student Right-To-Know Act, which would have required institutions to disclose the revenues and expenditures of each sport within the athletic department. Unfortunately, the NCAA—which has a vested interest in perpetuating the "trickle down" myth of big-time college sports—killed Henry's rider, partly on the ground that schools presently have such vastly different accounting schemes. Of course, one of the assumptions behind Henry's bill was that disclosure would foster greater uniformity in accounting methods.

Henry's financial disclosure bill is especially important now as American universities suffer through their worst financial crisis of the post–World War II era.[56] In 1991 at least thirty-three states cut services and raised taxes, and thirty-one states ended that fiscal year with a budget deficit.[57] As a result of the recession that has rocked state economies, about 45 percent of all colleges and universities suffered midyear cuts in their 1990–1991 budgets, which had a substantial impact at about 60 percent of those institutions; and many schools are predicting further deterioration of their finances.[58] With higher education being squeezed financially, how much longer can we afford to feed the sports monsters on our campuses?

Like almost all college athletic programs, Maryland was struggling financially even in apparently successful years and had no reserve for unanticipated losses. The "up side" of college sports is limited, but the "down side" can be disastrous. Thus, in 1990 when the NCAA hit the Terps with sanctions that included bans on postseason play for two years and on TV appearances for a year, the school faced revenue losses of up to $4 million over the next two years.[59] As Maryland Governor William Schaefer remarked to me at a joint campaign appearance in 1990, "I've restructured higher education to try to raise more money for the system, and now the NCAA has undermined my efforts."

The fiscal shakiness of college programs strengthens the hand of the NCAA, which holds the power of life or death over an athletic department. Just as NCAA sanctions generally fall heaviest on innocent athletes who were not attending the targeted school when the violations allegedly occurred, such sanctions often penalize innocent schools. For example, in 1990 Nebraska announced a $1.8 million deficit for the sports program, partly because two of its colleagues in the Big Eight Conference (Oklahoma and Oklahoma State) were ineligible for bowl games and TV appearances.[60] Because the Big Eight, like many conferences, shares revenue among its members, a financial penalty to one Big Eight school punishes all schools in the conference.

Viewed strictly as a business, big-time college sports are "fragile, risky, fraught with contradictions, and run according to expectations and practices that would be suspect in the business world."[61] Of course, few people view college sports strictly as a business. The argument is often made (and too often unchallenged) that college teams, as goodwill ambassadors, drum up substantial support—financial and otherwise—for their schools.

But the available research in the area has found no clear connection between the success of a college's sports teams and the generosity of its alumni.[62] As the national chairman of the Presidents Club, a fund-raising arm of the University of Maryland, which recently embarked on a $200 million campaign over five years, I have seen no link between our fund-raising success for the school's educational programs and the fortunes of our sports teams.

Indeed, a tremendously successful campaign was recently concluded by Johns Hopkins Hospital and University, which had targeted $400 million over five years. Without any sports programs at all, Hopkins exceeded its goal by collecting more than $650 million. Hopkins draws donations because of the excellence of its faculty, research, educational programs, and facilities. It did not build its reputation overnight, through gimmicks or with a Final Four appearance.

Unfortunately, a school that looks to its sports program for a quick infusion of money and prestige exacerbates the present imbalance between academics and athletics. All too often the quest for recognition through sports backfires on a school. The hungry institution spends too much on sports, presses too hard to win, recruits players who do not belong on the campus, bends the rules, and winds up on NCAA probation or worse, broke and disgraced.

Despite the sobering statistics on the crushing costs of big-time athletic programs, it cannot be denied that some schools are big financial winners in sports, with Notre Dame alone at the top of the heap. In college sports the rich, like Notre Dame, get richer while the poor get poorer.

Notre Dame seems to have it all—a glorious history on the field, which includes the winningest football record of any school in the country, eight national championships in football since 1936, and seven Heisman Trophy winners; the richest TV contract in college sports; an overwhelming advantage in recruiting; national exposure and popularity beyond any of its competitors; high academic standards (Notre Dame won the CFA's Academic Achievement Award in 1991, with a 92 percent graduation rate for its football players); and a relatively small athletic budget (for example, the athletic budget at Notre Dame is about $6 million less than the budget at the University of Michigan).[63]

Notre Dame is like the student who can letter in three sports, lead the student council, edit the school paper, and make straight A's without cracking a book. The problem surfaces when other students who are less gifted and blessed attempt to emulate her and adopt her practices.

After landing a $38 million TV contract with NBC in 1990, Notre Dame defended itself against charges of greed and hypocrisy, by insisting that it was simply cutting the best economic deal for itself. That is free enterprise, but it is not reform. It is certainly not a step toward deemphasizing athletics and breaking the connection between winning and the big payoff.

Notre Dame's deal is still sending tremors through the sports world. While no team can hope to match it, no team is safe from the blandishments of the networks and cable stations. In the cash-hungry world of college sports, when TV lines up against tradition, the smart money is on TV.

TRUTH #5: MERGERS AND ACQUISITIONS IN THE MERCENARY WORLD OF COLLEGE SPORTS

It is ironic that a college athlete is penalized for transferring to another school even for the purest motives, while an institution like Arkansas can ditch seventy-six years of Southwestern Conference tradition to jump to the Southeastern Conference for more money. Arkansas simply could not resist the temptations of the bigger stadiums, budgets, and paydays of the SEC. While SWC schools have annual sports budgets of about $8 million a year, Tennessee's men's athletics budget alone is $18 million annually.[64]

Welcome to the bigger leagues, Arkansas. Good-bye Rice. Hello 'Bama.

In the wake of Arkansas's desertion, SWC officials fear that its TV syndicator, Raycom, will insist on renegotiating the SWC's $16.5 million contract for broadcast rights from 1990 to 1995.[65]

"Television is part of it," said Dr. Gerald Turner about the SEC's designs on other schools.[66] Dr. Turner is the president of the University of Mississippi, the chairman of a committee formed to study SEC expansion, and a master of understatement. With Arkansas added to its stable, the SEC quickly cast its eyes toward other football heavyweights, such as South Carolina.

TV is the impetus behind the expansion and realignment of conferences, which is reshaping the football map by spurring a rash of highly publicized divorces and remarriages as schools promiscuously hop in and out of conferences.

Prior to 1984 decorum was maintained by the NCAA, which was the matchmaker between the networks and college football. In 1984, however, the Supreme Court condemned the NCAA's stranglehold on TV rights as an antitrust violation in *NCAA v. Board of Regents of the University of Oklahoma.* In a well-reasoned dissent, Justice Byron "Whizzer" White, an all-American football player and Rhodes scholar, argued that the NCAA's TV plan "fosters the goal of amateurism by spreading revenues among various schools and reducing the financial incentives toward professionalism."[67]

The Supreme Court's 1984 decision freed the colleges from certain NCAA restrictions, allowing them to become more capitalistic in their athletic departments. The fundamental flaw with the decision is that it relaxed the NCAA's restrictions on the colleges (the employers) without unshackling the college athletes (the employees), who are strictly prohibited by the NCAA from cashing in on the popularity of college sports. In other words, everyone in the world of college athletics—the colleges, the conferences, the coaches, and the TV executives—is freed from the pretense of amateurism, except the student-athletes.

After the Supreme Court decision, the CFA stepped into the void and negotiated a contract with ABC. The CFA was created as a bargaining unit to deal with the networks, but it too faces a serious antitrust challenge. The Federal Trade Commission brought an antitrust action against the CFA, alleging that it and Capital Cities/ABC had illegally conspired to limit the number of college football games on TV. An administrative law judge has, however, dismissed the FTC's claim on the ground that the CFA is a nonprofit organization (which deprives the FTC of jurisdiction), despite a credible argument that the CFA has by its actions forsaken its nonprofit status to chase TV dollars. The FTC has vowed to appeal.[68]

The courts may ultimately rule that a television contract with a body larger than a single conference violates antitrust law. Hence, each of the major conferences is pushing to package the strongest teams and largest TV markets to deliver to the networks, and every team is desperate to prove that it belongs in the prime-time world of the new superconferences. In the high-stakes game of musical beds, every team fears being left in the cold.

Arkansas's defection to the SEC, Penn State's absorption by the Big Ten, and Notre Dame's unprecedented TV contract have accelerated the pace of realignment. Perennial powers such as Florida State, Miami, Texas, Texas A&M, Oklahoma, and Nebraska are courted by conferences seized with the paranoid prescription to grow big or die.

While the shakeout is just beginning, Frank Broyles, Arkansas's athletic director, predicts that college football is moving in the direction of three superconferences. "Currently there are three networks—CBS, ABC, and ESPN—involved in televising major college football," Broyles explains. "The future may see each of the three superconferences with a major network partnership."[69]

In all the jockeying for bigger, stronger conferences with wider TV audiences, who has been overlooked in the stampede for greater revenues? The student-athletes, of course. When I played college ball, Georgia Tech and Florida State had not yet joined the ACC. Adding those two schools to the conference meant scheduling at least two more long road trips for Maryland.

When the Big Ten added a gold mine like Penn State to its fold, it undoubtedly boosted its stock in the networks' eyes, but it also increased the travel time and costs of its schools in all sports. For example, approximately fifteen hundred miles separate Penn State and Minnesota, both of whom will compete in the Big Ten.

Imagine the travel time between Texas and Florida State if both flocked to the SEC. Or the distance between Nebraska and the Pac-10 teams.

Even as colleges purport to lessen the time demands on their athletes, the conferences are expanding to a degree that will force the players to spend more time on the road and miss more classes. To counteract this trend, the athletic departments should be precluded from scheduling their athletes to be away from the school for more than one night a week.

Furthermore, when the distances are great between competing schools, the student body of the visiting team cannot afford to attend the game; but then, students are becoming increasingly irrelevant to college sports, which are geared toward the convenience of a TV audience of millions, not a few thousand students.

The configuration of the conferences is being decided not by history, tradition, or proximity but by TV ratings, and matchups will mesh with the schedules of the networks, not the students. "This may be a situation where you give up a great deal of tradition," admits Texas A&M Athletic Director John David Crow fatalistically. "Time marches on."[70]

And where has the NCAA been while this explosion has rocked college football? After the Supreme Court took the TV rights away from the NCAA, the shell-shocked organization has been little more than a spectator at the gold rush. NCAA Executive Director Dick Schultz characterizes the major cause of the realignment not as greed but as survival.[71] In doing so, he neglected to mention that realignment is necessary to survival only because annual athletic budgets have skyrocketed to $10 million or more. In other words, college sports empires cannot survive, at their present bloated sizes, without massive infusions of TV money.

While blithely assuring that the advent of the superconference will not decrease the study time of athletes, Schultz characterizes the NCAA's role as ensuring that realignment is achieved "in orderly fashion and with high ethical standards."[72]

What do those empty words mean?

The realignment will proceed with the single-minded goal of maximizing the bargaining strength of colleges and conferences vis-à-vis the networks. It will be down and dirty, with dozens of also-rans being cut out of deals by their former partners. Most of all, it will reinforce in the minds of the public, including athletes and nonathletes from kindergarten to college, that sports are about money. Nothing more. Nothing less.

For all its good intentions and worthy recommendations, the Knight Commission ultimately failed to grapple with the crux of the problem with college athletics, which involves the escalating incentives to cheat in order to win. The financial incentives for winning are rising to unprecedented heights. In the coming age of the superconference, the rich programs will get richer, and the poor will perish. The TV gods will not long tolerate a losing team. So clean programs at fine, small schools, such as Rice and Northwestern, will be banished to the Siberia of college ball. In the future, college teams will either hit the jackpot or hit the road.

While college football teams are scampering to squeeze into a fat-cat conference (or to avoid being squeezed out of one), college basketball teams face a different but related problem—as the pie grows, the big boys want to cut it into fewer slices. Presently Division I of the NCAA has a diverse membership, with enrollments varying from two thousand to fifty thousand and athletic budgets ranging from $600,000 to $20 million.[73]

After the NCAA cut a $1 billion deal with CBS to telecast the basketball tournament for seven years, the basketball powers of Division I-A plotted to reduce the number of mouths at the table. The powerhouses railed against the freeloading schools that allegedly belonged to Division I only for the basketball proceeds without making the same level of commitment (re: spending) to sports as the I-A institutions. In effect, the big boys want to pare down Division I and, thereby, reduce the number of slices of the $1 billion pie; and at the NCAA's so-called "reform convention" of 1991 in Nashville, the bullies got their way, not completely but close enough to portend disaster for the smaller schools in the division.

At Nashville, the delegates approved a sum for athletic financial aid that a school must meet or exceed in order to remain in Division I; and only by a one-vote margin did the small schools set that floor low enough to survive in the division without dramatically increasing their sports budgets. If not for the single deciding vote, as many as seventy schools would have been jettisoned from Division I unless they managed to raise large sums

for athletic scholarships during a recession while the NCAA pur-
ported to campaign for cost cutting in athletic departments.[74]

Despite their reprieve in 1991, the small schools cannot afford
to relax. There will be other attempts by the superpowers to
bounce the little schools from the division. Why? It has nothing
to do with tradition because there will be no exception to the
relegation for schools with long, glorious tenures in Division I;
nor will there be an exception for schools whose athletic programs
have never been tainted by scandal or who graduate high per-
centages of student-athletes. To the contrary, the small schools
with modest athletic budgets are in danger of expulsion precisely
because they embrace an outmoded, traditional belief that athletics is a sidelight at an academic institution and not an overriding
obsession.

TRUTH #6:
THE CONTROL OF COLLEGE ATHLETICS BY TV EXECUTIVES

Even though the public realizes that big-time college sports programs are out of control, the institutions delude themselves into
believing that they can harness the monster created by breeding
an insatiable athletic department with a TV siren. The Knight
Commission suffered a similar delusion by making "presidential
control" the linchpin of its entire reform platform without really
dealing with the influx of TV money into college sports.[75]

As TV dollars pour in, the colleges expand their programs,
becoming ever more dependent on TV money. Colleges anticipate
postseason appearances and factor the spoils from future bowls
and tournaments into their budgets. With big paydays tied to
winning, the temptation to cheat is overwhelming, and schools
justify their corner-cutting as a matter of survival.

Not every insider is blind to the corruption tainting college
sports. "Some programs are out of control," admits Big Ten Commissioner Jim Delany, the head of the committee overseeing the
NCAA basketball tourney.[76]

The networks, not the schools, are calling the shots. When the

NCAA uncharacteristically granted a one-year reprieve to UNLV, allowing the defending champions to compete in the 1991 tournament, there was much speculation that CBS had leaned on the NCAA with an eye to the ratings.[77] Apparently UNLV's presence in the tournament boosted CBS's ratings because the semifinal match, where the Runnin' Rebels were upset, was the highest-rated semifinal in the last five years, while the ratings for the championship (without UNLV) fell 3 percent from the ratings of 1990's championship with UNLV.[78]

In a giant step backward, the CFA struck a deal with ESPN to begin broadcasting college football games on Thursday nights, breaking the tradition of Saturday games and ensuring that even more student-athletes will miss another day or two of classes.[79] Where is the NCAA while these student-athletes are being yanked from classes by the TV programmers? And even if the NCAA is powerless to block the CFA, why hasn't Schultz mounted his bully pulpit to denounce the cynical deal?

Of course, the NCAA and the colleges have a thousand excuses for every mercenary move. Notre Dame can rationalize its abandonment of the CFA even as Notre Dame's vice president sat on the CFA's board, and Arkansas can explain its desertion of the SWC. The SEC's raids on other conferences are part of a long-range plan, and every other conference can justify retaliatory or anticipatory forays on its neighbors. Penn State has reasons for surrendering its cherished independence. With the world of college sports in a state of flux, it is not surprising to find the NCAA hunkering down in the bunkers.

Does anyone doubt that an end-of-the-season college football playoff is on the horizon? A 1989 study by the CFA estimated the haul from a sixteen-team playoff could be as high as $100 million.[80] Even if such a playoff system results in more missed classes by players and flies in the face of the need to deemphasize athletics, how long will the schools leave that TV money on the table?

In addressing the NCAA convention in 1988, Neal Pilson, the president of CBS Sports, attempted to downplay TV's control of college sports:

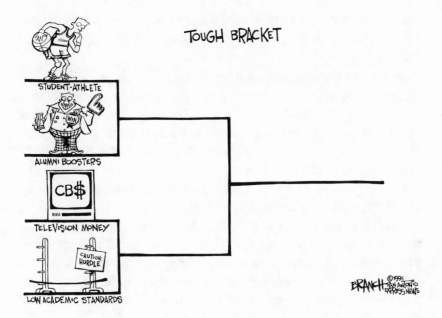

Please note that this revenue generated from television has no strings attached and may be used for any purpose. We do not tell college athletics how to spend their money, we do not tell the NFL, we do not tell the NBA, golf, tennis—they are free to spend that money as they choose.[81]

Despite Pilson's disclaimer, his audience realized that the speaker and his competitors deeply care about how the money from college sports is spent. If it is plowed back into the athletic departments to improve the "product," the networks will up the ante at the next round of contract negotiations. On the other hand, if the colleges devote the funds to libraries, books, non-athletic scholarships, and the like, with the result that the "product" suffers, the networks will punish the schools when their TV contracts expire.

Ostensibly to reduce the temptation to cheat to win, the NCAA established a new formula for the distribution of TV money from the basketball tournament beginning in 1991–1992, which will amount to an average of $143 million a year for the seven-year life of the deal with CBS.[82] This was a chance to send a powerful message about college sports and money to the nation, but the NCAA blew it.

In the 1990 NCAA basketball tourney, each team pocketed $286,500 for each game played, with Final Four participants taking home more than $1.4 million each. Thus, the payoff depended upon a team's progression through the tournament. The more victories, the greater the jackpot. Because of the NCAA's $1 billion TV contract, the pot for the winners would skyrocket to several million in the 1990s if a team's allocation were based solely on its advancement through the brackets.

Consider the impact if the NCAA now decided to distribute the pot more equally among its member institutions, regardless of their finish in the tournament or even whether they made the field of sixty-four. Or imagine the repercussions if the organization had decided to take into account nonathletic factors, such as the graduation rates of athletes at a school.

Characteristically, the NCAA did neither. Instead, it adopted a plan to distribute the bulk of the largesse to conferences in accordance with two predominant factors—the performance of their teams in the basketball tourney over a six-year period and the size of their athletic departments based upon the number of sports sponsored and athletic scholarships granted. An NCAA subcommittee specifically considered but eliminated a proposed graduation incentive, which was replaced by a fuzzier (and un-defined) concept of "academic enhancements."[83]

In short, the NCAA has timidly replaced a winner-take-all formula with a winner-take-almost-all plan. The new formula will continue to reward schools with the biggest, most expensive sports programs, which also historically perform well in the tournament. Thus, the rich will still get richer while the poor are eliminated.

"Under this proposal, a bid in the tournament is worth money for six years," pointed out Jeffrey Orleans, the executive director of the Ivy League. "You've just replaced one kind of financial pressure with another."[84]

Is this reform? Hardly. It is a sop designed to block true reform, which explodes the most dangerous sports myth of all—that the NCAA is really interested in reforming college sports.

I refuse to surrender our colleges to the TV moguls. This is not simply an issue of selling out a few thousand athletes every year, as serious as that breach of trust would be. If colleges become nothing more than money-grubbing enterprises, speaking in platitudes while filling their coffers, they have forfeited their highest calling, which is to teach youth the value of ethics and principles; and they will have reinforced the destructive lesson that money is the ultimate goal. Inevitably the corruption of our colleges filters down to our high schools, junior highs, and grade schools.

Imagine the powerful lesson conveyed to the public if our universities walked away from money on the table, if the colleges decided that certain principles were simply not for sale.

But because the NCAA has failed to push fundamental reform, Congress must be willing to force the issue. When the NCAA comes to Congress for relief from the IRS, as it has in the past and will in the future, Congress should condition any tax breaks on real reforms, such as a fairer distribution of the bonanza to all schools, regardless of their records. If the NCAA is unwilling to take such bold steps, then college sports should be treated and taxed as the big, cutthroat businesses they have become.

Jeffrey Orleans of the Ivy League sounded the warning:

My concern is that if we as an association are viewed as being capitalists—foremost—there are plenty of people in the Congress and the executive branch and in all sorts of state and local governments who will treat us as capitalists. And if they treat us as capitalists, they will tax intercollegiate revenues in ways that have never happened before—and they will regulate intercollegiate athletics in ways that have never happened before.[85]

Chapter 5

MUNICH, 1972

Olympic Reform

No EXPERIENCE IN my life has been as disappointing, bitter, and painful as the 1972 Olympics in Munich, which was the most controversial and tragic competition of modern history. For me, the games were almost over before they began. For eleven others, their lives were over before the Olympics ended.

When I was invited to try out for the Olympic squad at the Air Force Academy, I was riding high. During my sophomore year, I had flirted with a 4.0 grade point average; Maryland had won the NIT championship; and I had been named an all-American. Only a year ago our freshman team had been undefeated and nationally ranked, and a pro team had offered me a $1 million contract.

The tryout camp at Colorado Springs was brutal under the iron hand of Hank Iba, the former Oklahoma State coach whose credentials included guiding the Olympic gold medalist basketball teams of 1964 and 1968. He was a fanatic for "control ball" offense, a throwback to the era when teams were slaves to the "slow-down offense." Most of the players at the camp, including me, preferred a more freewheeling offense, but Iba drilled us to pass the ball sixteen times before taking a shot. At sixty-eight, he had not coached college ball for almost a decade.

From the outset I believed that Iba's methodical, low-scoring offense was unsuited for the talents of his personnel, but he was the coach. Since the elevation of basketball to an Olympic sport in 1936 at Berlin, the United States had won not simply every gold medal in the sport (seven) but also every single game in the Olympics through 1968 (fifty-five in a row). The pressure on us to uphold the tradition was tremendous.

In addition to imposing a slow-down offense on the team, Iba moved me from low post to high post. At Maryland Lefty had installed a double post offense, and I had become adept at working with Len Elmore to spring one or both of us free. Iba was positioning me farther from the basket and discouraging me (or anyone else on the team) from taking an outside shot. We were drilled to look for the pass, not the basket.

Despite the major adjustments to my game, I thought I had played well in the camp, and Iba told the press that I was one of the best players in camp. Then came the announcement of the twelve-man squad, and I was stunned at being named an alternate. I was devastated by my failure to make the cut and the lost opportunity to play for my country . . . ever.

While the Olympic team headed west for three weeks of training in Hawaii, I retreated east to lick my wounds at home. Because Hurricane Agnes was lashing the East Coast, I had been unable to call my parents with the bad news, and they had been unable to reach me with even worse news.

Upon arriving at Mansfield, I discovered that our home had been flooded and the floors were buried beneath silt. Everything in the basement was ruined, including scores of trophies and memorabilia collected by Jay and me over the years. What a depressing sight!

Suddenly my anticipated week of solitude and reflection was washed away, and I was pitching, bailing, and shoveling with the rest of the family to save our home. In retrospect the intense, grueling physical activity was probably the best tonic for me. It snapped me from depression and banded our family together in a common goal.

Several weeks later, after the house had been salvaged, I was focusing on the next season at Maryland when I was called by one of Iba's assistant coaches. Fed up with Iba's "boot camp" regimen at a military base near Pearl Harbor, UCLA's Swen Nater had quit the squad, and I was being asked to jet to Hawaii to fill the empty spot on the roster. I accepted the invitation, partly because Lefty was touting the Olympics as a "once in a lifetime" opportunity.

Missing much of the training camp hurt me, and it was a painful adjustment for me not to start but to wait impatiently on the bench for three or four minutes of playing time. Still, I was proud to be an Olympian and determined to make the necessary adjustments by honing my passing and defensive skills under Iba's tutelage.

We were the youngest basketball team the U.S. had ever fielded for the Olympics, with eight of us under twenty-one (in contrast, the youngest player on the Soviet squad that year was twenty-one); but we were also the tallest. The average height on the team was six feet seven inches, with Tom Burleson of North Carolina State at seven-four. (With Burleson at NC State and me at Maryland, we were destined to compete in the ACC for four years and would later become teammates in the pros.)

Other standouts on the squad included Doug Collins of Illinois State, who later became an outstanding NBA player and coach; Bob Jones of North Carolina, who went on to star for the Philadelphia 76ers; and other future pros such as Jim Brewer of Minnesota and Dwight Jones of Houston.

Despite our youth and inexperience in international competition, we were the heavy favorite to win the gold medal at the Twentieth Olympiad and maintain the U.S.'s unbeaten streak, with the USSR and Cuba posing the greatest threats to our preeminence. Iba repeatedly warned us that, although we could not be beaten by another Olympic team, we were in danger of beating ourselves.

When we arrived in Munich, all the pressures dissipated, at least for the moment. The Germans were determined to erase every trace of the 1936 Olympics, which had been Hitler's showcase for Nazism. As the birthplace of the Nazi party, Munich was especially eager to distance itself from Hitler's games. Our hosts had taken great pains to remove every vestige of militarism, even to the point of outfitting the police in civilian clothes. This was intended to be an Olympics unsullied by politics. "Munich is interested in neither records nor superlatives," insisted its former lord mayor, Dr. Hans-Jochen Vogel. "We are aiming at a festival dedicated to a peaceful encounter among nations."[1]

Trouble was the farthest thing from my mind as German President Gustav Heinemann opened the games on Saturday, August 26, 1972. To foster international goodwill, the Germans had arranged for four runners to accompany their torch bearer—Jim Ryun of the United States, Kip Keino of Kenya, Kinji Kinihara of Japan, and Derek Clayton of Australia.

As part of the throng of thousands of athletes from 122 nations who marched inside the stadium while eighty thousand spectators stood and cheered, I was deeply moved by the opening ceremony. It was a kaleidoscope of flags and colorful uniforms. The stadium was also awash in commercialism, with eye-catching logos and advertisements at every turn. Even the red-white-and-blue blazers of our U.S. team had been donated by Sears. It was ironic that the Olympics were so eager for corporate sponsorships while at the same time so defensive about the pristine image of the "amateur" athletes.

I was so touched by the spectacle that I almost forgot that politics had already intruded on the games. Not marching with us athletes were forty-three Rhodesians, who had been evicted from the competition and the Olympic Village by a recent vote of the International Olympic Committee (IOC), the governing body of the games. Faced with a threatened boycott by thirty-four African nations and the cream of the American track-and-field team, the IOC had banished the Rhodesians in a close vote (thirty-six in favor of expulsion, thirty-one against, and three abstentions), marking the first time in his twenty years as the IOC president that Avery Brundage had been on the losing side of a showdown.

Presiding over his last Olympics, the eighty-four-year-old Brundage was ending his long tenure on a note of defeat. He was convinced that the IOC had set a dangerous precedent by bowing to political pressures. On the officials' stand during the opening ceremony, he looked forlorn and out-of-place. Time had long since passed by Brundage, especially his outmoded belief in a rigid dichotomy between "amateur" and "professional," which was rooted in the English Victorian preoccupation with preventing the working class from competing against gentlemen of leisure. I was marching with thousands of athletes, the vast majority of whom were not amateurs in any meaningful sense. Most of the competitors were being supported by the state, a corporation, or a college, but Brundage was still clinging to the charade of amateurism.

The basketball entries were broken into two divisions, with the United States favored in one and the USSR in the other. We breezed through our division with a 7–0 record and were seriously challenged only by Brazil. For the first four games, I saw limited action and never broke into double figures in scoring. From the fifth game (against Egypt) on, however, I found my range and began playing substantial stretches, even breaking into the starting lineup for a few games. Despite Iba's conservative offense, I scored in double figures against Egypt (16 points), Japan (14 points), and Spain (10 points).

Wrapping up our bracket with a perfect 7–0 mark filled the team with confidence even though we did not have a single scorer in the top twenty in the sixteen-nation basketball tournament. But far from concerning Iba, the absence of a scoring leader delighted him. He focused on team statistics, not individual marks. And our team was averaging 77 points on offense while giving up only 44 points on defense.

More important, we were only two victories from the gold medal. Two teams from each bracket advanced to the medal round. While we were slated to face Italy in the semifinals, the Soviets and Cubans would tangle in the other semifinal match.

The predictions of a U.S.–USSR championship were looking good in this most politicized Olympics of all time.

For refusing to stand at attention during the playing of the national anthem, two black U.S. runners were banned by the IOC. Petitions were placed in the American dorms urging President Nixon to stop the bombing in Vietnam, but there were few signatures. Insulated by my "tunnel vision," I paid scant attention to these distractions.

On Tuesday, September 5, tragedy struck the Olympics and held the entire world hostage. In the early morning hours, eight terrorists from the Black September movement, a violent arm of the Palestine Liberation Organization, infiltrated the Olympic Village and stormed Building 31, a three-story structure that housed Israel's twenty-one-member contingent.

In a building across the Village, I was awakened by a commotion outside the room about 5 A.M. and later learned that two Israeli coaches had been killed in the bloody takeover. The body of one of the early victims was pushed onto the street for all of us to see, a bloody message that the terrorists meant business.

From the Village I watched the tragedy unfold with a front-row view of the terror. It was the longest day of my life and the most tragic day in the history of sports. By 9 A.M. thousands of German police and dozens of sharpshooters in sweatsuits surrounded Building 31; and by noon the terrorists announced their demands—the release of 236 Palestinians from Israeli jails and safe passage from West Germany. Inappropriately the IOC allowed the games to continue until late afternoon, almost twelve hours after the deaths of the first two Israelis. Most of the athletes blithely went about their business, as if nothing were happening in Building 31. Self-absorbed in their private sports world, they were oblivious to the horror before them. A few coaches and athletes insensitively suggested the demolition of the occupied building to teach the terrorists a lesson, even at the cost of the hostages' lives.

Rumors flew through the Olympic Village faster than the fleetest sprinter. A deal has been reached. No deal has been made.

Two dead. Ten dead. More terrorists sighted. The hostages were safe.

As the negotiations stretched out all day and into the night, I often thought I was trapped in a surreal nightmare. I could not believe my eyes. Every hour or so a masked terrorist stepped onto a balcony in plain sight of thousands of police and witnesses, and only a few hundred yards from me.

I was struck by the irony that, twenty-five years after World War II, German police were trying to protect Israelis on German soil. There was the further irony that the Germans, who had been so intent on removing all vestiges of militarism from the Olympics, had been forced to flood the compound with twelve thousand police officers. I could not shake my mind from the visit by our basketball team to Dachau only a week ago, and I feared the horror of more Jewish sacrifices.

The talks stalemated. Golda Meir, Israel's prime minister, refused to negotiate with the terrorists. Chancellor Willy Brandt rushed to the scene from Bonn to offer an unlimited cash ransom. He also proposed substituting German officials for the Israeli hostages, but the terrorists were adamant. The sky turned dark, and a sense of foreboding seized me. Around midnight I heard helicopters overhead and watched in horror as the terrorists herded nine hostages, bound and blindfolded, onto a bus. I feared that the terrorists had won.

After the terrorists departed with the hostages, I could not sleep. Anxiously I awaited a report on the fate of my fellow Olympians. Shortly after midnight a radio announcer assured us that all the terrorists had been shot and all the hostages were safe. My relief was, however, short-lived as later stories began to suggest that the initial report of success had been inaccurate.

About 3 A.M. on Wednesday I was sickened by the official word that all nine hostages had been killed. The kidnappers had taken the athletes by bus to three helicopters, which whisked them to a Boeing 727 at an isolated military airfield about fifteen miles from Munich. At the airport German sharpshooters had opened fire on the terrorists. When it became clear that the kidnapping had been thwarted, the terrorists lobbed grenades into the heli-copters holding the Israelis. In the bloodbath all nine Israelis, five terrorists, and a policeman were killed.

It was, as ABC's Jim McKay accurately described, "the worst day in the history of sport."[2]

In the aftermath of the massacre, everyone was in a state of shock. Many athletes, including me, assumed the Olympics were over; and although the events were resumed after a delay of twenty-four hours, the spirit of the games was dead. The Olympic Village assumed a different personality. Instead of the freewheel-ing accessibility that had made the competition so enjoyable, se-curity clamped down on the compound. Our hosts discontinued all efforts at downplaying their security measures and packed the compound with uniformed guards.

During the one-day delay, a memorial service for the slain athletes was held in the stadium. Unfortunately, Brundage was more interested in rearguing the Rhodesian expulsion than in honoring the Israelis. In his speech he linked the expulsion and the deaths as "two savage attacks" on the Olympics, as if the events were equally grave. When Brundage announced that "the games must go on," a knot tightened in my stomach. I was ap-palled by Brundage's heavy-handed attempt to convert the me-morial service into a pep rally.[3]

Despite Brundage's admonition, the games did not go on for everyone. Many athletes who had finished their events hastily departed, including seven-time gold medalist Mark Spitz, who is Jewish. Several dozen athletes pulled out before their events, including the entire Egyptian and Israeli teams. Although I wished the games had been cancelled, I abided by the consensus to resume the competition on Thursday.

On Wednesday I joined an American contingent in placing a wreath on Connollystrasse in front of Building 31, where the slain Israelis had lived. Inside Building 31, I saw bullet holes in the walls and in the door that Josef Romano, a courageous Israeli weight lifter, had tried to close on the storming captors until he was felled by their bullets.

The stench of fear and death hung like a cloud over the claustrophobic compound. Gone were the laughter, the banter, the friendly exchanges, and the exuberance of meeting and competing against the best in the world. Now there was only the mechanical drive to finish the charade and return home safely. There could be no happy ending to the Twentieth Olympiad.

Shana Alexander captured the surreal nature of the Munich Olympics:

> By then we had all—audience, journalists and participants alike— become too facile at snapping back and forth between tragedy and sport; we no longer quite knew the difference between game and reality. It was so easy to switch from timing milers to timing murderers.[4]

Even though our team was barely emerging from the shock of the massacre, we had little trouble with Italy in the semifinals on Thursday. In contrast, the Soviets were forced to come from behind to beat the tenacious Cubans, 67–61, in the other semifinal contest. The United States was now 63–0 in Olympic basketball competition, and only the USSR stood between us and our eighth straight gold medal in the sport of our invention. In four of the last five basketball finals, the United States had beaten the Soviets.

Stepping onto the court on Saturday night to face the Soviets, I had no idea that in a few hours I would be embroiled in one of the most controversial matches in Olympic history and suffer my bitterest defeat in sports. From the opening tip, we knew we were in a dogfight. The Soviets were big and strong, but we were quicker. Unfortunately, Iba's half-court game played into their strength and robbed us of our advantage in team speed.

The Soviets led for the entire game, building an 8-point cushion with six minutes to play; but we chiseled away at their lead. With three seconds in the game and down by only a point, Doug Collins drove for the basket and was hammered to the floor. He rose to his feet slowly, still reeling from the blow, and groggily made his way to the foul line. Collins calmly sank both free throws, and by a single point we led for the first time, 50–49.

With only three ticks left on the game clock, I was deployed to guard an out-of-bounds opponent with the ball. He threw a desperation pass, which was deflected at midcourt, and we had won. Iba's "kiddie corps" had done the job and brought home another gold medal. I was whooping it up and hugging my teammates when I noticed the confusion at the scorer's table.

An Olympic official in the stands, with no jurisdiction over our game, was instructing the scorer to reset the clock to three seconds and give the Soviets another shot at the basket. There was pandemonium on the court, and it took minutes to restore any semblance of order. In the melee Iba lost his wallet to a pickpocket.

After everyone had been removed from the court except the players, the Soviets were handed the ball and another chance. Again I was assigned the man with the ball out of bounds, and I harassed him so much that he threw short. The buzzer sounded, and again we began to celebrate.

As before, our celebration was aborted by an official's decision that, because the clock had been improperly reset, the Soviets were to receive a third shot at the gold. This time there was bedlam on the court. Because Iba and his assistants were arguing at the scorer's table, we were without a coach to position us for the upcoming inbounds pass.

I was still guarding the man with the ball, but this time the referee forced me to back away from the line. With the referee hovering over me, I feared a technical foul if I played too close to the line, and I would have died if we had lost our first Olympic game on a technical foul.

With mass confusion on the court, Aleksandr Belov shoved two American players out of the way, caught the inbounds pass and scored an easy lay-up. USSR 51, U.S.A. 50, the scoreboard read as the final buzzer sounded for the third time. Covering the game for ABC, Frank Gifford made the call, "And this time, it is over." Never before or since have I plummeted from such heights to such depths so quickly.

The gym was a madhouse as we players were hustled into the dressing room. One of the two officials actually working the game, a Brazilian referee, refused to certify the score; and Iba was lodging protests with anyone who would listen. Fights were erupting among the reporters covering the bizarre ending.

Tom Burleson and I broke away from the Olympic Village to drown our sorrows at a hofbrauhaus. The next day in the relative quiet of the compound, the team voted unanimously not to accept the silver medal because we felt we had won the gold. Twice.

The medal ceremony was postponed while the International Federation of Amateur Basketball (FIBA) heard the U.S. protest, which was skillfully pleaded by our attorney-commentator Howard Cosell and supported by the game referee who had, contrary to international rules, seen his authority usurped by a meddlesome official in the stands. Despite Howard's eloquence and the Brazilian referee's testimony, the score stood. The Soviets belatedly received the gold medal, and for the only time in Olympic history, no silver medals have ever been accepted. The vote on the FIBA jury of appeals was believed to be three to two, with representatives of the Communist bloc countries of Hungary, Poland, and Cuba siding with the Soviets, and judges from Italy and Puerto Rico ready to overturn the result.[5] A desperation appeal to the IOC also netted us nothing.

The disputed game sparked a firestorm and threatened to escalate into an international incident. At first the criticism was leveled at the Soviets, but later the guns were turned on Iba and his players. No one was harder on Iba than my college coach, Lefty Driesell, who was in the stands for the Olympic finals, sitting next to my apoplectic father. In an Associated Press story that was carried in every major paper in the country, Lefty slammed Iba for playing a slow-down game. "Our game is fast break," Lefty explained. "John Wooden or Dean Smith could have taken any college team in the top ten and whipped the Russians by 20 or 25 points."[6]

Lefty came down even harder on me and my teammates for refusing our medals, calling our protest "even more bush than the officiating."[7]

The basketball fiasco crystallized the frustration of the American competitors and viewers over a pattern of controversial officiating, especially in boxing, wrestling, and gymnastics. Many of our wounds, however, were self-inflicted. A sprint coach had forgotten the starting times of two world record–holders and overwhelming favorites for medals, Eddie Hart and Rey Robinson, who were scratched from the races for which they had prepared for years. American doctors had neglected to clear Rick De Mont's asthma medication, which cost him the gold medal in the 400-meter freestyle and a shot at the gold in the 1,500-meter freestyle, which was his best event.

Blunders marred the games, even down to the closing ceremony. When the electronic scoreboard saluted Avery Brundage for his twenty-year reign as the IOC president, the name was misspelled—"Brandage." This was a fitting end to the most tragic and controversial Olympics in history.

It was not, however, my last brush with the Olympics. In 1976 I was invited to attend the Olympic tryouts by the new American coach and my friend, Dean Smith, even though I was then earning about $80,000 a year playing pro basketball in Italy while attending Oxford as a Rhodes scholar. I was making a good salary but still had an AAU card, which allowed me to play in the Italian league and the Olympics. It made no sense. As much as I craved another shot at the gold, I was not ready to indulge in the hypocrisy that permitted some pros to play but denied others the opportunity to do so. For that reason I turned down Dean's invitation—the second time I had disappointed the talented Tar Heel coach, who led the U.S. team to the gold medal in 1976.

Since 1972 I have been an outspoken advocate of dropping the outmoded definition of amateurism preached by Brundage and opening the Olympics to the best athletes in the world—pro, amateur, or hybrid. Notwithstanding Brundage's frequent references to the ancient games, the earliest Greek games were amateur because only the well-heeled aristocrats could devote the time and resources to the competition. And over time the Greek city-states began subsidizing their leading athletes and munificently rewarding them.[8]

In 1894, as the modern games were being revived, the IOC promulgated its first ruling on amateurism, which directed that "[t]he tendency of every sport without exception must be towards pure amateurism, with no permanent motive existing in any sport to justify cash prizes. . . ."[9] But from the outset the distinction between amateur and professional proved elusive, and the issue was revisited almost every four years. The first serious attempt to abolish the distinction in the modern Olympics was spearheaded by Bo Ekelund of Sweden in 1946. Unfortunately, he was outflanked by Brundage, whose philosophy dominated for the next forty years.

Immediately after the 1988 competition, I circulated a resolution in Congress to allow pros to compete in the games. And now the IOC has dropped the pretense of amateurism for the 1992 Olympics and will permit professionals to compete, at least in certain sports such as basketball. In general, the IOC will now accept competitors if they meet the qualifications of the international federations of their sports.

With NBA players eligible for the Olympic basketball team in 1992, Chuck Daly, the Olympic coach who guided the Detroit Pistons to back-to-back NBA titles in 1989 and 1990, will lead the strongest team in Olympic history onto the court in Barcelona—a dream lineup that includes Michael Jordan, Magic Johnson, Larry Bird, David Robinson, Patrick Ewing, John Stockton, Charles Barkley, Scottie Pippen, Chris Mullin, and Karl Malone.[10]

Ironically, at the 1992 games, the NBA superstars and other wealthy pros may be competing solely for the trophy while the so-called amateurs will still receive remuneration for their Olympic efforts. Brundage's world will have been turned on its head. One of Brundage's oft-repeated assertions was that he had never known of an athlete who was unable to compete in the Olympics for financial reasons—a highly dubious claim in 1946 and utter nonsense by the time of the Munich games in 1972. Opening the Olympics to professionals will relieve some of the financial pressure in the "money" sports, such as basketball and hockey. To the extent that our Olympic roster is filled with superstars such as Michael Jordan, a subsidy is not necessary. But in less glamorous sports, such as rowing and water polo, it will have little effect.

A 1989 report overseen by George Steinbrenner, vice president of the United States Olympic Committee (USOC), concluded that about 90 percent of U.S. amateur athletes were struggling financially.[11] Moreover, of the 167 countries in the Olympic movement, the USOC is the only Olympic committee that receives no sustaining government subsidy.

Compared to competitors from other countries, U.S. Olympians are underfunded, and the results of the medal derby reflect this. In 1968 the United States won 20 percent of the medals, compared to only 13 percent in 1988.[12] The sad fact is that the U.S. Olympic team is not competitive today and is becoming even less so over the years. Furthermore, in this era of austerity, we cannot ask the taxpayers to foot a massive bill to fund our athletes. And while the IOC has recently become more forthright about the fuzzy line between pros and amateurs, the NCAA has not. Too many college athletes refuse any assistance from Olympic committees, fearful of disqualification from intercollegiate competition by the NCAA.[13]

Moreover, the USOC has a checkered history of managing our Olympic effort, and much of the money raised by the umbrella organization is diverted to the myriad of sports federations, never reaching the individual athletes.[14] Rife with power struggles, inadequate management techniques, and excessive administrative expenses, the USOC has failed to develop a long-range plan to train and assist our Olympic athletes.[15]

Internecine warfare is not new to our Olympic effort. In 1974 I testified before the Senate Committee on Commerce, which was considering the Amateur Athletic Act of 1974, on the lack of representation by athletes on the governing boards of the NCAA and the Amateur Athletic Union (AAU). The NCAA and the AAU had long been sniping at each other, with American Olympians caught in the cross fire. In this connection the Senate Committee expressly found in 1974 that

> these on-going disputes among sports organizations are highly detrimental to individual American athletes and to teams representing the United States in international competition. The Committee rec-

ognizes further that both the AAU and NCAA have established a
system of inflexible rules and regulations, reflecting in a significant
way their antagonistic attitudes toward each other. Both groups tend
to look upon athletes as "property," rather than as individuals who
have voluntarily agreed to participate in organized programs and
competition.[16]

In the Amateur Sports Act of 1978, Congress created the present incarnation of the USOC to oversee our Olympic activities.
Unfortunately, Congress has failed to monitor the USOC, which
was rocked in 1991 by the resignation under fire of its president,
Robert Helmick, amid charges that he abused his volunteer post
with the USOC to benefit his private law practice.[17] There has
been no major congressional review of the body responsible for
our Olympic effort since its creation in 1978.

To improve and promote our Olympic team and to ensure that
the USOC is performing its intended functions, Representative
Ben Nighthorse Campbell of Colorado, who is the only Native
American and one of only three Olympians in Congress, approached the other two Olympians—Senator Bill Bradley and
me—to form an Olympic Caucus in Congress to apprise elected
officials of the USOC's activities. Campbell had competed on the
Olympic judo team in 1964, and Bradley had captained the Olympic basketball team the same year.

Since 1988, we have begun working toward the goals of encouraging youth participation in sports, improving training facilities for our Olympic athletes, identifying potential problems with
the Olympic organization, and exploring legislative initiatives in
the area. Although the federal government does not directly support the Olympics, its support of the Olympic Coin Act has helped
raise millions for the USOC.

Congress is rightfully disinclined to pump massive public mon-
ies into the U.S. Olympic effort. The ultimate irony is that, while
U.S. athletes are suffering financial hardships and falling farther
behind the field, money from American networks is fueling the
Olympics and flowing to other host countries. The gargantuan
Olympics could not exist without the frenzy of bidding by the

American networks, which pay far more than their foreign counterparts for the TV rights to the spectacle.

For example, ABC paid a whopping $309 million for the U.S.
rights to televise the winter Olympic games in Calgary in 1988,
over 95 percent of the total revenues received by the IOC for
broadcast rights, while all of Western Europe (with a population
larger than the United States and an economy of roughly the same
size) paid only $5.7 million, Canada forked over $3.65 million,
and the Soviet Union and Eastern Europe chipped in $1.2 million.
For the 1988 summer games in Seoul, NBC paid the IOC $300
million for broadcast rights, almost 75 percent of the IOC's total
take, while Western Europe anted up only $28 million.[18]

The overpayment by American networks to the IOC will continue into 1992. NBC bid more than $400 million for the summer
games in Barcelona (while all of Western Europe will receive the
TV rights for only $90 million), and CBS sank $243 million into
the rights for the winter competition in Albertville, France.[19]

Why do U.S. networks pay such disproportionate fees for essentially the same TV feed enjoyed by their foreign counterparts
at much cheaper rates? The answer is simple. American networks
bid against each other, while the rest of the world largely avoids
such cutthroat competition. For example, the bid from all of Western Europe is lodged by a single body—the European Broadcasting Union (EBU), whose members are mainly public
broadcast networks.

Who benefits from the bidding frenzy of the U.S. networks?
Apparently not the networks, because both ABC and NBC lost
millions from their 1988 deals. There are estimates that CBS may
lose as much as $75 million on the 1992 games.[20] Moreover, TV
viewers in this country suffer because the U.S. networks must
pepper their broadcasts with commercials in an attempt to recoup
their staggering investments. NBC inundated its 1988 coverage
with more than five thousand commercials, which consumed about
23 percent of the viewing time.[21]

In the future, U.S. audiences may discover that more and more
of the Olympics are being carried by cable or pay-per-view channels, again in an effort by the networks to recover their invest-

ments or at least cut their losses. NBC has developed a plan to sell more than six hundred hours of programming on the 1992 summer Olympics to pay-per-view subscribers.[22]

It is conceivable that cable will outbid the beleaguered networks for the broadcast rights to the 1996 Olympics in Atlanta, which will be the hundredth anniversary of the modern games. It will be ironic if the American networks—which have largely funded the Olympics for the benefit of other countries and their citizens for decades—will then be limited to carrying over free TV what cable decides to sell.

Concerned that the networks' current economic woes may affect their bidding on the rights to the 1996 games, the Atlanta Committee for the Olympic Games (ACOG) has conducted discussions with at least five groups of television producers (including Turner Broadcasting) about the possibility of providing the world feed for the games.[23] This would be a break in past practice under which the network with the rights to the games in the United States has served as the originator of the television signal for the world feed. And this would be another sign that the networks' grip on sports broadcasting is slipping.

While American networks and consumers have paid a heavy price for the networks' bidding wars, the IOC has received a hefty windfall, most of which has been channeled to the host cities, into administrative costs, and even to other countries to fund their Olympic efforts. Because of the payment to the host city to defray the massive costs of constructing an Olympic infrastructure (both the costs to Atlanta and the IOC allocation to the city are still undetermined for 1996), the Olympics makes sense economically to the United States only if the games are being held here.

The funneling of money from American businesses to foreign host countries will be even more politically sensitive in connection with the winter games in Japan in 1998. It is likely that American citizens will be very touchy about sending American dollars to Japan to construct Olympic buildings.

According to the USOC, it will receive back from the IOC only about 10 percent of the revenues paid to the IOC by U.S. networks in 1992; but the formula will change for 1996, with the USOC pocketing 10 percent of the first $400 million for U.S. broadcast rights and 50 percent of the excess above $400 million. Thus, to increase its cut in 1996, the USOC has a strong incentive to drive up the costs to U.S. networks of the TV rights, courting the twin dangers of commercial overkill and flight to pay-per-view channels.

In 1990, I introduced The Olympic Television Broadcasting Act to benefit the networks by curtailing the destructive bidding wars, the viewers by improving the broadcasts, and the athletes by increasing their funding.

At the request of Dick Pound of the IOC, I withheld my bill from the 1991 session of Congress to avoid harming the chances of Salt Lake City to host the winter games in 1998. Unfortunately, Utah lost its bid to Japan. So the bill was reintroduced in 1992, with my request for hearings before the Telecommunications and Finance Subcommittee of the Energy and Commerce Committee, on which I serve.

My Olympic burden-sharing bill interposes a middleman—the USOC—into the negotiations between the IOC and the U.S. networks. The networks would submit their bids for Olympic broadcast rights to the USOC, which would exact limits on the timing of commercials (no interruption of live action), the overall amount of commercials (no greater than the average for prime-time programming), and the sale of Olympic coverage to cable or pay-per-view channels. In return for accepting such conditions, the networks and cable would be granted by Congress an antitrust exemption in bidding on the rights to the Olympics. In effect, the networks and cable would be allowed to pool their bid for broadcast rights and share the coverage and the financial risk.

The USOC would then negotiate a TV contract with the IOC, much as Western Europe and the rest of the world now do; and the USOC would tailor its bid to be commensurate with those of other countries. It is anticipated that the USOC would not pass through to the IOC the full bid of the networks but would retain a substantial cut (at least 35 percent) to train and support our Olympic athletes.

In 1990 I met with Harvey Schiller, the executive director of the USOC, who has mixed feelings about my bill. On the one hand, he realizes that the USOC must work with the IOC, and both organizations fear the loss of their windfalls if my bill reduces the networks' bids by bringing them in line with the payments of other countries. The USOC apparently prefers the present situation in which negotiations are open between the IOC and the networks, and between the IOC and the USOC. On the other hand, the USOC understands the advantage of using my bill as leverage to pressure the IOC into sweetening the pot for the USOC.[24]

If the IOC fails to remedy the present imbalance in funding soon, Congress may do so, through either my proposal or others. Several years ago Congressmen Charles Rangel of New York and Guy Vander Jagt of Michigan introduced a bill to impose a tax of 10 percent on an entity receiving payment for U.S. television and radio broadcast rights for the Olympics. Under their proposal, the payor is to withhold the tax, which will be earmarked to train and assist U.S. Olympic athletes.

Both the Rangel–Vander Jagt bill and the USOC's acquiescence in the status quo leave untouched the present proliferation of commercials during Olympic coverage and the encroachment of cable and pay-per-view. The American consumer deserves better.

The USOC, our Olympic athletes, the U.S. consumers, and the American networks will all benefit under my bill. In fact, the only clear loser under my proposal is the IOC, which would be stripped of its leverage over the U.S. networks. The IOC will argue that it will be difficult if not impossible for it to offset the loss of TV revenues under my proposal, and this is true to a point.

But the Olympics, like many college sports programs, have become a bloated bureaucracy, which invests far too heavily in massive infrastructures and far too sparingly in the athletes. If the U.S. networks were no longer the patsies of the IOC, it might be impossible to maintain the games at their present size and scale, but there are a number of ways for the Olympics to cut costs significantly.

The most important reform is to select a permanent site for the Olympics, perhaps in Greece. After all, the Greeks invented the

Olympic games in 776 B.C.; and when the modern games were revived in 1896, they were held in Athens. Switzerland is also a good candidate for a permanent site because it could host both the winter and summer games.

It may no longer be economically feasible to move the Olympics to different locales, sparking massive investments in a new infrastructure and bloody political battles every four years. It would be much less expensive and wrenching to settle on a fixed site, and the savings could be channeled to the training and assistance of athletes.

And a permanent site could reduce the political problems associated with moving the games and increase the security of the athletes. As one who will be forever scarred by the tragedy in Munich in 1972, I would be inclined to adopt a permanent site for security considerations alone.

Chapter 6

SOUND BODY

The Physical Fitness of Our Nation

DURING MY SENIOR season in 1974, I played in one of the most memorable college basketball games of all time—the Atlantic Coast Conference championship between Maryland and North Carolina State. I was only a few months from graduating with a premed degree with honors; I had been selected as a Rhodes scholar; and I had led the Terps in scoring for the past two seasons. Only the national crown had eluded me, and I was down to my last shot. Although we had won the NIT tournament in 1972 (which was a much more prestigious event before the NCAA tournament expanded to sixty-four teams), we were hungry for the NCAA title.

So was North Carolina State, which had not lost a game the previous season but had been barred from the NCAA tournament. My college basketball nemesis was David Thompson, the superb forward for the Wolfpack. With his forty-two-inch vertical leap, Thompson played much bigger than his six-foot-four-inch frame, and he had an abundance of offensive weapons. Thompson was the most gifted athlete I ever competed against, and the Pack boasted outstanding talent to complement his considerable skills, including Tom Burleson and playmaker Monte Towe.

Although North Carolina State had gone undefeated in 1972–1973 and had won the ACC tourney (with Thompson easily winning ACC Player of the Year honors), the NCAA bounced the Pack from the national tournament that year for recruiting violations. As the runners-up in the ACC tourney, we replaced the suspended Wolfpack in the NCAA tourney in 1973, where we lost in the regional finals to the Providence Friars, who were led by a trio of future pro standouts—ball-handling wizard Ernie DiGregorio, Marvin Barnes, and Kevin Stacom. As excited as we were to play in the tourney, we hated to sub for the team that had beaten us in the ACC finals—a squad that had bested everyone but the NCAA that year.

Although the ACC had been brutally strong in 1972–1973, the conference was even deeper in talent the following year, so deep that three of its teams would finish the season in the Top Ten—Maryland, North Carolina, and North Carolina State. Indeed, Billy Packer and Roland Lazenby rated the 1973–1974 lineups at Maryland and North Carolina State as two of the twenty-five greatest college teams of all time.[1] Unfortunately, throughout my college years, only one team from the ACC qualified for the NCAA tourney. In contrast, today a strong conference like the ACC might place five or six of its teams on the sixty-four-squad field for the NCAA tournament.

As if we did not have enough problems within our conference, we opened my senior season on the road against UCLA, which had won the last seven national championships and was enjoying a seventy-five-game winning streak. This was the first of two West Coast road trips for us in December, and I was very reluctant to leave the East Coast because my father was gravely ill. It was a tough time for me.

Pauley Pavilion at UCLA was a madhouse when we stepped onto the court against the awesome Bruins, coached by the legendary John Wooden and led by Bill Walton. With only seconds to play, UCLA held the ball and a one-point lead, forcing us to foul intentionally. When UCLA's Richard Washington missed the free throw, we had a chance to pull off the biggest upset of the decade. Unfortunately, John Lucas was bottled up in a corner with the ball, and he never fired a shot or a pass before the buzzer sounded. By a single point, the Bruins preserved their amazing streak.

Instead of demoralizing us, however, the near-upset pumped us with confidence. We rolled over the next nine teams before running into North Carolina State. Like us, the Wolfpack had lost only one game, also to unbeaten UCLA. Our first of three contests with North Carolina State was televised to a huge audience on a Super Bowl Sunday, and Thompson lit up the scoreboard with 41 points to spark the Pack to an 80–74 victory.

We finished the regular season with only four defeats (two losses to North Carolina State, one each to UCLA and North Carolina), while the Wolfpack had lost only to UCLA early in the year. Like the Terps, the North Carolina Tar Heels had four losses (three to North Carolina State and one to us). All three teams were destined to finish the year in the Top Ten, but only one of the ACC powers would move on to the NCAA tournament.

We easily dispatched our first two opponents in the 1974 ACC tournament, winning by 20-point margins over Duke and Dean Smith's Tar Heels. Now only North Carolina State stood between us and the NCAA tournament. The ACC tournament was staged in Greensboro, North Carolina, which was hostile territory for us but almost home to the Pack; and the championship was our third game in three days, while North Carolina State, which had drawn a bye in the first round, had enjoyed an extra day's rest.

Both teams played at exceptional levels, each committing only four turnovers in the first half, at the end of which we led 55–50. In the second half we fell behind 66–61 and then surged ahead 77–72. With five minutes in the game, the score was knotted at 89–89, but State pulled ahead by four with two minutes to play. We hit two quick baskets, and John Lucas launched a desperation shot at the buzzer for the victory. It fell short, and the score was 97–97 at the end of regulation.

In the overtime we ran out of gas. We led 100–99 with a shade over two minutes left in the overtime and Lucas on the line. He missed, and we never scored another point. The Wolfpack won 103–100, behind 38 points for Burleson and 29 by Thompson. Maurice Howard and I led the Terps with 22 points each, with Lucas and Elmore contributing 18 apiece.

Norm Sloan, the Wolfpack coach, was gracious in victory, calling Maryland the second best team in the country. "His [Driesell's] team shot near 60 percent, they scored 100 points, they had few turnovers and they still lost," Sloan said. "Maryland didn't get to go to the NCAA Tournament. They were one of the best teams of the decade, one of the best ever."[2]

So was Thompson's Wolfpack, which advanced to win the 1974 national championship by beating UCLA in double overtime in the semifinals and rolling over Al McGuire's Marquette in the championship, all without ever leaving its home state for a playoff game. In a tribute to Maryland, Wolfpack guard Monte Towe said after his team won the national crown, "Nothing can compare to beating Maryland in the ACC finals."[3]

With only one defeat over the past two seasons, North Carolina State ruled the basketball world in 1974; and so did its high-flying star, David Thompson, who was named the NCAA tournament's outstanding player and AP's national Player of the Year as a junior.

Even though the Wolfpack did not make it back to the NCAA tournament during Thompson's senior year, he averaged over 29 points a game during the 1974–1975 season and was again tabbed as the national Player of the Year. The honors poured in, and he became the first player selected in the NBA draft of 1975. Drafted by Atlanta, he signed instead with Denver of the ABA and starred in the new league for several seasons as an All-Star. He was the ABA Rookie of the Year and the Most Valuable Player in the ABA All-Star game in 1976.

Thompson was like a meteor in basketball. He blazed brightly across the scene and then disappeared; and despite his many honors and awards, I believe that he could have achieved much more. He could have been another Dr. J or Michael Jordan. The eleventh of eleven children in a struggling family, Thompson rose to the top of his sport by talent and effort. In college no one had worked harder than the Wolfpack star to become an all-around player; but in the pros, after a few years of stardom, he began to slide. Drugs accelerated his fall from grace.

I was never blessed with the natural gifts of David Thompson, but we shared the same work ethic. I carved a steady but unspectacular career spanning eleven seasons in the NBA. If Thompson could have lasted eleven strong seasons, he might have rewritten the record books.

John Lucas, one of my teammates at Maryland, was almost a match for Thompson in the talent department. John was so athletically gifted that he was a college all-American at both basketball and tennis and was the first pick in the 1976 NBA draft—a year after Thompson had been the number one draft pick.

During his pro career, John played for the Houston Rockets, Golden State Warriors, Washington Bullets, San Antonio Spurs, and Seattle SuperSonics. But he became so hooked on cocaine that he was banned by the NBA. With tremendous strength and courage, however, John fought back to kick his drug habit and resume his basketball career. Today he lectures nationwide on the importance of rejecting drugs and is the president of Students Taking Action Not Drugs (STAND), a nonprofit group dedicated to deglamorizing drugs, and the John Lucas Regional Treatment and Recovery Center in Houston, where former Dallas Maverick Roy Tarpley (the seventh player to be banned for life by the NBA) is being treated.[4]

In the pros I watched drugs destroy individual careers and entire teams. The Atlanta Hawks, for whom I played six seasons, had great young athletes and appeared to be poised to break into the NBA elite; but drug abuse crippled several players and sabotaged the team. When I was traded to Atlanta in 1983, Ted Turner often boasted about having a Rhodes scholar on his team, but then again he also boasted that he had the lowest payroll in professional sports. Ted did not, however, boast about his team's personnel problems.

Our coach on the Hawks was the hard-charging Hubie Brown, who was convinced that the performance of several players was suffering from drug use. He was constantly berating these players—chiefly John Drew, Armond Hill, Terry Furlow, and Eddie Johnson, an All-Pro guard who was arrested with cocaine in his car and was later discovered to have a lithium imbalance.[5]

Some of the Hawks were sleepwalking through the games; and during a contest at Indianapolis, Drew actually fell asleep on the bench as he was coming down from drugs. Later he recognized the seriousness of his drug problem and sought treatment. Furlow would die in an auto accident, with traces of cocaine in his blood.[6]

I never actually witnessed drug use on any of my NBA teams, but I saw its effects. My closest encounter occurred after a playoff game when I was an Atlanta Hawk. I knocked on a teammate's door to ask about the departure time for the team bus. When the door was opened, I was hit by a cloud of smoke. I left without asking any questions.

In my maiden campaign for Congress in 1986, during my transition from the NBA into politics, I was looking for imaginative ways to create excitement and raise money. A fund-raising event was organized around a number of basketball stars from the NBA and local colleges who were supporting me. One of these stars was Len Bias, an all-American at my alma mater playing under my old coach, Lefty Driesell. Bias had recently been the number one pick of the Boston Celtics and was destined for NBA superstardom.

On the night of the fund-raiser, a number of luminaries gathered, including several congressmen and Washington Bullets; but Bias was a no-show. I was troubled because Bias was responsible and took his commitments seriously, but I assumed that an emergency had intervened. The next morning I learned that he had OD'ed on cocaine while celebrating his multimillion-dollar contract with the Celtics, which had been signed that day.

The ink on his contract with the Celtics was still wet as his death certificate was being signed. One day he was the envy of millions of sports fans and the NBA's newest multimillionaire, and the next day he was stone cold on a slab. Dead at twenty-two. There would be no second chance for Bias, as there was for John Lucas.

It is a tragic irony that athletes, whose livelihood depends upon their mental and physical conditioning, would destroy their minds and bodies with drugs. Another sad irony is that our society, though obsessed with sports, is woefully unfit. We spend so much time watching sports or arguing about sports but so little time playing sports. As a nation, we have little respect for our bodies, and this is particularly true of our children.

Only 40 percent of adults in the United States exercise or play sports regularly, with less than 20 percent exercising at levels vigorous enough to produce cardio-respiratory benefits.[7] The picture is even bleaker for our kids.

Among our youth, fitness has not improved in the past decade and is in some cases declining. Fifty percent of girls from six to seventeen and 30 percent of boys from six to twelve cannot run a mile in less than ten minutes; and 55 percent of girls and 25 percent of boys between six and twelve cannot do even one pull-up.[8] According to a 1989 study, the proportion of children meeting or exceeding the minimal standards on four fitness tests has declined from 43 percent to 32 percent.[9] A shocking 40 percent of American youngsters between the ages of five and eight already have at least one heart-disease risk factor—physical inactivity, obesity, elevated cholesterol, or high blood pressure.[10]

Obesity among our children has increased greatly since the 1960s.[11] Tragically, most of our children are overweight, and overweight kids turn into overweight adults.[12] Nearly one in three kids between the ages of three and eighteen have above-average blood cholesterol levels; and researchers have discovered a link between high cholesterol levels among youth and their hours of TV watching, during which they are physically inactive, are bombarded with ads for junk food, and are susceptible to nonstop snacking.[13] According to Newton N. Minow, former chairman of the Federal Communications Commission, television viewing has increased from an average of 2.2 hours a day in 1961 to 7.3 hours a day now.[14]

So the myth of sports stardom has seduced kids away from not only the libraries but also the gyms. The myth divides the world into stars and spectators and confuses the distinction between sports and fitness. Athletes shortchange their minds and abuse their bodies with steroids in the quest to become stars and, upon failing to reach that plateau, abandon fitness entirely.

Although blessed with about five hours a day of leisure time, many Americans complain about a lack of time to exercise. The flimsiness of this excuse is illustrated by a few examples of exceptionally busy people who make the commitment to fitness, including many of my colleagues in government.

A congressman's life is a nonstop whirl of meetings, hearings, receptions, and fund-raisers. But almost every afternoon at 3:30, the House gym is the site of a basketball game that draws ten to fifteen "regulars" from Congress. Dan Rostenkowski, the powerful chairman of the House Ways and Means Committee, derisively refers to these jocks as "wetheads," because they regularly return to their seats with their hair still plastered from the shower. Perhaps the most famous of the "wetheads" was Dan Quayle, who was rumored to enjoy the gym more than the committee room while in the House and later the Senate.

When I was first elected to Congress in 1986, the "wetheads" invited me to play. Although I participate in a game or two a month, I never became a regular. An ex-pro like me faces a real quandary in deciding on the level of intensity for a pickup game, especially the annual congressional Democrat-versus-Republican grudge match.

Do I play all-out, seek to dominate the court, and risk censure as a bad sport? Or do I stifle my competitive instincts and jeopardize my reputation as a jock? What if I have a bill before an important committee, such as Ways and Means, and a key member of that committee is driving for the basket? Do I try to stuff the ball down his throat, or do I surrender the basket for the good of my constituents?

Although I have occasionally allowed certain colleagues a break when a committee assignment was at issue, it is difficult for me to curb my competitive instincts.

Another reason for not becoming a regular wethead is the craziness of my schedule. Although it is often difficult for me to escape in the afternoon, I make time in my schedule for a daily workout. If I have a free half hour or more, I enjoy basketball or tennis; and if my schedule for the day is tight, I usually resort to more solitary activities such as lifting weights, climbing the StairMaster, or running with my two Labrador retrievers—Chocolate and Licorice.

After my election to Congress in 1986, one of my close advisers suggested that I abandon basketball to avoid the "jock" stereotype, much as Bill Bradley had reportedly done following his election to the Senate. Only rarely will Bill pick up a basketball, apparently because he wants to be known as a hard-working statesman and not as a former NBA star. Nonetheless, even the cerebral senator from New Jersey deigned to play a few basketball games in the House gym when his Tax Reform Bill of 1986 needed shoring up in Congress. Who says politics and sports do not mix?

In committing myself to a daily workout, I am inspired by the example of President Bush, who is probably the most physically active president of this century. Fishing, boating, tennis, golf, paddle ball, and jogging are all part of his fitness regimen; and the President is a frequent visitor to the House gym, where he plays paddle ball with his close friend, Representative Sonny Montgomery of Mississippi. On many occasions I have had an opportunity to chat with the President during his workouts there.

During the week before President Bush was hospitalized with atrial fibrillation in May 1991, I worked out with him twice—once in the House gym and again on the lawn of the White House during National Fitness Week with a group of congressmen under the stern guidance of Arnold Schwarzenegger, the chairman of the President's Council on Physical Fitness and Sports (PCPFS).

When I was an eighteen-year-old high school senior, I was no-
tified by the White House of my appointment as the youngest
person ever to serve on the President's Council. James Lovell,
the former astronaut, was its chairman at that time; and Judy
Ford, Miss America, also served with me on the Council. At that
point the Council had been in existence almost fifteen years and
was slipping into the background as the crisis behind its creation
became old news.

In 1955 Hans Kraus, a prominent New York physician, published the results of his study showing that American children
were unfit compared to their European peers, and the report
triggered an outcry from which the President's Council emerged.
The following year President Eisenhower founded the Council
(first known as the President's Council on Youth Fitness) through
an executive order. The Council enjoyed its heyday under President Kennedy but has since degenerated into a small federal
agency with little funding or hoopla. The twenty private citizens
on the Council are appointed by the President and report to the
President and the Secretary of Health and Human Services.

The Council was almost moribund until the energetic Schwarzenegger seized the helm, reinvigorating the body and bringing
fitness to the forefront of the nation's thinking. One of the actor's
goals is to visit all fifty states during his chairmanship to promote
fitness. While President Bush was exercising in the House gym,
he bragged to me that Schwarzenegger was traveling across the
country "on his own dollar" to promote health.

I informed the President that recently Schwarzenegger, the
"Kindergarten Cop," had visited an elementary school in Mill-
ersville, Maryland, which is in my congressional district, and had
generated great excitement among the kids (and the adults as
well). I told the President that his muscular chairman had warned
the children of the danger of "chunck" food, and President Bush
(who has a weakness for fried pork rinds) admitted that Arnold
had given him the same lecture.

Like President Bush, Schwarzenegger has an extremely hectic
schedule and could tender a thousand excuses for missing his daily
workout, but the world's top box office draw makes fitness a

priority. "I haven't lost more than twenty days in the last year with my fitness schedule," Schwarzenegger boasted. "I make it a priority, a part of life. There is no excuse today of 'I don't have time.' That's crap. Everyone can find time."[15]

In naming Schwarzenegger as the head of the President's Council, George Bush made an excellent choice. If Schwarzenegger surrenders the crown, President Bush should look no further than his home state of Texas for the next chairman of the President's Council—Nolan Ryan, the fortysomething phenom of the Texas Rangers. In his twenty-five-year pitching career, Ryan has amassed a string of impressive statistics—more than three hundred victories; more than five thousand strikeouts; and a record seven no-hitters, the final gem pitched at the grand young age of forty-four.

Ryan would be a great pick for the Council not because of his staggering statistics but because of his devotion to the ideal of a sound mind and a sound body. He owes his longevity in the big leagues to his fitness regimen. After Big Tex became the oldest pitcher in the history of baseball to toss a no-hitter, the TV cameras followed him to the clubhouse. What an inspiring and instructive sight for all sports fans! As millions of Americans watched, Ryan mounted his stationary bike and performed his postgame exercise ritual.

The first order of business for Arnold and the Council is to stress the difference between fitness and sports. While sports should enhance fitness and encourage respect for the body, they have not always done so in our society. Instead, we have perverted sports by overemphasizing competitive contests and underemphasizing lifetime fitness. Only in recent years have the tests used by the Council been modified to reflect fitness (endurance, flexibility, and strength) rather than athletic ability.[16]

We need to be less preoccupied with honing the skills of the varsity quarterback or developing the hook shot of the star center and more concerned with the health of the large class of couch potatoes. Our sports-obsessed society invests great time, resources, and attention in sports such as football, which can generally be played only by the young, when we should be encouraging participation in activities such as tennis, which can be played by most individuals for their entire lives.

To elevate the level of youth fitness in our country, we must return physical education to our schools; and under Schwarzenegger's leadership, the Council has made this goal its first priority. Presently only about one in three schoolchildren receive daily physical education; and only one state—Illinois—requires daily P.E. in all its schools from kindergarten to twelfth grade.[17]

Furthermore, the knee-jerk reaction of many financially strapped school districts is to jettison their P.E. programs in the first wave of budget cuts. Too many school administrators lose sight of the Greek ideal of the sound mind and the sound body. Instead of cutting or scaling back our P.E. programs, we need to make them more relevant by emphasizing lifelong activities such as tennis, hiking, and cycling.

Cutbacks in physical education programs represent a false economy for several reasons. To begin with, a good exercise regimen is not necessarily expensive. Running, jumping, hiking, calisthenics—these are not expensive activities. Moreover, the same school districts that cry poverty when pressed to provide a comprehensive P.E. program for the benefit of all students will often lavish money and attention on state-of-the-art sports programs for their elite athletes. And it costs no more to stock snack machines with fruit instead of candy bars.

Finally, the failure to educate our children on the importance of a sound body will cost us in the short and long runs by reducing the quality of their lives and driving up health costs. The nation's health costs skyrocketed from $230 billion in 1980 to $606 billion a decade later; and they may triple in the next ten years if our sedentary kids become sickly adults.[18] Aware of the connection between greater fitness and lower health costs, Schwarzenegger hopes to persuade a coalition of insurance company executives to fund his media campaign for fitness.[19]

Politicians frequently warn of the catastrophes that inevitably unfold from the failure to invest in the "infrastructure," which became the political buzzword of the 1980s. But our children are the true infrastructure; and if we fail to teach them the importance of a sound mind and a sound body, our society will suffer for generations to come.

Parents must pressure their schools to return P.E. to the curriculum and not surrender to the will of "penny wise, pound foolish" school boards. Parents must also realize that schools are not the sole answer to the fitness crisis. A parent who exercises regularly with his child is triply blessed. Not only has the parent spent precious time with his offspring, but he has also furnished the child with a role model for life. And he has maintained his own fitness.

It is shortsighted for people to fail to develop their bodies and even more shortsighted for them to abuse their bodies with drugs, whether performance enhancing or so-called recreational. Perhaps the most extreme example of short-term thinking was uncovered by Gabe Mirkin, who reported that more than 50 percent of the athletes he surveyed were willing to take a drug that would guarantee them a gold medal in the Olympics, even if it was certain to kill them within a year.[20]

This is the most extreme manifestation of the myth of sports stardom, which beckons an athlete to sacrifice everything—his education, his health, and even his life—for a few years, months, or even minutes in the spotlight. In our society, steroids are the closest thing to Mirkin's magic potion or alchemic formula. Derivatives of the male hormone testosterone, these drugs increase protein synthesis, which may (in conjunction with a high-protein diet and an intensive training regimen) increase lean muscle mass. They promise a new body capable of greater strength and faster speed, a transformation from human to superhuman. They offer an edge or, at least, negate the edge of an opponent who is also "on the juice."

Although some doctors are skeptical that steroids really work, many athletes subscribe to the slogan of "Better Bodies by Du Pont." They have seen the pills transform a five-foot-eight-inch 135-pound kickboxer into a 185-pound bodybuilder.[21] Or a 219-pound football lineman into a 241-pound monster with a 35 percent increase in strength.[22]

A former football player described the attraction of steroids as follows:

No single element of physical training has had as much impact on sports as anabolic steroids. They are the genie's third wish to thousands of athletes who have slaved on the track and in the gym all their lives. Just that little pill, or that quick injection, and training results leap to a new dimension. Every football player on "the juice" chuckles as doctor after doctor tells him that there's no proof steroids really work.

I took steroids. I wanted that extra something to make my body that much more potent on the field. Some people "add" to their resumes, football players "add" to their bodies.[23]

Steroids have been used by athletes since the 1950s, mainly in track and field and bodybuilding; but their use is growing more pervasive, spreading to other sports and reaching younger kids. An estimated 500,000 adolescent boys are using steroids to gain a competitive advantage in sports or merely to look better.[24] Moreover, it is feared that the nonmedical use of steroids by teenagers is growing, with more than half of the users starting by the age of sixteen.[25]

Dr. Louis Sullivan, the Secretary of Health and Human Services, fears that "some adults who are charged with our young people's welfare might be passively accepting or even tacitly approving the use of these dangerous drugs."[26]

According to a 1990 study by Professor Charles Yesalis of Penn State, steroid use among college athletes may be higher than previously estimated by the NCAA, which in a 1989 report found that fewer than 5 percent of college athletes admitted steroid use. By asking universities to estimate the steroid use of their opponents, however, Professor Yesalis's research team projected a rate of almost 15 percent for male college athletes (and 29 percent for college football players) and nearly 6 percent for females.[27] The football world was rocked several years ago by the allegations of a former Notre Dame football player that "almost half" of the lettermen on his team used steroids despite an NCAA ban.[28] The

American Heart Association estimates that 50 percent of Division I college football players have used steroids.[29]

The Seoul Olympics in 1988 was called the "Drug Olympics" in many quarters because random testing discovered ten competitors who tested positive for performance-enhancing drugs, including Canadian sprinter and gold medalist Ben Johnson. As pointed out by Dr. Gary Wadler, the coauthor of *Drugs and the Athlete,* Ben Johnson offers a "double-edged lesson" in that, despite being detected and stripped of his Olympic medals, he proved to many that steroids really work.[30]

A subsequent, more sophisticated test uncovered more than fifty additional athletes at Seoul who had used steroids in the six months before the games but who had successfully masked their drug use.[31] Currently a game of cat-and-mouse is escalating between officials (IOC, NCAA, NFL, and others) and athletes in which science is simultaneously refining the drug testing procedures and the tricks to beat the tests. In this endless game of technology versus technology, which is the drug equivalent of the arms race, the chemical epitestosterone, which is used to mask the results of steroid testing, has recently appeared on the black market and in the possession of athletes.[32] Of course, a test will be devised to detect epitestosterone, which will then be replaced by a new masking agent. And so it goes.

The drug of choice today appears to be human growth hormone (HGH), which cannot presently be detected by testing.[33] Lyle Alzado, the former All-Pro defensive lineman of the Los Angeles Raiders, took HGH during his aborted comeback bid with the Raiders; and he easily passed the team's drug tests.[34] Now he suffers from an inoperable brain cancer that he attributes to two decades of using hormones to improve his performance on the football field. Describing NFL drug testing as "minimal and light," Alzado estimates that 80 percent of NFL players are taking steroids or HGH—a figure that the league calls far too high.[35]

Alzado attributes to steroids not only his present illness but also his violent brand of play.[36] One of the well-documented side effects of steroids is greater aggressiveness, which exacerbates the risk of injury.[37] In football the general rule is that the incidence of injuries rises with the size and speed of the players.[38] Thus, to the extent that steroids and HGH succeed in building bigger, faster bodies, we can expect an increase in the number and severity of injuries in the sport—at every level of drug use, from the pros to junior high schools.

As players become bigger and stronger (whether due to steroids or not), contact sports such as football and basketball have become rougher and more violent. Unfortunately, we have almost come to expect violent behavior during athletic contests. Indeed, we have gone so far in condoning violence in sports that we are surprised when an assault during an athletic match is treated seriously by the authorities.[39] There have been assaults on referees, coaches, and players; and in Los Angeles there were so many fights connected with prep soccer—on the field and off—that the sport was placed on probation.[40] In recent years athletes at all levels from high schools to the pros have been involved in a disturbing number of sexual assaults.[41]

No one claims that steroids are responsible for all or even most of the violent episodes by athletes. Nonetheless, because the incidence of steroid use is unknown, the drug may be a contributing influence in much violence on and off the athletic field. Other contributing factors are the general level of violence condoned in society at large and the extent to which athletes have been coddled into believing they are above the law.

Drugs—both performance-enhancing and recreational—are destroying sports, which is a small cost compared to the toll on the lives of the human guinea pigs who swallow them. In the beginning, the chief concern of the IOC and the NCAA in banning steroids was maintaining the competitive balance among athletes and between teams, but now the fear of dangerous side effects to the athletes is paramount.

Among the side effects of steroids in adult males are acne, aggressiveness, kidney dysfunction, reduction of sperm production, breast enlargement, baldness, enlargement of the prostate gland, and prostatitis.[42] The drugs can also cause heart disease, liver cancer, sterility, and impotence.[43] In addition, they can lead to severe personality disorders, sometimes resulting in aberrant sexual and criminal behavior. An athlete who cycles on and off steroids may display two distinct personalities, both of which differ from his presteroid self.[44]

The side effects for women, which may be even more devastating and some of which may be permanent, include masculinization, abnormal menstrual cycles, excessive hair growth on the face and body, and deepening of the voice.[45]

In the quest for the scientific key to the better body, steroids are only the beginning. The future will bring more sophisticated technology, such as implants, to produce the bionic athlete. The "brave new world" of implants has already been scouted by East Germans, who, prior to the reunification of Germany, experimented with harvesting the organs of living patients for transplants.[46] If we cannot cope with the proliferation of steroids now, how can we handle the technological "advances" of tomorrow?

Even if steroids had no serious side effects, however, they confer an unfair advantage to the takers; and for that reason alone, drug testing would be warranted. I am not enthusiastic about universal drug testing but recognize that in some form it will be a necessary evil of sports for years and probably decades. In their obsession with sports, the fans and gamblers will demand the testing of thoroughbred athletes.

In this area, the NBA is far ahead of the other leagues. When I was playing pro ball, the viability of the NBA was threatened by drugs, but the league adopted a sane testing policy that has helped to remedy the situation. The NBA has successfully combined testing upon suspicion with generous doses of counseling and a set number of violations before a player is banned from competition. By admitting its serious problem with drugs early, the NBA is a model for other leagues.

Nonetheless, it seems ludicrous that, in a society that is ravaged by drugs from top to bottom, we are more concerned with the mandatory testing of athletes rather than those in positions of greater responsibility—CEO's, lawyers, doctors, teachers, and even congresspersons. Because of the cult of sports, Len Bias's death hits the nation's newspapers and air waves while thousands of addicts die anonymously. Similarly, Magic Johnson's announcement that he was infected with the AIDS virus belatedly focused the attention of the world (and especially young black men) on the terrible toll of AIDS and the importance of safe sex. Magic made it impossible to ignore AIDS or pretend that it was "their" problem—meaning gays and drug users; and he has become the most forceful advocate for AIDS education in the world.

The purpose of sports should be to enhance fitness and to encourage everyone to strive for the ideal of a sound mind and a sound body. But occasionally sports and fitness erupt into open conflict, as in the present furor over alcohol and tobacco companies that link their products to sports figures, teams, and events.

When I played pro ball, some of the arenas were so smoke filled that it was hazardous to compete there. Certain images were indelibly stamped on sports. For example, Red Auerbach, the legendary coach and general manager of the Boston Celtics, ritualistically lit his victory cigar near the end of a Celtic win. I recall watching Phil Jackson, my teammate on the Knicks and the coach of the 1991 NBA champion Chicago Bulls, smoking in the locker room after a game. Ironically today Red is banned from firing up in the stands, but Phil can still smoke in the locker room, which is practically the last haven for cigarette-starved athletes, since most sports arenas have banned smoking.

Rightly or wrongly, kids idolize athletes, and sports have become the medium for transmitting values to the next generation. Alcohol and tobacco producers are profiting from this connection. In the not-so-distant past, we were bombarded with ads of athletes hawking beer and cigarettes. Since 1971, no one—not even star athletes who have been placed above the rules all their pampered lives—can pitch cigarettes on radio or television (and smokeless tobacco ads were banned from radio and TV in 1986). So the tobacco companies, unwilling to abandon the lucrative association between sports and nicotine, began to subsidize entire sporting events.

The tobacco industry pours $500 million into sports for advertising every year.[47] It is almost impossible to watch a sporting event—whether football, baseball, tennis, or racing—without catching a tobacco ad. Some sports circuits—particularly the Virginia Slims women's tennis tour—owe their existence to cigarettes, which are the leading cause of premature, preventable death in the United States. Almost 500,000 Americans a year die from tobacco-related disease.[48]

Dr. Alan Blum, the outspoken founder of Doctors Ought to Care (DOC) and an antismoking activist, described the dangerous link between sports and tobacco:

> Through billboards picked up at key camera angles on television, the tobacco companies have found a way to juxtapose their cigarette brands with the athletes—without even having to pay an endorsement fee. Some of the best TV camera angles—the runner leading off first base . . . for example—pick up a huge billboard for Marlboro in the background. Dozens of such images, totaling several minutes, occur during each telecast, in violation of the law against advertising on television. The health warnings, difficult to read at the ballpark, are invisible on the TV screen.[49]

In recent years, however, two high-ranking federal officials have attacked the alliance between the tobacco industry and the sports establishment—former Surgeon General C. Everett Koop and Dr. Louis Sullivan, Secretary of Health and Human Services. The former championed a ban on all cigarette advertising, and the latter is urging a boycott on sports events backed by tobacco companies, including ballparks plastered with cigarette ads.

In 1991, the Federal Trade Commission (FTC), which enforces the ban on TV ads for smokeless tobacco, brought the first complaint that based the alleged violation upon the display of a brand name and logo during a sports telecast. Although the case was settled, it raises a host of questions about similar sports programs sponsored by cigarette companies and may prompt the Department of Justice (with jurisdiction over the ban of cigarette ads on TV) to become more aggressive in enforcement.[50]

The movement in this country for an outright ban on cigarette ads continues. A handful of countries have already banned cigarette advertising, including Canada.[51] Although Canada's ban was overturned by a judge in 1991 on the ground that it violated the right to free speech, the case is expected to reach the Supreme Court of Canada.[52] In the past five years, several bills have been introduced in Congress to follow the example of Canada and other countries, and these bills have come before the House Committee on Energy and Commerce, on which I serve.

But an outright ban troubles me, chiefly for First Amendment reasons. If we ban cigarette ads, where do we draw the line? Do we also ban movies and books that portray smokers in a positive or flattering light? Young people may be much more strongly influenced by a movie featuring Julia Roberts with a cigarette in hand than by any ad from the industry. I prefer to stress the importance of educating the public to the dangers of smoking, taxing the sale of cigarettes, curbing the threat of passive smoke, and toughening the laws forbidding the sale of tobacco (or alcohol) to minors.

There is momentum in Congress to increase the federal tax on cigarettes in order to reduce both consumption and the deficit— a move that received a boost from a 1990 study suggesting that raising the taxes on cigarettes reduced their consumption.[53] Indeed, cigarette taxes were raised in 1990 and will increase again in 1993. In addition, there are a number of congresspersons, including Mike Synar of Oklahoma, who have long criticized the association between the tobacco industry and sports.[54]

With or without Congress, citizen initiatives in this area will press forward. For example, Minnesota activists pressured the public body that runs the Metrodome Stadium, home of the Twins and Vikings, to purge the already smoke-free stadium of cigarette ads as soon as contracts with the tobacco sponsors expire.[55] Similarly, the owners of the Oakland A's baseball team issued an edict against smoking in their ballpark.[56] In 1991 the NCAA banned the use of all tobacco products in its postseason baseball tournament.[57]

But even if the fans and governmental bodies purged sports of its ties to the tobacco and alcohol industries, the battle for our youth has only begun. Parents are still the front-line soldiers in the fight to convince kids of the importance of a sound mind and a sound body. If a child's role models are overweight, slothful spectators who abuse their bodies and minds with inactivity, alcohol, and tobacco, the child will follow in the parents' tracks—from the refrigerator for a beer, the pantry for potato chips, and the purse for a cigarette, to the TV room for afternoon doubleheaders all weekend.

Chapter 7

GLOBAL GLADIATORS

New Worlds to Conquer

In 1978, I was traded by the New York Knicks to the Atlanta Hawks. I had heard and read much about Ted Turner, the brash, colorful owner of the Hawks, a billboard business, and a fledgling television company. By this point the controversial entrepreneur had attracted a slew of nicknames—"Captain Outrageous," "the Mouth from the South," and more than a few that are unprintable.

During my first meeting with Ted, he was a whirlwind of activity. He pumped my hand and gushed with excitement about landing a Rhodes scholar on his team. The next day he ushered me into his car and whisked me to the Atlanta countryside. Beckoning me from the car, he proudly pointed to a stretch of land littered with twisted metal, which he grandly described as his "satellite farm." Although the area looked more like a junkyard, this was where Turner was arranging his uplinks to send signals to his satellite, which would relay them to cable stations across the country.

"This is where I will send my signals to the stars," Turner intoned reverently. Turner's "SuperStation," which is now beamed into half the homes in the United States, was only a pipe dream then.

My initial reaction was that Ted was completely bonkers, but before long I began to appreciate the strategy behind his grand scheme. The "satellite farm" was the beginning of his cable empire. Ted was at the forefront of the revolution of sports and television in this country and in the world, realizing early that sports and TV were shrinking the globe. While other owners of independent stations were struggling to hold on to their share of the local market, Ted set his sights first on a national audience and then on an international audience.

Turner's SuperStation and HBO were the first cable stations to uplink to satellites. Ted has often said, "I was in cable before cable was cool." While other station owners were fighting cable in the 1970s, Ted joined the cable association and angered his fellow owners of independent stations by testifying before Congress in favor of cable.[1]

Over time Ted and I became close friends—so close that shortly before his divorce from his first wife Jane, he jokingly offered me $1,000,000 to marry her and take her off his hands. Of course, I laughed at his tongue-in-cheek suggestion; but many times since, I have estimated in jest how much I could have saved Ted if he had not been kidding. After all, his divorce settlement cost him many times more than his seven-figure offer to me, and Ted was always looking for a way to save a buck. For example, while league rules dictated that his basketball team fly first class, Ted traveled coach on team trips.

Because so many of our Hawk games were carried by WTBS to all parts of the country, I received tremendous exposure. We were the most watched sports team in the world; and to this day I run into sports fans from small towns thousands of miles from Atlanta who followed me on WTBS. To a budding politician, such exposure was gold.

I was also fortunate to be around Ted, whose ideas are ambitious and enthusiasm infectious. He led me to invest in the telecommunications industry in which I am still involved. Will Sanders, Ted's former chief financial officer, and I were among the early pioneers in the cellular telephone industry.

As I was settling into Atlanta, I was becoming more deeply involved with politics and especially the Democratic party. In 1981 I was appointed an assistant to the finance chairman of the Democratic National Committee (DNC), and my jobs included recruiting sports stars to the fold and devising innovative ways to raise funds for the party, which had been depleted and demoralized by Reagan's landslide victory in 1980. Suddenly the idea of a political cablecast hit me. If the SuperStation could beam basketball stars into millions of living rooms, it could do the same for political stars such as Bill Bradley, Gary Hart, and Walter Mondale.

I sold the idea of a telethon to Ted Turner and Charles Manatt, then the chairman of the DNC. On June 10, 1982, a two-hour program entitled "We Are the Democrats" aired from 8 P.M. to 10 P.M., with Manatt and me as cohosts. There was no way the party could have afforded two hours of prime time on one of the networks, even assuming a network would have sold us such a block of time. With our coffers depleted, this was the most effective way to take our message to the nation.

The telecast cemented the marriage between politics and cable. And the wedding of cable and sports was not far behind, with Ted Turner again serving as the best man. Ted was among the first to realize that cable, with its proliferation of channels, had an insatiable appetite for sports. He also understood the advantage of owning both the sports franchises (the Hawks, Braves, and Chiefs) and the SuperStation (WTBS)—of owning the message and the medium.

While traditional team owners were still depending on the live gate for much of their revenue, Ted gambled on satellite distribution and won. And the Atlanta fans were the real winners. Atlanta viewers receive hours of free sports programming a day on Ted's stations because he controls the program costs for team rights and relies on a mass advertising base and subscription fees for revenue. The combined revenues of broadcasting and sports franchises result in savings to the fans and extra funds for team development. It is ironic that the fans and press in Atlanta have often blasted Ted for everything from meddling with his teams to cheerleading on the sidelines—without realizing that Ted's innovative operation made it possible to maintain three major sports franchises in a medium-size sports market.[2]

Years ago Ted told me that someday he would not need a live audience at his sports events to make money, and that in the not-so-distant future the only people in the stands would be spectators who were paid to provide local color and background noise, much like a "laugh track" for a sitcom.

Ted was a pioneer "narrowcaster." Realizing that the television dial had become clogged with fifty or more channels, he targeted discrete audiences by offering highly specialized fare—sports on one channel, news on another, movies on a third. With a multitude of channels, Ted understood that no single channel had to be all things to all people—a lesson that the networks are learning today, much to their distress.

In 1990 he outbid the networks for the rights to NFL games. Ted forked over $445.5 million for the rights to Sunday night games for the first half of four seasons. In the process he broke ESPN's stranglehold over the NFL on cable and emboldened the NFL to extract the richest TV programming deal in history from the networks.

During the negotiations, Ted impressed the NFL brass by promising to make NFL games international events. He boasted, "Sports are becoming international; we're international."[3] Ted told me years ago that if he could beam his signals to the people of the Soviet Union, the entire country would be transformed; and he was probably right.

It is no accident that a cable magnate like Ted Turner is also promoting the internationalization of sports, that a television pioneer is also the genius behind the Goodwill Games, which is a mini-Olympics. The two phenomena—the explosion of cable TV and the globalization of sports—are linked; and Turner's vow (or threat) to take the NFL worldwide is part of his plan to shrink the world.

The ramifications for our sedentary society are sobering. In the past decade broadcasters have gambled that there is an insatiable hunger for sports on TV. In effect, they have hooked viewers on TV sports and in the process have created an army of sports junkies. For Arnold Schwarzenegger to succeed in reinvigorating the nation, he will have to coax adults and children away from the tube. There is, of course, an irony in using a media star like Schwarzenegger to counter an addiction that has been fed by the media.

And our national sports addiction, which is difficult to control today, will be even harder to harness in the future, because it is being fueled by technology. The paging industry now caters to sports fans who will pay for updates of sports scores. And over the next few years, advances in cable technology—especially in fiber optics and digital video compression—will expand the number of cable channels from an average of thirty-three today to as many as three hundred.[4] While perhaps fifty of these new channels will be devoted to pay-per-view movies, a chunk of them will be dominated by sports.[5]

This is a staggering prospect in light of the present saturation of sports on TV. Whereas in 1970 the networks offered the fans less than eight hundred hours of live sports events, in 1990 the junkies were bombarded with seventy-three hundred hours of sports programming on broadcast and cable television, excluding the fare carried on regional and local cable channels and local broadcasts.[6] One hundred eighty-four more games and ten thousand more commercials will air over the course of the new sports contracts with the three networks, ESPN, and Turner than were carried under the terms of the previous agreements.[7] In 1979 ESPN became the first national cable network to provide sports programming exclusively. Today ESPN provides more than fifty-two hundred hours of live sports programming a year and is available to more U.S. homes (approximately 61 percent of all television households in the country) than any other cable network. In addition, there are about ten national cable networks that devote all or part of their air time to sports.[8] Dozens of regional cable sports networks (RSN's), which serve a limited geographic area, have sprouted in the major media markets in the last decade.[9] Two of these—SportsChannel and Prime Network—now compete on a national level. And the flood of sports telecasts will increase with the privatization of television in Europe.

In May of 1990, the House Subcommittee on Telecommunications and Finance, on which I serve, held hearings on the role of TV and sports. Among those testifying were the commissioners of the major sports leagues and Dick Schultz, the executive director of the NCAA.

Paul Tagliabue, the NFL commissioner, testified that in the 1989–1990 season, a Redskins fan in D.C. had available a total of eighty-five NFL games on broadcast TV alone, while NBA Commissioner David Stern stated that the NBA's exposure on national network television had more than doubled in the last decade. On the college level, Schultz claimed that coverage of both football and basketball is increasing on both broadcast and cable. In 1989 nearly five hundred college basketball games were available to viewers in most TV markets, through a combination of broadcast and cable stations, RSN's, and local stations.[10]

The established networks anticipated a shot in the arm from all this sports programming. In 1988 the third-place network, CBS, launched a $3.5 billion buying spree for rights to four baseball regular seasons, four All-Star games, four baseball playoff series in each league, four World Series, seven thirty-two-game NCAA basketball tournaments, two Olympics, four NFC regular seasons, four NFC playoff series, one Super Bowl, and one Masters golf tournament.

CBS's strategy was to replicate the feat of ABC in 1976, which jumped from last among networks to first, partly on the strength of its Olympic coverage. The theory is to hook the viewer with a big sports event and then induce him to sample the regular shows, which are plugged ad nauseam during the sports telecasts.

CBS's high-risk plan has been, at best, a limited success and, at worst, a financial bust. During CBS's "Dream Season" of 1990—during which the "Tiffany Network" aired more than 50 percent of network sports programming, including the Super Bowl, the NCAA basketball tournament, the NBA All-Star game, both of baseball's league championship series, the World Series, tennis's U.S. Open, the Masters golf tournament, and the Daytona 500—it paid an astronomical price and gained only a little ground on NBC and ABC.[11]

On the first year of its baseball contract alone, CBS lost somewhere between $55 million (the network's official word) and $100 million (the estimate of industry analysts).[12] CBS is reeling from the double whammy of a decline in viewer ratings and a softening of the advertising market in a recession.[13] The loss was so heavy that CBS unsuccessfully begged Major League Baseball to restructure its four-year, $1 billion deal—a contract that then-NBC-chief Brandon Tartikoff described as "the worst deal ever made" and that author Curt Smith called "the Exxon Valdez of sports network contracts."[14]

Stunned by the magnitude of the loss, CBS Sports president Neal Pilson plaintively asked, "How far can free TV go to support the major sports league?"[15] In the wake of this financial disaster, CBS's CEO Laurence Tisch has apologized to his stockholders for the network's "mistake," and NBC has indicated that it may not even bid for the next baseball contract when CBS's deal expires after the 1993 season.[16]

And CBS is not alone in losing money on sports. In 1990 Capital Cities/ABC Inc. lost money on baseball on its cable network (ESPN), and Turner Broadcasting System Inc. lost at least $34 million on the Goodwill Games. Although General Electric Co. did not report separately on its broadcasting subsidiary (NBC) in 1990, the "Peacock Network" reportedly suffered a loss, partly due to its football package. All the networks are losing money on their latest deal with the NFL.[17] Sports News Network, an all-sports news cable channel, lasted only a half year.[18]

If so many broadcast and cable networks are losing money on sports programming, why is sports coverage increasing? The answer to that apparent anomaly illustrates the distinction between broadcasting and narrowcasting. As the number of channels increases tenfold over the next few years, there will be a dire need for product for these new channels, and sports provides ready programming.

Not all sports programs, however, will attract a mass audience on network TV and, thus, justify a whopping rights contract. Many of them must find a "niche" audience on cable. Moreover, certain sports that did not survive the ratings wars on broadcast TV (for example, hockey) will capture a hard core of fans on a narrowcasting cable channel. The rationale for the premium channels—whether dedicated to sports, movies, or music—is to cater to a loyal core audience.

Nonetheless, the leagues cannot blithely assume that the fees paid by TV for sporting rights will continue to escalate. In the past the leagues have looked to the networks to more than offset the rising operating expenses of the teams, but the networks may balk at bailing out the leagues in the future, particularly if the demand declines for advertising time on sports broadcasts. Largely because of the proliferation of sports coverage, the average rating for a sports event broadcast has dropped by one-third during the past decade, according to Nielsen Media Research.[19]

The rising costs of running a team have been driven in large measure by the escalation of players' salaries. Every new wave of player contracts is more mind-boggling than the previous agreements. While Kareem Abdul-Jabbar was a star center at Power Memorial High School in New York, the great coach Joe Lapchick predicted that Jabbar would someday command a salary as high as $50,000 a year. Who could have predicted then that Jabbar would be pulling down closer to $50,000 a game during the twilight of his glorious career?

Recently Rony Seikaly, the center for the Miami Heat in the NBA, signed a nine-year deal for about $31 million, which averages about $3.5 million a year. Cavalier forward John "Hot Rod" Williams also makes about $3.5 million a year, with Chicago Bulls superstar Michael Jordan close behind at $3.2 million. Knick

Patrick Ewing jumped to the top of the list in 1992 with a two-year contract extension worth $18.8 million.

Basketball is not alone in the escalation of players' salaries. In 1991 Major League Baseball, which has an average player salary of $900,000, rewarded more than two hundred big leaguers with contracts worth more than $1 million a year, and more than thirty stars with an annual salary in excess of $3 million.[20] Two pitchers—Roger Clemens and Dwight Gooden—make more than $5 million a year.[21] By signing a five-year contract worth $29 million with the New York Mets, Bobby Bonilla became the highest-paid player in baseball—at least until the next big free agent tests the market.[22]

There is, however, nothing inevitable about the escalation of salaries in sports, at least not at the current rate. If expenses, such as players' salaries, are to continue rising, then revenues must increase as well. From present indications the networks and cable stations may be almost tapped out. In a harbinger of hard negotiations to come, the National Hockey League in 1991 became the first major league to sign a national TV contract that was less lucrative than its previous deal: a one-year agreement with SportsChannel America for $5.5 million (about one-third of the fee received by the NHL annually under its previous three-year deal).[23]

"Hockey is the first chapter in what will become a story in a book that will be concluded two years from now in mid-1993, when we go back to the baseball and football contracts," warned Dick Ebersol, president of NBC Sports. "The most radical change is yet to come, and I think that will be in baseball."[24]

As Neal Pilson of CBS Sports pointed out, "I think all the leagues and all the franchises have to be aware now that there is a big change in the economics of television sports . . . Certainly all of the networks have said they can no longer accommodate sports as a loss leader. We've had as much experience as anyone on that subject."[25]

For some sports stars, it will be painful to learn that their salaries are not recession-proof. In the ongoing struggle between labor and management, the pendulum swings both ways. In the

1980s it swept in favor of the players; but from the mid-'80s it has swung back toward the owners.[26]

Furthermore, it is doubtful that the leagues can wring much more from the live gate. Basketball, football, and hockey already sell more than 90 percent of their seats, and baseball attendance has been setting records for the past several years.[27] To raise ticket prices too much would place a sports outing beyond the reach of the average family.

And the goodwill of the fans is the bedrock of the entire enterprise. The danger of alienating the public is exacerbated when their loyalty is taken for granted by prima donna athletes who pull down seven-figure salaries while arriving at training camp overweight and out of shape—as did John Williams, who was suspended by the Washington Bullets in 1991 for weighing in at 305 pounds when his optimum playing weight is 245 pounds.[28]

If the major networks scale back their bids for sports rights and the gate is unlikely to increase dramatically, the teams will intensify their efforts to tap into new sources of revenue, particularly the international market and pay-per-view TV. On the international front, the world is shrinking for all businesses, including sports; and the NBA has been the trailblazer in the globalization of sports, largely due to the foresight of Commissioner David Stern.

It is difficult for me to believe that only a decade ago, when I was laboring in the NBA, it looked at times as if the league might fold or perhaps limp forward as a shadow of its former glory. In the 1980–1981 season, only five of the NBA's twenty-three teams made money, and total attendance had plummeted by one million from the previous year. The teams were drawing an average of only about ten thousand fans a game, and some of the franchises were playing before practically empty bleachers.[29] Worse still, the league had the rap of being drug infested, culminating in a report in the *Los Angeles Times* that 75 percent of NBA players were on drugs.[30]

On the brink of financial collapse, the NBA had one thing going for it in the early '80s—the league was so desperate that it was willing to adopt radical proposals. Shortly before David Stern became commissioner, the owners and players agreed upon the most enlightened drug policy in pro sports. And to end the protracted, bitter warring between the owners and the players, both sides accepted a landmark agreement in 1983, which established a salary cap for the teams and guaranteed the players 53 percent of the gross revenues, including the gate and TV fees. The players and owners became partners in the league, with both groups sharing in its successes. Both the NFL and Major League Baseball—where the owners have resisted revenue sharing with the players—should take a cue from the NBA on this score.

As the NBA's first general counsel in 1978, its first executive vice president in 1980, and its commissioner since 1984, Stern has masterminded the boom in NBA basketball since the mid-'80s. Under Stern's regime attendance has risen every year, reaching in 1990–1991 an average of more than fifteen thousand a game (almost 90 percent of capacity); and while television ratings for all other major sports have fallen in the last decade, the NBA's ratings are up by more than 20 percent.[31] During the past decade the average value of an NBA franchise has more than tripled (to about $65 million), and the average player's salary has jumped from $325,000 to $900,000.[32] Under Stern the NBA leaped ahead of the NFL and Major League Baseball in internationalization and labor relations.

Stern has also grasped what I had glimpsed during my brief stint in Italian ball—basketball is one of the most popular sports in the world. Under Stern's five-pronged strategy—broadcasting, licensing, sponsorship, exhibition games, and clinics—the NBA has jumped far ahead of the NFL, NHL, or Major League Baseball in international popularity.[33]

Of course, basketball has a great advantage because it, unlike football and baseball, is already played and appreciated around the world. There is a worldwide market for basketball talent. There are more than two dozen foreign-born players competing in the NBA; and each year scores of U.S. players migrate to foreign countries to play ball. In the past the Yanks abroad tended to be either has-beens or never-wases; but in recent years more top stars, such as Danny Ferry (the second pick in the first round of the 1989 NBA draft) and Brian Shaw (a first-round pick in the 1988 draft and a starting guard for the Boston Celtics) have spurned the NBA for bigger money overseas.

It was during my foray into European basketball that I first realized the tremendous international potential of the sport. While a full-time student at Oxford in 1974, I wanted to sharpen my basketball skills. Unfortunately, basketball in England was very primitive then. So I contracted to play for Virtus Sinudyne of Bologna in the Italian professional league, which was highly competitive and could probably hold its own against a very good college team in the United States.

When I first arrived at the Milan Airport, I was met by a car and chauffeured to Bologna. As my car reached the outskirts of Bologna, I was stunned to see thousands of fans lining the streets to herald the arrival of their new American player. The throngs followed my car as it wound through the city and to my apartment.

Thousands of fans flocked to my first practice and mobbed me throughout my initial visit to the city. Our games were sold out in a stadium that seated nine thousand at ticket prices that topped those of some teams in the NBA. I will never forget the Italians' hospitality, their love of basketball, and their fanatical support of the team.

The initial hoopla, however, soon faded into the realities of commuting all over Europe. I was living in two worlds—as a scholar at Oxford and as an athlete in Italy—that were one thousand miles apart. It was much harder being a student-athlete in Europe than it had been at Maryland. Moreover, my Bologna team played about fifty games a year—less demanding than an NBA schedule but almost twice as many games as a college team plays in a season.

I spent weekends in Bologna and also made two all-night commutes each week between Oxford and wherever the team was playing, sometimes as far away as Tel Aviv and Leningrad. It became common for me to jump a plane to Milan, drive three hours to Bologna, play at 9 P.M., leave the stadium at 11, reach Rome at 4:30 A.M., hit London around 7:30, and drive to Oxford by 9 A.M., in time for another day of classes. Traveling consumed sixteen to thirty-two hours a week.

Studying and sleeping in cars and on planes, I managed to maintain my academic requirements while absorbing the rarefied atmosphere of Oxford. At the outset I was afraid that college officials might rule me in violation of Oxford's stringent residency requirements because of my frequent absences, and for a few weeks I went to great lengths to cover my tracks. But it turned out that everyone in the college had been aware of my Italian connection from the day I set foot in Oxford. Once I asked an Oxford don if I could leave our tutorial ten minutes early, and he asked where I was flying this time. "Tel Aviv," I answered sheepishly as I slipped out the door.

My nomadic existence prepared me well for the travel grind of the NBA. And because European basketball is much more physical than college ball in the United States, my stint in the Italian league toughened me under the boards.

Basketball has another advantage over football and baseball: It has been an Olympic sport since 1936; and the decision of the International Basketball Federation (FIBA)—with its 176 member-countries—to allow pros to compete in the 1992 games will provide another boost for the popularity of the NBA and basketball. While the NBA commissioner is not counting on European-based NBA teams in the near future, he envisions the McDonald's Open becoming a world club championship, perhaps as early as 1994, which will pit the NBA champions against the victors from every other major league in the world. The NBA strategically selected Paris to host the McDonald's Open in 1991 because France was largely untapped by the league, and the selection was a huge success. Spinoffs from the tournament included an NBA trade show, which attracted six hundred retailers from all over Europe; plans to air taped NBA games to pay-per-view channels in France; and intense interest by a number of countries—including Australia, Canada, Israel, and Sweden—to host the McDonald's Open in 1993.[34]

In addition, Stern advocates a world championship to be modeled after soccer's World Cup and held every four years.[35] In 1990 the NBA began playing the opening game of its regular season in Japan.[36]

The NBA's investment in the overseas market is already returning handsome dividends. Presently the NBA is regularly televised in about seventy countries, including Russia.[37] Revenues from the licensing of NBA broadcasts and the marketing of NBA properties outside the United States, though only a small fraction of the league's $1.7 billion in gross revenues today, are expected to grow exponentially in the near future.[38] NBA superstars are as recognizable worldwide as the most popular entertainers in movies and music.

At a small, private lunch hosted by Bill Bradley in the summer of 1991, Stern described to me the international popularity of Michael Jordan and the Chicago Bulls, the NBA champions of that year. According to Stern, Michael is even idolized in Red China, where his team is known as the "Red Oxen." As Stern rushed away from the lunch to preside over the NBA draft in New York, he bragged that the draft now outdraws in TV ratings many of the regular season games.

Other professional leagues are also mining foreign markets. For example, in the summer of 1990, shortly after the fall of the Berlin Wall, I watched an NFL exhibition game in Berlin with Jack Kemp, the Secretary of HUD and a former pro quarterback. To spread the gospel of football to Europe, twenty-six of twenty-eight NFL owners in 1991 kicked off the World League of American Football (WLAF), with teams based in the United States, Canada, England, Germany, and Spain. Football is, however, a tough sale overseas because of the widespread unfamiliarity with its rules and intricacies; and the TV ratings for the WLAF during its first season were disappointing.[39]

Baseball will be a medal sport at the 1992 Olympics, and during the 1980s the number of countries with baseball federations increased from thirty-nine to sixty-five.[40] All-star teams from the pro ranks in basketball, football, baseball, and hockey regularly tour Europe and the Far East, especially Japan.

But the leagues are not gambling their existence entirely on overseas money. Instead they will explore other sources of revenue, including pay-per-view TV. In the near future a consumer will be able to pick up a phone and order the game of his choice for a fee. While sports coverage on TV will increase, more and more sporting events will migrate from free TV to cable and pay-per-view channels. This threatens our concept of an open society in which information is available to the haves and the have-nots. So any significant siphoning of programs from free TV will be carefully monitored by Congress. Allowing pay-per-view to scuttle free TV would be equivalent to charging for access to public libraries.

Teams and leagues are vulnerable to the bidding of cable companies, which have two streams of revenue—advertising and subscription fees—while the networks are dependent solely upon advertising. Because the networks have, by and large, lost so much money recently, they may scale back their bids when their sports contracts expire, allowing cable to land the broadcast rights of many major sporting events practically by default. Squeezed by increasing competition and falling revenues, the local broadcast stations are pushing Congress to require cable companies to obtain consent (presumably in return for consideration) for retransmitting network signals. This retransmission consideration allows network and cable to work out an arrangement for carrying the broadcast signals on cable, And, in my view, this retransmission consideration may be the key to keeping more sporting events on network television.

When Congress passed the Cable Communications Policy Act in 1984, which deregulated the cable industry, it was expected that competition would increase and prices would fall; but this has not happened. According to one of my colleagues, Representative Christopher Shays of Connecticut, today more than 99 percent of all cable systems in the country are operating without direct competition; and as a result, consumers are being overcharged about $6 billion a year.[41] In Shays's opinion, the cable barons are reaping a windfall in the absence of competition and regulation.

The cable industry counters that it has increased the quality and quantity of its programs by, for example, adding expensive sports broadcasts. For example, George Steinbrenner sold broadcasting rights for all Yankee games to the Madison Square Garden cable network for twelve years, beginning in 1991, at a whopping tag of $550 million—although only a fraction of the households in the Bronx and Brooklyn are wired for cable.[42] America's pastime may become a thing of the past for many youngsters who will not be able to afford to follow the game.

Likewise, as part of ESPN's $400 million purchase of the rights to 175 baseball games a year for four years, Major League Baseball agreed to preclude free broadcasts of other major league games on Wednesday nights and almost all games on Sunday nights.

The trend toward cable is not limited to baseball but has swept across basketball, football, hockey, and even down to collegiate sports. But this shuts out households that are not wired for cable and those that cannot afford it. A billboard in Los Angeles summed it up: NO CABLE, NO GRETZKY.

Moreover, there is little reason to believe that the owners will be sated with their windfall from regular cable if they smell a bigger killing on pay-per-view. Pay-per-view has attracted little controversy so far, mainly because it has largely been restricted to boxing, which is not a staple of free TV. The powers of pro and college sports, however, took notice of the $55 million in revenues generated by the Evander Holyfield–George Foreman fight in 1991—the highest-grossing event in pay-per-view history at that time. Robert Wussler, former president and CEO of Comstat Video Enterprises, president of CBS Sports, and executive vice president of Turner Broadcasting, recently told me that the day of the $100 million purse for a fighter is not far away.

If a relatively obscure champ and a forty-two-year-old challenger can pull in $55 million, how much would the Super Bowl fetch on pay-per-view? Or the World Series? The Final Four?

Every major sport is exploring the potential of pay-per-view. The San Diego Padres already offer some home games on pay-per-view, as do the Dallas Mavericks of the NBA and the Minnesota North Stars of the NHL. Indeed, the North Stars jumped to pay-per-view for their playoff games during their championship season of 1991, leaving behind the poor and the unwired who had followed the team's progress throughout the regular season. The NFL will experiment with a pay-per-view "regional" package, perhaps as early as 1993.[43] For example, a Redskins fan will be able to follow the team free only if he lives on the East Coast; otherwise, he must pay.

The most closely watched barometer of the future of pay-per-view will be the 1992 Olympics. As a harbinger of the future of sports, NBC will offer three channels of Olympic coverage on pay-per-view, while also airing the 1992 games on its free broadcast. Realizing it cannot recoup its costs solely from advertising, NBC is gambling that there are three million homes that will pay for round-the-clock coverage of the Barcelona Olympics, from which the network expects to rake in $100 million.[44] NBC will offer three options to viewers—a fee of $95 (for weekends or the first seven days' events), $125 (for all fifteen days), and $170 (for all fifteen days plus merchandise such as medals and T-shirts) for twenty-four-hour coverage (twelve live and twelve tape-delayed).[45]

NBC's pay-per-view triplecast is an important experiment to recover part of its investment in the summer games, including the $401 million paid for broadcast rights. The network's foray into pay-per-view demonstrates that the networks and cable are not necessarily competitors but can work together.

Unfortunately, NBC has experienced difficulty in finding national cable channels on which to air the pay-per-view events.[46] And another major challenge is to offer enough top-notch events to lure viewers to the pay-per-view format without diluting the coverage of its free broadcast. "As much as we want to make sure that people know they'll get what they've always got on over-the-air," said Dick Ebersol, the president of NBC Sports, "we also want people to know that pay-per-view won't be a dumping ground."[47] According to NBC, pay-per-view will not siphon programming from free TV but will supplement the standard fare.

To the extent that pay-per-view channels carry programs or events that were not broadcast on free TV in the past, they increase the viewers' options. Similarly, by catering to the distant fan (for example, a Boston Celtics fan in Los Angeles), pay-per-view can add to his choices.

Still, there are dire predictions that the Barcelona games will be the last Olympics on free TV.[48] Alarmists (or realists?) insist that the enormous profits of pay-per-view will be too great for team owners in all sports to ignore, especially as salaries continue to escalate while ticket prices, attendance, and advertising revenues stabilize or even fall.

Over time, the alarmists warn, all the big events will migrate to pay-per-view—the World Series, the Super Bowl, the Final Four, the NBA playoffs, the Olympics, and the college football bowl games. This will leave behind those who cannot afford the programming charges and those who live in unwired areas.

Congress, concerned by the prospects and ramifications of a significant shift from free to pay-per-view TV, launched a series of hearings on the issue. Among the witnesses appearing in May 1990 before the House Subcommittee on Telecommunications and Finance, on which I serve, were the commissioners of the major pro sports leagues and Dick Schultz of the NCAA.

The commissioners roundly denied the charge that cable was siphoning games from free TV, insisting that cable was adding options instead of subtracting them. Claiming there are far more baseball games than free TV can possibly absorb, Baseball Commissioner Fay Vincent couched the issue as one of scheduling, not availability. He minimized the significance of the exclusive broadcasting rights that ESPN had been contractually granted over Wednesday and Sunday nights.[49]

At the same hearing NFL Commissioner Paul Tagliabue assured us that "[t]he decision to expand the use of basic cable was made only after a careful assessment of the television marketplace, including changes in television technology, the reaction of NFL fans to our cable programming during the last three seasons, and the depressed state of television revenue available to the NFL clubs during 1987–1989."[50] He repeated his pledge that the Super Bowl would not be placed on pay-per-view for at least the rest of this century.[51]

On behalf of the NBA, David Stern stated that he did not anticipate any significant shift of games from free TV.[52] He also pointed out that the number of pro basketball contests on free TV had more than doubled in the last decade.[53] Stern understands that sports addicts are made, not born.

Dick Schultz, the executive director of the NCAA, also reminded the panel that coverage was increasing on both cable and broadcast.[54] Schultz claimed that, in general, institutions deal with cable companies only after being turned down by the networks.[55] Finally, in defense of schools that limit their exposure on free TV by selling out to cable, he resorted to the time-dishonored claim that the windfall from football and basketball often funds the less-popular sports—a defense that is trotted out to justify every pernicious practice of big-time college athletics.[56]

Despite the assurances of the commissioners, I left the hearing with lingering doubts. What happens if, as expected, the next round of TV contracts is not as generous to the leagues? How long can the owners, who have spent ungodly fortunes to buy franchises and are pressed by rising salaries (current and deferred) and other escalating costs, withstand the temptation of pay-per-view revenue? Downstream liabilities may force owners to choose between bankruptcy and pay-per-view.

Always the maverick, the outspoken Ted Turner departed from the "party line" in his testimony before the Senate Judiciary Committee's Subcommittee on Monopolies and Commercial Law by predicting that pay, cable, and subscription TV would soon dominate sports broadcasting. Turner further predicted that only the World Series and the Super Bowl would long remain on free TV and only because Congress would prevent their migration to pay TV.[57]

Pay-per-view is a young, growing industry that can add to a viewer's choices and may prove a salvation for free TV, which may in the future be able to bid on sporting events only because part of the coverage will be carried on pay TV. Neither the industry nor its proponents should be vilified. Pay-per-view should not, however, be viewed as a panacea by owners who cannot control spiraling costs. I believe in pay-per-view, but I also believe in network TV. Part of my job as a public policymaker is to maintain a balance between them. Congress cannot allow the networks to become dinosaurs, with the result that the haves are gouged for their programming and the have-nots face a blank screen.

The technology that will usher in pay-per-view is ready, and all the major sports leagues are experimenting with pay-per-view now. Within a few years the NBA, NFL, and NHL may be pushing packages of pay-per-view games—for the NFL, perhaps one a month and perhaps as early as 1993.[58]

Tagliabue's announcement of the NFL's plan sparked an immediate response from Representative Ed Markey, the chairman of the House Subcommittee on Telecommunications and Finance, who warned: "We will take a close look at whatever plan the NFL or any of the other major sports puts together. It is important that we maintain a policy that does not create a nation of the information-rich versus the information-poor."[59]

Some members of Congress suspect that the NFL's blackout of nonlocal games is geared not so much to protect the gate for local teams but rather to develop a pay-per-view format by restricting access and not fully marketing its product at this time. Also some believe the NFL is pricing its games to avoid sellouts and the lifting of blackouts, thereby conditioning consumers not to expect games to appear on free TV.

The primary concern of Congress, and particularly those of us on the Telecommunications Subcommittee, will be to ensure that, as the commissioners assured the subcommittee in 1990, cable is truly adding choices by carrying games that were not previously offered, rather than simply siphoning games from free TV. If the owners attempt to sell out the public by siphoning games from free to pay TV, their inevitable resort to a "free market" defense will likely fall on deaf ears in Congress because the owners are quick to abandon free market principles by seeking to retain or extend their protection from antitrust regulations. Pro sports have repeatedly and successfully sought congressional protection from the free market, as well as subsidies from local governments. Indeed, federal, state, and local governments have added millions of dollars to the value of many pro franchises through special status under antitrust and tax laws (for example, by allowing owners to use teams as tax shelters) and through the public financing of stadia and other improvements.[60]

The owners cannot have it both ways. They cannot declare their teams to be public treasures when begging Congress for antitrust exemptions (or local governments for public financing for a new stadium) while treating the teams as private toys by selling TV rights to the highest bidder, regardless of the interests of the fans. Similarly, a franchise ought not be permitted to soak the public of tax revenues to finance a new stadium and then hold the city hostage by threatening to move.

By threatening to revoke the antitrust exemptions enjoyed by the sports leagues, Congress has tremendous leverage over them. Seventy years ago the Supreme Court ruled that baseball was exempt from antitrust laws and, thus, could determine its own rules covering everything from free agency to franchise location. Congress has left untouched the Court's ruling, which has accorded baseball the most extensive protection from antitrust regulation of any sport and perhaps of any business.

Despite repeated runs at Congress, football has never been given the blanket exemption of baseball but has benefited from limited exemptions that, for example, have enabled the NFL to pool revenues from TV contracts. Furthermore, in the Sports Broadcasting Act of 1961, Congress granted to every organized sport the rights to negotiate as a league on broadcasting fees, pool its sales, and share the revenues.

In 1985 Howard Cosell eloquently argued before the Senate Judiciary Committee that pro sports should not enjoy any antitrust exemptions but should be forced to run their businesses like any other in this country.[61]

Even if one does not accept Cosell's cogent argument, there is considerable doubt whether the 1961 Act protects the sale of games to cable or pay-per-view. Senator Arlen Specter of Pennsylvania believes that games telecast on cable or pay-per-view are not "sponsored telecasts" within the language of the 1961 Act and, thus, are not outside antitrust regulation.[62] Senator Specter, a member of the Senate Judiciary Committee, has declared that the loss of their antitrust exemptions is "a distinct possibility" if the leagues reduce the amount of free sports programming on TV.[63]

To hammer home his point, Senator Specter sent a letter to NFL Commissioner Tagliabue in 1991 in which he flatly stated, "I do not believe it is appropriate for the NFL to have pay-per-view as long as the league enjoys antitrust exemptions."[64] Even more forcefully, Senator Specter introduced a resolution in the Senate in 1991, chiding the professional leagues for cable deals that "demonstrate disregard for the public's interest compared with the owners' financial interest" and calling on Congress to limit or curb the existing antitrust exemptions "unless big league sports franchise owners demonstrate reasonable concern for the public's interest."[65]

But Congress finds itself in the ironic position of exerting more leverage over the pros than over colleges. If the NFL shifts its games to pay-per-view, Congress can revoke the antitrust protection enjoyed by the league; but what does Congress do if a college jumps to pay-per-view, as Louisiana State University has already done?

In the absence of legislation, such as the Collegiate Athletic Reform Act, which I introduced in 1991, Congress can do little. Moreover, during a congressional hearing in 1991, Gerald Turner, the chairman of the NCAA's Presidents Commission, admitted that the NCAA is presently powerless to stop or even regulate the migration of college games to cable or pay-per-view channels.

In the end, a balance must be struck among the interests of the owners, players, broadcasters, and fans. First, we have a strong public interest in the free flow of information, and anything that restricts it should be strictly scrutinized.

Second, we do not want a society divided between the information-rich and the information-poor. Television has demonstrated for decades an ability to unite the people of this country, despite barriers of race, creed, age, health, politics, geography, and wealth. We cannot allow TV to rip asunder the traditional fabric of our society by blacking out families on low or fixed incomes or those who happen to live in unwired areas.

Third, it will be short-term profits but long-term folly for teams to alienate the fans who have supported them, over good years and lean, through the purchase of tickets, concessions, and souvenirs and the payment of taxes to construct stadia. The public is already restless about high ticket prices, prima donna athletes, drug scandals, and owners who bolt to a new city at the drop of a dollar. Will the fans sit still while being gouged in the living room?

Finally, the people own the air waves used by both free and cable TV. We have a duty to ensure that TV executives use the air wisely and fairly.

Congress will not sit on the sidelines as viewers are trampled in the gold rush by team owners and cable moguls. There are presently a number of proposals before Congress to reregulate cable and spur competition within the industry.[66] The harder the owners and cable barons squeeze the fans for money and the more they exploit the national addiction to sports, the heavier will be the flurry of bills to check their greed.

In a thought-provoking article in *Sports Illustrated*, William Oscar Johnson described the "brave new world" of sports in the year 2001—when pay-per-view will have gobbled up all sports programming on TV, with the poor receiving "Sports Aid stamps" from the government (akin to food stamps), which allow them to watch certain events; gambling on sports from the home is heavily taxed and strongly encouraged by the local, state, and federal governments; corporate sponsorships have attached themselves to games from the high school level to the pros; fans can immerse themselves in a flood of games at a wide array of prices and with a menu of interactive options; viewers receive credits (like frequent flyer miles) on their pay-per-view fees for suffering through commercials; and pseudo-fans are paid to attend the games, fulfilling Ted Turner's prediction to me of years ago.[67]

In fact, the "brave new world" of sports gambling is here today, in Cerritos, California, where the GTE Corporation has installed a state-of-the-art fiber optic cable system. From a home in Cerritos, an individual can shop, bank, order books, choose from hundreds of movies, and even play a game called "QB1."

QB1, which is licensed by the NFL, tests the frequency with

which a player makes the "right" decision during a live NFL telecast—run, pass, and so on. The winner is the one who picks correctly most often during the game. While QB1 is a benign version, the game could easily be adapted to incorporate gambling on NFL contests. For this reason the NBA has refused to license a similar version for basketball, fearful of tainting its image.

In the future, technology will permit viewers to place bets on games and automatically debit their bank accounts—all from the comfort of their living rooms. (Steve Ross, the CEO of Time Warner, the huge cable-telecommunications-publishing empire, briefed me on his company's future cable system, which includes fiber optics and government channels and which features consumer interaction that could be easily adaptable to gambling.) There would be no bookies, and everything would be aboveboard and, thus, taxable, adding a great boon to local and state governments (and, of course, the team owners). Safeguards could be added to cap the potential losses of a viewer (for example, to the cash in his account) or to prevent a person from betting on games involving home-state teams.

These safeguards, however, may not be enough to protect the integrity of sports in an era of rampant home betting, and the scandals of the past may be dwarfed by the scandals of the future.

While the NFL has skirted dangerously close to gambling, with its fascination with Jimmy the Greek and injury reports, the NBA wisely shuns sports gambling as a threat to public trust in the games. Sports gambling is a $1.8 billion business in Nevada, the mecca for legal gambling in the United States.[68] Estimates of illegal sports betting run as high as $100 billion a year.[69]

In 1989 Oregon launched a sports lottery. But it dropped its basketball lottery after only one year because of lack of interest, and its football lottery has fallen short of original projections.[70] Oregon's experience with a sports lottery mirrors a nationwide trend in which lotteries are not generating the anticipated riches. Presently thirty-three states and the District of Columbia have lotteries, which produced $19 billion in revenues for the 1991 fiscal year (a 5 percent decline from the previous year); and there are predictions that ten more states will add lotteries by 1994.[71] But nine state lotteries experienced declining sales in 1990, with revenues from the California lottery falling 14 percent from the previous year.[72] Though sports lottery games have not proven to be the "quick fix for flat sales" that many predicted, about thirteen deficit-ridden states are considering a sports lottery to ease their budget woes.[73] The danger exists that states are becoming as addicted to their lotteries as the customers are.[74] But gambling is not the answer for chronically unsound government budgets.[75]

Representative John Bryant of Texas and Senator Dennis DeConcini of Arizona have introduced similar bills to prohibit state-sponsored sports gambling. Compulsive gambling is the fastest-growing addiction of our day; is the most hidden of mental disorders; has been identified as the "addiction of the '90s"; and is likely to become even more widespread with the proliferation of legalized gambling.[76] Because wagering threatens the integrity of sports, undermines public confidence in the games, and instills the wrong values in our children, I support the ban on state-sponsored sports lotteries.

Fortunately, on June 26, 1991, the commissioners of the major sports leagues appeared before the Senate Judiciary Committee's Subcommittee on Patents, Copyrights, and Trademarks to support the proposed ban on sports gambling. Paul Tagliabue, Fay Vincent, David Stern, and Gil Stein, the general counsel for the NHL, were unanimous in their opposition.

But I wonder how long the sports establishment will resist the temptation of gambling revenues. Within the next decade or two, when the sports juggernaut needs new revenues, the sports leagues may well switch sides, banding with the states to push for sports gambling. I believe that the commissioners sincerely oppose legalized sports gambling on principle.

The commissioners, however, are hired by the owners, and they can be fired by the owners. If the money from TV contracts levels off or even declines and the international marketing boom is not a pot of gold for one or more of the sports leagues, the hard-pressed owners—who probably overpaid for their franchises and their talent—will be sorely tempted to exploit the sports addicts' compulsion to gamble on the games.

Jim Wimsatt, the director of the New Hampshire Sweepstakes, believes that the commissioners are merely holding out for a cut of the action. "As soon as any state sports gambling operation volunteers to share revenues with the leagues," predicts Wimsatt, "it will not only be accepted, it will be blessed. They [the professional leagues] simply want a slice of the pie."[77]

It remains to be seen whether Congress can stand up to the combined forces of the cable industry, local and state governments, and team owners, all of whom may soon be clamoring for the revenues from sports gambling.

Cable, pay-per-view, internationalization, and gambling are all about money and the insatiable appetite of the sports leviathan. We have not yet learned to tame the sports beast. When sport crosses the line from a diversion into an obsession, our priorities are thrown out of whack, and our most important institutions, such as our schools, are threatened.

One of the most chilling passages in William Oscar Johnson's article on sports in the year 2001 involves his prediction of a national high school basketball tournament along the lines of the NCAA tourney:

> But much of the falloff in viewership (of the NCAA basketball tournament) occurred because the nation had been sated a week earlier with all the fresh and exciting basketball it could take during the third annual *USA Today* High School Final Four. This increasingly popular event features an elimination tournament among *USA Today*'s 32 top-rated high school teams, and the spectacle of these excitable teenagers playing their innocent young hearts out has completely captured the American imagination. Of course, there are the inevitable rumors in the media (*USA Today* excepted) that some of these players are neither so innocent nor so young, but so far nothing has been proved and I personally am accepting the whole thing at face value, acne and all.[78]

Whether our schools will return sports to their proper perspective or sell out to TV and cable moguls remains to be seen. Stay tuned.

Chapter 8

LIFE AFTER SPORTS

The Road to Reform

ONLY A FEW months after my election to Congress in 1986, a writer from *Sports Illustrated* contacted me about a story on pro athletes who had gone into politics. In addition to me, the article would focus on Senator Bill Bradley, the former Knick and NBA Hall-of-Famer; Jack Kemp, an ex-quarterback for the Buffalo Bills; Mo Udall, who had played pro basketball; and Jim Bunning, a former pitcher in the major leagues. Except for Bradley, the rest of us were then in the House of Representatives.

For the story *SI* wanted a photo of the five of us—dubbed the "Jock Caucus"—on the steps of the Capitol. Running from appointment to appointment, I arrived five minutes late for the shoot, whereupon Bradley immediately fined me $40, as if we were playing together on the Knicks again. Without protest I paid the fine to Mo Udall, our unofficial treasurer, who had not lost his sense of humor despite a painful, protracted battle with Parkinson's disease that made it difficult for him to climb the steps for the photo.

As we pros-turned-pols jockeyed for position on the Capitol steps, I was in awe of my present company. Two of the quintet (Kemp and Udall) had already been serious presidential candidates, and Bradley was emerging as a contender for the highest office in the land. It was a symbolic commentary on American politics that a jock could vie for the top spot in government.

There was also an irony at play. We had all undoubtedly been boosted by our athletic fame, but each of us had, to some extent, been forced to overcome the stereotype of the dumb jock to make the jump into politics.

Whether Republican or Democrat, we five shared a strong interest in burying the stereotype for good; and the informal Jock Caucus (which could also include ex-athletes not pictured in the *SI* article, such as Congressman Ben Nighthorse Campbell of Colorado, a former Olympian, and Congressman Ed Towns of New York, with whom I have collaborated on legislation) provides a broad base for initiating sports reform in Congress. President Bush, a former congressman with a lifelong devotion to sports, could play a role as powerful as Teddy Roosevelt's in reforming athletics.

The banter on the Capitol steps that day in 1986 was light, good-natured, and sports-oriented. Surrounded by colleagues whose careers had transcended sports, I was reminded of the importance of keeping athletics in perspective and preparing for a life after sports.

There are many tragedies of "stars" who had no life after sports, and act one of the tragedy often begins in the schools. True reform of college sports will be a long, hard process with many false starts. The roots of the problem lie in skewed societal values that are widespread and deeply held. And reform will impinge upon powerful forces not only within our educational institutions but also outside the schools, such as TV executives, boosters, and agents.

As a result of our misplaced priorities, we have allowed vast entertainment complexes to reshape our schools and deflect them from their true educational missions. It is sheer folly to think that school officials have the time, energy, or resources to educate their charges and to run vast, multimillion-dollar entertainment empires at the same time.

Sports reformers often speak of restoring the balance between academics and athletics, but this does not mean that athletics and academics should be equally weighted. Athletics are not as important as academics for the individual, the school, or our society. Under the proper circumstances, sports can play an important role in the schools—the key is to ensure that athletics are serving educational aims and not subverting them.

Because of the vast sums of money washing through the sports system, it is more accurate to assume that there is a natural disequilibrium, rather than a balance, between academics and athletics, and that the system will require great energy and commitment to correct. Reform will be won not by a short flurry of corrective measures but by a constant battle against our national sports addiction.

There is a tendency to romanticize a distant age, when the sporting lion lay down with the academic lamb. Yet, as the Carnegie Report of 1929 makes clear, the "good old days" of college sports were not all that good, and most of the evils that bedevil college sports today were rampant then, long before the age of television. A key issue is whether the NCAA can reform itself. History is replete with examples of its inability to do so. And the NCAA will continue to be unable to reform unless it controls the money generated by college sports; but only Congress, through an antitrust exemption, can restore the power of the purse string to the NCAA, since the Supreme Court stripped the NCAA of control over the football broadcasting contracts in 1984. Even that would not, however, guarantee fundamental reform.

The NCAA's abysmal treatment of women's sports is perhaps the most graphic example of its callousness and commitment to the status quo. In 1971 the Association of Intercollegiate Athletics for Women (AIAW) was founded, and a year later Congress passed Title IX, which mandated:

> No person in the United States shall, on the basis of sex, be excluded from participation in, be denied the benefits of, or be subjected to discrimination under any education program or activity receiving Federal financial assistance. . . .

Faced with the spectre of a fundamental reform that threatened the economic primacy of men's sports, the NCAA launched an intense lobbying effort to exclude athletics from Title IX. Failing that, the NCAA fought Title IX in the courts and again lost.[1]

Saddled with Title IX, the resourceful NCAA changed strategies and launched a predatory plan to assume governance of women's programs by destroying the AIAW. By controlling both men's and women's programs, the NCAA could thwart the intended effect of Title IX. The coup de grace for the AIAW came in the early 1980s, when the NCAA began to televise the women's basketball finals. By offering incentives to schools to defect from the AIAW, the NCAA buried its shoestring competitor in 1982.[2]

The NCAA has largely succeeded in nullifying the broad reach of Title IX for almost two decades. Instead of working toward a true gender equity in intercollegiate sports, the NCAA has maneuvered to preserve the well-financed fiefdoms of big-time football and basketball while relegating all other sports (men's and women's) to second-class status. The NCAA and its members have consistently treated the revenue and nonrevenue sports differently under Title IX, even though its statutory language does not warrant such differential treatment.[3]

Women's sports have made progress since the enactment of Title IX, but there is still far to go. I have been heartened by the pride of parents in the athletic accomplishments of their daughters and by the excitement of young women who win athletic scholarships. Unfortunately, too many of these "winners" wind up in programs that are forced to take a backseat to the men's teams. According to the NCAA's statistics, even though women represent about 50 percent of college students, women's sports receive only 18 percent of the athletic budget.[4]

Although the number of female college athletes has almost tripled since the passage of Title IX (from over thirty-one thousand in 1971 to more than ninety-one thousand in 1990), the percentage of female coaches and administrators running women's programs is steadily declining.[5] By bringing more money into women's sports programs, Title IX has attracted men into the field, with the unintended effect of driving women from administrative jobs. In 1972 women coached more than 90 percent of women's teams whereas today fewer than 50 percent of the coaches of female teams are women. In contrast, men coach more than 99 percent of male teams.[6]

Likewise, in 1972 women ran more than 90 percent of the female programs as compared to fewer than 20 percent of those programs today; and there are no women involved in the administration of almost one-third of the women's programs.[7] There are no women among the conference commissioners of the nineteen major Division I conferences.[8] Significantly, the median salaries of female athletic administrators are more than $10,000 less than those of their male counterparts, and coaches of women's basketball make only 39 cents on the dollar of the money pulled down by coaches of men's basketball.[9]

Title IX has proven only a marginal success because, in the absence of NCAA initiative, enforcement generally requires costly court action; and female coaches and administrators, as employees of the universities, have proven reluctant to litigate.[10]

Moreover, the Reagan and Bush administrations have treated Title IX as a low priority. Since 1972 the Department of Education's Office of Civil Rights (OCR), which is charged with monitoring compliance with Title IX, has initiated only three reviews of college programs.[11] After passing Title IX in 1972 (and the Civil Rights Restoration Act of 1988 to overrule the Supreme Court's decision in *Grove City College v. Bell,* which effectively exempted athletics from Title IX from 1984 to 1988), Congress has not followed through for female student-athletes by pressuring the OCR to be more aggressive in this area and by prodding the

NCAA to tackle greater gender equity. Congress has twice criticized the OCR for its failure to enforce Title IX—in 1985 and
again in 1988—to little avail.[12]

Unfortunately, the women's programs are at a competitive disadvantage within the NCAA precisely because they embody many
of the elements of amateurism that in theory should define college
sports. The Knight Commission Report stated that the "continued
inattention to the requirements of Title IX (mandating equitable
treatment of women in educational programs) represents a major
strain on institutional integrity."[13]

Whenever the NCAA grouses about increasing funding to low-
profile women's sports, it should be reminded that it gobbled up
women's programs years ago, when those programs were run by
women at a profit. According to a critic of the NCAA, "[a]ny
current problems were brought on by arrogant men who refused
to allow women to run their own show."[14]

Another needed reform toward which the NCAA has been
dragged, kicking and screaming, involves its enforcement apparatus, which fails to provide sufficient due process protections to
individuals and institutions under investigation.

The NCAA metes out draconian punishments that destroy individual careers and cost institutions and taxpayers millions of
dollars. Nonetheless, the targeted athletes and schools are not
allowed to face and cross-examine their accusers. And before
1991, when the NCAA belatedly began to tape interviews on an
experimental basis, the only records of the interviews were the
notes of the NCAA investigators, which were often unreliable
and contained hearsay.[15] Even today the individuals and institutions in jeopardy are not given a transcript of the entire hearing
before the Infractions Committee.

Wint Winter, Jr., a lawyer and state senator from Kansas, declared that individuals and schools under an NCAA investigation
have "limited access to evidence used against them, have no real
means to appeal decisions, and, most important, are subject to
an incredible penalty system that punishes the innocent student-
athletes, often lets free the guilty and flip-flops on high-profile
cases."[16]

The unfairness of the present system is revealed by the fact that the NCAA investigators have a 100 percent conviction rate before the Infractions Committee and that no major penalty levied by the Infractions Committee has ever been reversed on appeal before the NCAA Council (which, not coincidentally, appoints the Infractions Committee whose decisions are rubber-stamped on appeal).[17]

The capriciousness of the NCAA's enforcement procedures has prompted critics to ask who is in charge of the docket—the NCAA or CBS? For example, whereas Kansas University was placed on probation by the NCAA and not allowed to defend its 1988 national basketball championship, the NCAA reversed its previous ruling to allow UNLV—a media favorite—to defend its 1990 championship.[18] Similarly, shortly before a televised game against Notre Dame in 1991, seven suspended Syracuse basketball players were reinstated by the NCAA.[19]

In part because of doubts about the fairness of NCAA investigations, the Oversight and Investigations Subcommittee of the House Committee on Interstate and Foreign Commerce held a series of hearings in 1978, instigated by Representative Jim Santini of Nevada because of NCAA investigations of two institutions within his state. The hearings mushroomed to encompass all aspects of the NCAA—recruiting, enforcement, finances, leadership, and academic integrity.

In January of 1979, the Subcommittee on Oversight and Investigations issued its final report, focusing on the NCAA's enforcement process. The Subcommittee recommended that the NCAA appoint an independent, blue-ribbon committee "to be charged with the responsibility of reviewing and assessing the entire NCAA enforcement program with a view toward essential fairness in the system, and to report its findings and recommendations in sufficient time to be considered in full by all NCAA members in January of 1980."[20]

The Subcommittee followed its suggestion with the threat "to reexamine its present posture with respect to federal intervention in intercollegiate athletics" if the blue-ribbon commission were not created.[21]

The reaction of the NCAA (and its executive director at the time, Walter Byers) to the congressional hearings and the Subcommittee's report bordered on contempt. No commission was appointed in the wake of the report. Moreover, the NCAA did not implement any of the Subcommittee's major recommendations, such as the separation of the enforcement apparatus from the adjudicative body, the provision of complete transcripts of infraction hearings to interested parties, and the recodification of its substantive rules with an eye toward simplicity and clarity.

Under the leadership of Dick Schultz, the NCAA finally appointed a committee to study its enforcement procedures in 1991—a belated reaction not to the 1978 hearings but to the recent spate of bills in the federal and state legislatures to regulate the NCAA. The committee made a number of worthwhile recommendations, including (1) encouraging summary dispositions of cases by seeking agreement on the relevant facts; (2) opening hearings to the public; (3) hiring retired state and federal judges to decide cases, replacing the current system in which NCAA employees are both prosecutors and judges; and (4) tape-recording interviews and proceedings to maintain an official record of each matter.[22]

These recommendations are a step in the right direction, but it remains to be seen whether they will be adopted, in whole or part, by the organization. Some of the more far-reaching proposals will not come up for approval by NCAA members before 1993.[23] Moreover, the recommendations do not address the larger issues of simplifying the rules and treating punished schools more consistently.

It is also unclear whether the committee's recommendations will slow or derail the various due process bills winding through Congress and the state legislatures. Representative Ed Towns of New York has introduced one such bill—"The Coaches' Bill of Rights"—which would require the NCAA to accord due process protections to coaches, players, and institutions under investigation. In addition, there are about eight bills mandating varying degrees of due process in NCAA investigations, which have been passed or are pending in state legislatures.[24] Rather than working cooperatively with these elected bodies, the NCAA has generally resorted to impugning the motives of legislators working for NCAA reform and threatening to expel schools in states that pass due process bills.[25]

Burton Brody, a law professor at the University of Denver and a witness at the 1978 and the 1991 hearings, testified that the NCAA has not shown the will to clean its own house. Characterizing the enforcement procedures as "unfair, one-sided, arbitrary, demeaning, insensitive and without any of the procedural safeguards Americans expect when facing charges that can result in serious punishment," Brody pointed out that the NCAA "has had ample time and opportunity to do so and has not only failed to act, but has on numerous occasions gone on record as saying there is nothing wrong with its present system."[26]

Congress must not allow the NCAA to stall major reforms any longer. "Seventeen years ago, the NCAA said it needed a little more time," noted Cardiss Collins, the chair of our House Subcommittee on Commerce, Consumer Protection, and Competitiveness. "I'm still hearing the same thing."[27]

The role of college presidents in overseeing their athletic fiefdoms offers yet another example of the NCAA's reactionary attitude toward reform. The NCAA has always fought efforts by the presidents to seize real control from the coaches and athletic directors.

For example, in 1983 the American Council on Education (ACE), convinced that the NCAA would not reform itself, proposed the creation of a board of presidents with ultimate authority to impose, veto, or modify NCAA rules, subject to review by a mail vote of all presidents. Led by Walter Byers, the NCAA attacked ACE's model of presidential control, which was modified by the reformers to allow the actions of the board of presidents to be overruled by a majority vote of the NCAA convention. Even this watered-down version of ACE's proposal was defeated at the NCAA convention in 1984.

To co-opt the reform-minded presidents, however, the NCAA established the Presidents Commission, whose powers are merely advisory.[28] The Commission has enjoyed limited successes in recent years, especially in the important areas of strengthening the academic requirements of student-athletes and cost containment of athletic programs. But it is not proof, despite the NCAA's claims, that the presidents now control the organization.

NCAA Executive Director Dick Schultz overstated his case by claiming that "[i]f anybody questions whether the presidents are in charge of intercollegiate athletics, they are not doing a very good job keeping up on what's going on."[29]

During congressional hearings in 1991, I questioned Gerald Turner, the chairman of the Presidents Commission, at length about the extent to which the advisory body controls the NCAA. According to Turner, the Presidents Commission does not review budget line items, even on such sensitive matters as the lobbying by the NCAA of state and federal legislatures; and although the NCAA Executive Committee has the authority to conduct such a budget review, only one of its twelve members is a college president. Thus, the NCAA can sink substantial sums into an all-out lobbying effort to defeat the Student Right-to-Know Act without the knowledge (much less approval) of the Presidents Commission.

The NCAA convention in Nashville in 1991 has been bally-hooed as the "reform convention" because the major agenda items were proposed by the Presidents Commission, which lob-bied heavily and successfully for their passage. Nonetheless, the Nashville convention did not address the systemic, fundamental problems in college sports. An observer of the 1991 convention aptly described what took place there:

> So while this year's NCAA convention seemed to make more pro-gress than in previous years, the interest of the decision-makers, whether athletic directors or college presidents, seems to be pri-marily containing costs and maintaining the current bureaucratic structure.[30]

Indeed, in surveying the "reforms" pushed through the NCAA convention by the Presidents Commission in 1991, Gene Corrigan, the commissioner of the Atlantic Coast Conference, concluded that the new rules would have "zero effect on the quality of competition."[31] In other words, the Presidents Commission had done nothing to dilute the product of college sports in the eyes of the TV executives and the rabid fans.

Furthermore, there are already moves afoot to "roll back" some of the reforms passed by the presidents in the 1990 and 1991 conventions. The Presidents Commission has some powerful detractors, including Georgetown coach John Thompson, who claimed that "[t]hey [the Presidents Commission] probably know least about what is going on."[32] And Frank Deford, the noted sports commentator and a keen observer of college sports, has said that "by now, it must be painfully obvious that the one group that *can't* handle college athletics is college presidents."[33]

And while the NCAA and the Presidents Commission mustered the courage and commitment to convene "reform conventions" in 1990 and 1991, they have not heeded the call of women's advocates for an "equity convention" to equalize men's and women's athletic scholarships and opportunities.[34] And although a "gender-equity" study is being undertaken, it will not be available until 1993.

At its heart the NCAA operates chiefly as a trade association for athletic directors and coaches. A former athletic director himself, Schultz was elevated to his present position mainly by athletic directors and has remained sympathetic to his fellow AD's. According to Murray Sperber, although Schultz sincerely wants to help correct the problems of college sports, he was appointed mainly to protect the interests of athletic directors and coaches, who are largely responsible for those problems.[35]

We should not overlook the contributions of the many athletic directors and coaches who want reform, such as Dean Smith and Joe Paterno, but today they are like ants trying to move an elephant. Even a reform-minded moderate like Schultz finds himself mired in controversy, caught in an NCAA investigation of a series of questionable loans to athletes at the University of Virginia, some of which were made while he was the athletic director there.[36]

Ironically, the organization is losing the clout to effect fundamental change. The NCAA has done little to check the "balkanization" of college sports, which faces a war for the broadcast pie not only among its divisions but also between the haves and have-nots within a division. Eventually the NCAA will lose its grip on the riches of college sports and, hence, its "stick" over the out-of-control programs. The NCAA will probably awaken to the need for real reform only after it is too feeble to curb its unruly members.

With the NCAA fiddling while Rome burns, scores of blue-ribbon panels have tackled the thorny issue of college sports in this century. The Knight Commission held hearings over eighteen months before issuing a forty-seven-page report in 1991 entitled "Keeping Faith With the Student-Athlete: A New Model for Intercollegiate Athletics." The crux of the report was its "one-plus-three" model—the "one" being presidential control of college sports and the "three" being academic integrity, financial integrity, and certification.

My qualms about the Knight Report stem from its failure to follow its recommendations to their logical conclusions. As with most blue-ribbon panels, which are bursting with talent, intelligence, and good intentions, there was a strong push to issue a unanimous report; and at the outset, I fully expected to endorse without qualification the final recommendations.

During the hearings, however, I became more strongly convinced that college sports are doomed without radical, fundamental reform and that financial reform is the linchpin of the entire reform movement. Moreover, it became clear that many members of the Knight Commission (which included the NCAA's Dick Schultz) harbored far more trust in the NCAA to embrace true reform than I did.

At the final meeting of the commission, I urged my fellow members not to "pull our punches" in the final report but to hit the NCAA hard for the way it conducts its business. Unfortunately, my colleagues opted instead generally to ratify the direction and efforts of the NCAA.

So I departed from my illustrious colleagues by inserting a series of footnotes in the final report. I could not sign it without registering my qualifications.

The fundamental flaw of the report was its failure, after insisting

that college presidents assume control of their athletic departments and the NCAA, to explain how they could do so. Indeed,
even if all the specific reforms in the report were adopted, many
college presidents would still not be able to gain control of their
athletic departments from powerful coaches and boosters.

I proposed in my first footnote to the report that the NCAA
be restructured so as to ensure presidential control of the organization.[37] This can be accomplished either by requiring that presidents make up a majority on the NCAA Council or by creating
a higher body that is controlled by presidents and possesses power
to establish broad policy for the conduct of intercollegiate sports.[38]

Today college presidents theoretically control athletics through
the selection of delegates to the NCAA conventions, but the
reality is far different. Even absolute presidential control of the
NCAA, however, is no panacea. To begin with, any model of
governance that requires college presidents to devote the bulk of
their time to athletics is fundamentally flawed. College presidents
ought not be forced to choose between an out-of-control athletic
department and inattention to the other facets of university life.
Moreover, on some campuses college presidents have been part
of the problem; and presidential interest in athletic reform, while
hot now, will inevitably cool in the coming years.

College presidents come and go; blue-ribbon panels burst onto
the scene and quickly burn out; and even congressional interest
waxes and wanes—but the product becomes glitzier and more
expensive every year.

True presidential control will have little long-term impact on
college sports unless the incentives for winning (and cheating to
win) are removed or greatly reduced. The NCAA has failed to
accomplish this, and the Knight Commission was too timid in
pursuing this necessary goal. The central difference between the
majority on the Knight Commission and me was the focus of our
reform effort. In the "one-plus-three" model of the Knight Report, the "one" was presidential control. In my view, however,
the big "one" should be financial reform.

For example, in 1991 the NCAA distributed nearly $73 million
from the basketball tournament to Division I schools under a

formula that was weighed heavily toward the ACC, the Big Ten, and other traditional powers.[39] "When 66 percent of the money still goes back to the traditional powers," charged Jeffrey Orleans, the executive director of the Ivy League, "some individuals will see this as solely a commercial enterprise."[40]

Representatives of Division I-AA schools, which include many of our nation's historically black colleges and universities, testified before our House Subcommittee on Commerce, Consumer Protection, and Competitiveness in 1991 that their schools now receive "little more than the shells and crumbs" from the big money in college sports.[41] In response to my questioning, Florida A&M President Fred Humphries expressed doubts that the NCAA could bring about financial reform because the big programs control the distribution of revenues.[42]

In a letter to Representative Cardiss Collins, the chair of the House Subcommittee, Dick Schultz stated that the Mid-Eastern Athletic Conference (MEAC) and the Southwestern Athletic Conference (SWAC), two conferences whose seventeen members are historically black colleges or universities, would receive the largest sums allotted to any Division I schools from the $3 million needy student fund in 1991.[43] Schultz did not point out, however, that in the 1991 disbursement, each school in the ACC would receive almost as much as the total payout to all the schools in the MEAC or the SWAC.[44]

In short, at the same time that the NCAA purports to call for a deemphasis on winning and a downsizing of athletic departments, it shovels dollars toward schools that do the opposite. Faced with the NCAA's hypocrisy in this regard, the Knight Report merely suggested that "the [distribution] plan be reviewed annually by the Presidents Commission during the seven-year life of the current television contract and adjusted as warranted by experience."[45]

Convinced that here again the Knight Commission had not been bold enough, I inserted my second footnote into the final report:

I do not fully agree with this report's recommendation regarding the revenue distribution plan that presidents need only "review" the new formula. This is the most important reform necessary in intercollegiate athletics—without it, all other reforms will be difficult, if not impossible, to enact. While the NCAA and this Commission have focused primarily on the basketball revenues, we have not begun to address conferences' and institutions' revenues from athletics, including bowl games. I recommend that an independent panel review this issue and propose a new model for revenue distribution that eliminates the "winner-take-all (or most)" mentality that results in violation of NCAA rules, exploitation of student-athletes, and the commercialization of college athletics.[46]

As further evidence that the Knight Commission was too "soft" on the NCAA, the final report failed to address the fairness of its enforcement procedures. In 1991 the NCAA belatedly established a commission to study the enforcement process and make suggestions to change it. This effort, however, may be too little, too late. My third and final footnote in the report urged outside entities, including the government, to devise fairer rules of enforcement and not to count on the NCAA to clean its own house.[47]

Like presidential control, due process reform is important but no panacea. Making the enforcement system fairer will not check the widespread cheating in college sports unless the financial incentives are drastically changed. In an effort to evade the real problem of financial incentives, the NCAA generates reams of rules, many of which are unenforceable.

Today's NCAA is like a traffic cop in a "speed trap" town. Like the NCAA, the cop can arrest practically anyone because of the maze of picayune rules and regulations; and upon arrest, conviction is a foregone conclusion. While hauling his quota of "law-breakers" before a kangaroo court, the cop closes his eyes to the big crimes and festering corruption in his jurisdiction. Of course, it would be an improvement to replace the kangaroo court with a fairer tribunal; but fairness alone will not change the incentives to deter the big crimes and root out the corruption.

I fear that the failings of the Knight Report may consign it to dusty shelves that are already buckling under the dead weight of scores of fading treatises. Georgia Tech President John Patrick

Crecine may be justified in predicting that the Knight Report will have a "relatively minor" influence on college athletics.[48]

Still, the Knight Commission was an effort to head off federal intervention in college athletics. At a press conference marking the release of the Knight Report, Father Ted Hesburgh warned: "We may be up to bat for the last time. If the colleges don't do the job themselves, then the politicians may do it for us. They read polls. They like to do what's popular. But they'd turn the whole thing into a disaster."[49]

The Knight Report predicted that college sports faced one of three possible futures—reform from within; reform from without through government regulation; or the wholesale destruction not only of the sports programs but also of the credibility of the schools.[50]

At recent NCAA conventions, delegates have been warned to swallow proposals rather than have the government ram more drastic reforms down their throats. The terrified cry of "The feds are coming!" has frequently sounded from the podium. Referring to the government pressure swirling around college sports, Dick Schultz gravely asked the delegates at the 1991 convention, "Do you want to regulate yourself or do you want to be regulated?"[51]

The reform measures passed at recent NCAA conventions were due to outside pressure on the organization. Without the credible threat of intervention, the NCAA would lapse back into domination by those who profit from the status quo. After all, not only does the NCAA owe its existence to federal intervention but also it, its members, and its affiliates regularly solicit government help. Seeking tax breaks, antitrust relief, or other favors, the NCAA, its member institutions, and their high-powered lobbyists frequently comb the Hill for friends. I have never heard the NCAA or its members complain about "beneficial" federal intervention.

Far more important than the fate of any of the special bills and favors sought by the NCAA or its members, however, are the billions of dollars invested by governments in educational institutions. Each year the United States invests $160 billion in higher education, more per student than any nation in the world except Denmark; and 45 percent of this money comes from the federal, state, and local governments.[52] Congress cannot allow athletic corruption to jeopardize the taxpayers' investment in the future.

I echo the sentiments of Donna Shalala, the chancellor of the University of Wisconsin:

> We ought to have no complaints (about congressional intervention): We came too slow to the issue, and there is clear evidence that we have not sufficiently cleaned up our act. We're finally waking up and paying attention to it, and I think that prodding from Congress is useful.[53]

Frank Deford, who testified before the Knight Commission, reached the same conclusion:

> McMillen himself believes it's time the government stepped in. That is always an unpopular position, and we can be sure the NCAA and the rest of the college sports lobby will urge us to be vigilant in protecting their area from the evil "government control." Self-serving officials in the private sector always play that tune. But after a failed century of NCAA and presidential rule, "government control" is clearly the sensible alternative.[54]

And the public is in Deford's camp. A recent Harris poll indicated that the more strongly a group favored the reform of college sports, the more critical it was of the NCAA.[55] Sixty percent of the public also believed that legislative intervention, either federal or state, was necessary to effect meaningful sports reform.[56]

Aware of public sentiment in this area, Congress has reacted with a vengeance. After passing the Student Right-to-Know Act in 1990, Congress has turned its attention to a slew of additional measures, including a bill by Representative Paul Henry of Michigan to force schools to publish their revenues and expenditures on athletic programs; Ed Towns's bill to mandate due process protections for coaches and athletes undergoing an NCAA investigation; a resolution by Richard Weal of Massachusetts to endorse the recommendations of the Knight Commission; and a bill by Mervyn Dymally of California to establish a National Commission on Intercollegiate Athletics.

At least three House and Senate subcommittees are conducting separate but related hearings on college athletics. At my request in 1991, John Dingell, the chair of the House Energy and Commerce Committee, and Cardiss Collins, the chair of the Subcommittee on Commerce, Consumer Protection, and Competitiveness, launched a series of hearings on the spiraling revenues in intercollegiate athletics and the fairness of the NCAA's enforcement process.

At the suggestion of Senator Robert Byrd of West Virginia, a National Review Board has been established to spur the service academies into the forefront of the reform movement. Senator Byrd hopes that the service academies, by implementing measures such as those advocated by the Knight Commission, "can serve as excellent role models for civilian colleges and universities struggling with the proper place of athletics in higher education."[57]

Congress now realizes that sporadic federal involvement will not work. What is needed from Congress is not short-term grandstanding, but a full-court press for systemic, fundamental reform. And true reform will be impossible as long as each school is free to pursue its competitive, commercial advantage, which has been the case since the Supreme Court's 1984 decision stripping the NCAA of the power to negotiate a comprehensive football broadcast contract for its members. As Charles Young, the chancellor of UCLA and a longtime advocate of sports reform, testified before the House Subcommittee on Oversight and Investigations in 1984:

> [T]he precedent has now been established that a major extracurricular activity program of higher education establishes a property right that is to be regarded as a consumer product similar to those produced for profit alone. This is a new and, I submit, dangerous state of affairs for intercollegiate athletics.[58]

What is needed in this area is not more democracy and self-rule by colleges but a "benevolent dictator" of college sports. Congress is the only body that can restore the NCAA to its pre-

1984 power over TV contracts. In this regard I am not deterred by Dick Schultz's claim that the NCAA membership does not favor an antitrust exemption and a restoration of the NCAA's former powers.[59]

It is not surprising that NCAA members do not want to reinstate the NCAA as the bargaining unit for college TV rights because the Supreme Court's 1984 decision freed the schools (management) to compete for TV dollars in college sports, but did not free the athletes (labor) to do likewise. If the schools persist in treating college sports as a business, the athletes should be allowed to treat them as a business as well; and if the entire enterprise is merely a business, it should be taxed, and the athletes are entitled to all the rights of employees in other businesses, including workers compensation, minimum wages, and collective bargaining. Ultimately female athletes may force the NCAA's hand, using Title IX to block the organization from opting for the business route.

Partly to overturn the Supreme Court's 1984 decision and avoid the anarchy it portends, I have introduced the most comprehensive sports reform bill presently pending before Congress—the Collegiate Athletic Reform Act. The purpose of this act is to restore education as the primary goal of our institutions of higher learning by assisting college presidents in reining in the money-hungry monsters on their campuses.

I do not make great claims for the originality of my bill. Instead I take comfort in the realization that many of its components have been around for years or even decades. Some of my proposals appeared in the Knight Report; some were tendered by college presidents in 1983, only to be defeated by the NCAA convention the following year; some are being pressed by the American Association of University Professors; and the general spirit of my bill dates back to 1929, when the Carnegie Report concluded that corruption and commercialism were rampant in college sports.

My bill dovetails nicely with the call by the American Association of University Professors in 1991 to end the college athletic "arms race" through a series of reforms, including the adoption of the same criteria for special admissions of athletes as for other students and transferring control of athletic department finances to the central administration.[60]

The structure of my bill is simple. Upon its passage the NCAA will be granted an antitrust exemption for five years to negotiate and approve all major TV and radio contracts for college football and basketball (to the exclusion of individual schools or conferences, which would be dropped from the organization if they insisted on striking their own TV deals). The antitrust exemption is necessary to overcome the 1984 Supreme Court decision.

My bill would place a presidentially controlled NCAA in charge of broadcasting, as opposed to the present situation in which TV executives can pit the schools and conferences against each other. The Federal Communications Commission will conduct a study to determine the extent to which college sports programs are migrating from free TV to cable and pay-per-view systems. It is doubtful that the NCAA can presently stop or even regulate the migration of college sports from free TV. But under my bill, the NCAA will be empowered to control it.

In return for the antitrust exemption granted by my bill, the NCAA is required to enact various reform measures, including the establishment of a more powerful Board of Presidents to set major policy, which can be overruled only by a two-thirds majority of the organization's membership; the formulation of a more equitable revenue distribution plan, which does not depend on the win-loss record of an institution but takes into account the school's efforts to downsize its athletic programs and facilities, the academic performance of its student-athletes, and its compliance with Title IX; and the provision of due process protections to athletes, coaches, and institutions. If the NCAA fails to enact the reform measures within a year of the passage of my bill, the IRS will be authorized to tax the revenues produced by intercollegiate athletics.

The Collegiate Athletic Reform Act meshes with and complements pending bills offered by my colleagues Paul Henry and Ed Towns by requiring schools to report to the Department of Ed-

ucation their revenues and expenditures on sports and by requiring the NCAA to conduct its investigations according to the
dictates of due process.

Finally, my bill furnishes greater protection for student-athletes.
Schools are authorized to pay student-athletes a stipend of up to
$300 a month. And athletic scholarships will no longer be renew-
able on a year-to-year basis but will be extended to cover up to
five years and cannot be withdrawn by the school as long as the
student-athlete is enrolled in good standing at the institution.

To those who portray me as an outspoken critic of the NCAA
and big-time college sports, I point out that my bill actually confers
greater powers on the NCAA to handle the negotiation of broadcast contracts. Without such control, the NCAA is powerless to
effect fundamental reform. Indeed, my bill is necessary because
the NCAA presently lacks not only the will but also the strength
to champion real reform. I am an advocate of big-time sports but
under a new model in which the NCAA will be a "benevolent
dictator" and its executive director will hold a real hammer for
reform and report directly to the presidents.

Without my bill I fear that the power of the purse strings will
continue to devolve upon the strongest conferences and schools
and the NCAA will wither into a "paper tiger." If the NCAA
were to exercise its dwindling power today to seek real reform,
the most powerful conferences and schools would bolt from the
organization and thrust college sports into a Darwinian "survival
of the fittest."

I believe that the NCAA can be salvaged and forged into a
vehicle for reform. I do not share the view that the NCAA should
be abolished, as advocated by Anita DeFrantz, a 1976 Olympic
oarswoman and one of two U.S. members of the International
Olympic Committee:

I would abolish the NCAA. It's created and perpetuated a lot of
these problems. It is the "owner" at the collegiate level. It tells the
kids that they can become campus idols, but they can only have
$25 in their pocket. It tells them that they're not to be seen with

boosters, and yet boosters constantly give them money. It has taken opportunities away from parents to control their kids, it's taken opportunities away from universities. Abolish it.[61]

Under my proposal schools and conferences could still defect from the NCAA to cut their own TV deals, but they would do so at the heavy price of subjecting their athletic programs to the IRS. If a school or conference insists upon running its sports programs simply as a business, it must do so openly and accept the consequences, in taxes and otherwise.

I introduced the Collegiate Athletic Reform Act in July of 1991, and it has been referred to four congressional committees, including the Energy and Commerce Committee on which I sit. Already the bill has attracted much attention and, more important, a growing list of supporters inside and outside Congress. I do not delude myself that passage of the act will be quick or easy. It was difficult to push the Student Right-to-Know Act through Congress, and it was a much more modest piece of legislation. The Collegiate Athletic Reform Act is years ahead of its time.

In supporting my bill, the chancellor of the Regency Universities System in Illinois concluded:

By addressing the root cause of the problem, the McMillen legislation will enable us to take effective steps to restore public confidence in higher education and intercollegiate athletics. As such, it deserves our support. There's a time to fight your critics and a time to join them and this is the latter.[62]

But I do not exaggerate my bill's potential effect for good. Sports reform is necessary at all levels of our educational process, not merely at our colleges. And even at the college level, Congress cannot achieve fundamental reform on its own. Only through a concerted, long-term effort by Congress, the NCAA, college officials, athletes, the media, and the public can we redress the present imbalance between academics and athletics.

To stress the proper role of sports at all levels of our society, from cradle to grave, I suggest the following ten commandments of sports reform:

1. Encourage everyone to make a greater commitment to fitness, starting with youngsters in preschool, and encourage families to exercise together.
2. Do not allow untrained officials and overcompetitive parents to dominate kids' programs, where the games should be fun, safe, and belong to the youngsters.
3. Do not permit a student to play sports without doing schoolwork first. Academics must come first.
4. Integrate student-athletes into the academic and social life of a school, and make them follow its policies on admissions and curriculum.
5. Place the university presidents firmly in control of college sports and the NCAA.
6. Decommercialize college sports by emphasizing education and broad-based values over winning.
7. Create pathways (other than colleges) for athletes to enter the pros.
8. Make the Olympics a festival of sports, not a festival of money. The United States should shoulder its fair share of the financial burden of staging the Olympics, but no more than its fair share.
9. Remember that education does not end with the expiration of college eligibility. In recognition of the reality that athletes are role models in our society, professional leagues should create financial incentives for their players to continue their educations and explore ways to support younger student-athletes (such as the surcharge on ticket sales to professional games in San Francisco that is earmarked for high school athletics).
10. The American sports juggernaut thrives on the loyalty of the fans and the integrity of the games. Gambling, over-commercialization, prima donna athletes, and exorbitant pricing of events may eventually destroy this loyalty and the integrity of sports.

Sports reform comes in many ways—through the prodding of concerned academics, coaches, politicians, private individuals, and reporters. Sometimes a seminal event seizes the attention of the nation or even the world—the eighteen deaths of college football players in 1905; Jesse Owens's performance at the 1936 Olympics in Berlin; Jackie Robinson's breaking of the color barrier in baseball; the 1966 basketball finals between a segregated Kentucky dynasty and no-name Texas Western (now UTEP) with five black starters; Muhammad Ali's refusal to be drafted in 1967; the massacre of the Israeli athletes at the 1972 Olympics in Munich; Len Bias's tragic death; and Magic Johnson's announcement that he had contracted the HIV virus.

I watched Texas Western's triumph at the 1966 finals from the stands without realizing its significance at the time; witnessed the massacre in Munich, which will never be erased from my memory; was privileged to compete against Magic Johnson; and waited for Len Bias to arrive at my campaign fund-raiser on the night he overdosed. And, like millions of others, upon learning of his death, I asked myself again and again—Why?

Reform will not come easy, but reform will come.

NOTES

CHAPTER 1. SURVIVAL OF THE FITTEST

1. Cathy Harasta, "Young Athletes on Losing End of Sports Myth," *The Dallas Morning News,* July 1, 1990, p. 12.
2. Peter Alfano, "Visions of the Pros Come Early," *The New York Times,* March 9, 1989, p. D27.
3. Gerald Eskenazi, "Arena of Big Time Athletics Is Showcasing a Younger Act," *The New York Times,* March 5, 1989, p. A30.
4. William Oscar Johnson, "How Far Have We Come?" *Sports Illustrated,* August 5, 1991, p. 41.
5. Harasta, "Young Athletes on Losing End," p. 2.
6. Ibid., p. 12.
7. Henry Louis Gates, Jr., "Delusions of Grandeur," *Sports Illustrated,* August 19, 1991, p. 78.
8. James A. Michener, *Sports in America* (New York: Random House, 1976), p. 282.
9. Larry Hawkins, "Keep Profit Motive Out of High School Sports," *The New York Times,* February 16, 1989, p. B5.
10. H. G. Bissinger, "Kids Are Being Exploited by Our Interest in Sports," *The Dallas Morning News,* November 25, 1990, p. J9.
11. Eskenazi, "Arena of Big Time Athletics," p. A1.
12. Jay P. Goldman, "Who's Calling the Plays?" *The School Administrator,* December 1990, p. 13.
13. Ibid., p. 10.
14. Alexander Wolff and Armen Keteyian, *Raw Recruits* (New York: Pocket Books, 1990).
15. C. Anthony Mosser, "Camps Give Prospects Opportunity to Excel," *The Dallas Morning News,* July 13, 1990, p. B1.
16. Mick McCabe, "It's Not the Shoes," *The Detroit Free Press,* July 11, 1991, p. D1.
17. Eskenazi, "Arena of Big Time Athletics," p. 30.

18. Phil Taylor, "The Summer Game," *Sports Illustrated,* July 15, 1991, p. 51.
19. Ken Denlinger, "Coaches Not Happy Campers," *The Washington Post,* July 11, 1991, p. B1.
20. Robin Finn, "For Tennis Prodigies, Camp Becomes Job," *The New York Times,* November 21, 1991, p. A1; David Casstevens, "Tennis' Net Gain Can Tax Its Youngest," *The Dallas Morning News,* July 3, 1990, p. B1.
21. Barry McDermott, "He'll Make Your Child a Champ," *Sports Illustrated,* June 9, 1980, p. 28.
22. John M. Hoberman, *Sport and Political Ideology* (Austin: University of Texas Press, 1984), p. 201.
23. Jean-Marie Brohm, *Sport: A Prison of Measured Time* (London: Inks Links, 1978), p. 85.
24. Marc Fisher, "Merged German Sports: A Juggernaut in Limbo," *The Washington Post,* April 29, 1991, p. B1.
25. Hoberman, *Sport and Political Ideology,* p. 213.
26. Marc Fisher and Steven Pickman, "East German Sports: Ruled by Steroids," *The Washington Post,* September 7, 1991, p. A1.
27. Ibid.
28. "USOC Looks to Buy E. German Savvy," *The Washington Post,* June 18, 1990, p. D2.
29. John Tagliabue, "Political Pressure Dismantles East German Sports Machine," *The New York Times,* February 12, 1991, p. B10.
30. David Childs, "The German Democratic Republic," in *Sport Under Communism,* ed. by James Riordan (London: C. Hurst & Co., 1981), p. 94.
31. "German Sports Machine Sputtering," *The Sun* (Baltimore), November 9, 1991, p. C11.
32. Alfano, "Visions of the Pros Come Early," p. D27.
33. Howard L. Nixon, *Sport and the American Dream* (New York: Leisure Press, 1984), p. 33.
34. Edward C. Devereux, "Backyard Versus Little League Baseball: The Impoverishment of Children's Games," in *Social Problems in Athletics,* ed. by Daniel M. Landers (Urbana: University of Illinois Press, 1976), p. 39.
35. Ibid., p. 38.
36. Ibid., p. 37.
37. Edmund J. Burke and Douglas Kleiber, "Psychological and Physical Implications of Highly Competitive Sports for Children," in *Sports Psychology and an Analysis of Athletic Behavior,* ed. by William F. Straub (New York: Movement Publications, 1978), p. 205.
38. Michener, *Sports in America,* p. 106.
39. Christine Brennan, "Youth Sports Officials Rein In Parents, Coaches," *The Washington Post,* May 5, 1991, p. B1.
40. Ibid., p. B11.
41. Ibid.

42. Tara K. Scanlan, "Competitive Stress and the Child Athlete," in *Psychological Foundations of Sport,* ed. by John M. Silva and Robert S. Weinberg (Champaign: Human Kinetics Publishers, Inc., 1984), p. 125.

CHAPTER 2. TICKET TO RIDE

1. Letter from Dean Smith to Tom McMillen, September 21, 1970.
2. Paul Attner, "Basketball Elite Rush to Mansfield, Pa.," *The Washington Post,* February 3, 1970, p. D3.
3. "McMillen Inks Unusual Grant," *Greensboro News & Record,* June 25, 1970, p. D1.
4. Ibid.
5. Lawrence Linderman, "The Tom McMillen Affair," *Playboy,* November 1971, p. 234.
6. Letter from Dean Smith.
7. "ACC Outlook: Gamecocks and 7 Others," *Richmond Times-Dispatch,* November 29, 1970, p. F6.
8. Linderman, "The Tom McMillen Affair," p. 234.
9. William C. Rhoden, "Recruiting Extends Its Reach," *The New York Times,* March 6, 1989, p. C1.
10. Ibid., p. C4.
11. Katrine Ames, "A High School Fouls Out," *Newsweek,* June 10, 1991, p. 66.
12. Ibid.
13. Jonathan Yardley, "The Spectators' Sports Obsession," *The Washington Post,* May 6, 1991, p. B2.
14. Donald Huff and Neil H. Greenberger, "Keeping Up With Joneses May Usher In a New Era: Recruiting," *The Washington Post,* May 1, 1991, p. D3.
15. Francis X. Dealy, Jr., *Win at Any Cost* (New York: Birch Lane, 1990), p. 174.
16. Bobby Bowden, "Tension, Pain, Satisfaction: Inside the Recruiting Game," *The New York Times,* February 14, 1988, p. 57.
17. Ibid.
18. Dealy, *Win at Any Cost,* pp. 181–183.
19. See, for example, Wolff and Keteyian's *Raw Recruits* (see chap. 1, n. 14); and Dealy, *Win at Any Cost,* pp. 168–196.
20. Howard James Savage, *American College Athletics* (New York: The Carnegie Foundation, 1929), p. 9.
21. Dealy, *Win at Any Cost,* p. 181.
22. Michael Janofsky, "Report Applauds Universities," *The New York Times,* September 26, 1991, p. B14.
23. Dennis Kelly, "Students Say Sports Is Key to College Aid," *USA Today,* November 26, 1990, p. 1A.
24. "Student Athletes: Information on Their Academic Performance," Report by the United States General Accounting Office, May 1989, pp. 47, 50.

25. A. E. Housman, "To an Athlete Dying Young," reprinted in *Seven Centuries of Verse,* ed. by A. J. M. Smith (New York: Charles Scribner's Sons, 3rd ed., 1967), p. 550.
26. Bruce Springsteen, "Glory Days," *Born in the USA* (New York: Columbia Records, 1986).

CHAPTER 3. SOUND MIND

1. NCAA Tax Returns for 1987 and 1988.
2. Transcript of Hearing Before Congressional Subcommittee on Postsecondary Education, May 18 and 24, 1989, p. 31.
3. Ibid., pp. 28, 31, 51.
4. Ibid., pp. 45, 48, 50.
5. Ibid., p. 53.
6. Ibid., p. 28.
7. Murray Sperber, *College Sports Inc.* (New York: Henry Holt and Company, 1990), pp. 298–299.
8. Erik Brady, "Players: 46% Earn Degrees in Five Years," *USA Today,* June 17, 1991, p. 2A.
9. Ibid.
10. "Student Athletes: Academic Performance" (see chap. 2, n. 24).
11. Ibid., pp. 4–5.
12. Ibid., p. 5.
13. Douglas Lederman, "College Athletes Graduate at Higher Rate Than Other Students," *The Chronicle of Higher Education,* March 27, 1991, p. A1.
14. Gerald Eskenazi, "Athletes Lead Nonathletes in Graduating, Survey Says," *The New York Times,* March 28, 1991, p. B14.
15. Lederman, "College Athletes," p. A38.
16. Transcript of Hearing, p. 49. An example illustrates the potentially misleading nature of the NCAA's adjusted figures. If a college team starts with ten freshmen, five of whom later leave the school "in good academic standing" and five of whom ultimately graduate, the college can claim a 100 percent graduation rate according to the NCAA's adjusted figures, regardless of the fate of the five who withdrew from the program.

    Moreover, because schools have different interpretations of "leaving in good academic standing," it is difficult and often misleading to compare the NCAA figures from one school with another. For example, some institutions limit those who "leave in good academic standing" to athletes who leave with some eligibility, but the NCAA permits colleges to count those who leave the school without any remaining athletic eligibility but who are still eligible to return to the institution.

    Furthermore, in an effort to impress high school players and their parents, image-minded recruiters may manipulate the graduation figures by, for example, basing the percentages only on seniors and ignoring those from the original class who left the school. Occasionally recruiters will shade the statistics by counting walk-ons, practice players, and student managers. Elliott Almond, "Colleges Play Number Games With Athletes," *Los Angeles Times,* January 9, 1990, p. C7.

17. Lederman, "College Athletes," p. A38.
18. Of the Division I-A schools, forty-seven (or almost half) logged graduation rates of 25 percent or less for their men's basketball players. Similarly, twenty-four of the Division I-A schools (or approximately one-quarter of the total) had graduation rates for their football players of 25 percent or less. For both men's basketball and football, about 75 percent of the Division I-A schools reported graduation rates of 50 percent or less. "Student Athletes: Information on Their Academic Performance" (see chap. 2, n. 24), pp. 47, 50.
19. Lederman, "College Athletes," p. A38.
20. Douglas Lederman, "Black Athletes Who Entered Colleges in Mid-80's Had Much Weaker Records Than Whites, Study Finds," *The Chronicle of Higher Education,* July 10, 1991, p. B1.
21. Ibid.
22. "Foul," *Time,* April 3, 1989, p. 55.
23. *Ross v. Creighton,* No. 89-C-6463 (N.D.Ill., June 14, 1990). For an excellent discussion of this case, see Timothy Davis, "An Absence of Good Faith: Defining a University's Educational Obligation to Student-Athletes," *Houston Law Review,* vol. 28, no. 4, July 1991, pp. 743–790.
24. David Letterman, *The "Late Night With David Letterman" Book of Top Ten Lists* (New York: Pocket Books, 1990), p. 16.
25. Clifford Adelman, "Light and Shadows on College Athletics," Report by the United States Department of Education, December 1990, p. 12.
26. Ibid., p. 18.
27. Eskenazi, "Athletes Lead Nonathletes," p. B14.
28. Ibid.
29. Douglas Lederman, "College Officials Worry That Graduation-Rate Data May Be Misread and Misused," *The Chronicle of Higher Education,* March 27, 1991, p. A38.
30. Louis Barbash, "Clean Up or Pay Up," *The Washington Monthly,* July/August 1990, p. 40.
31. William Oscar Johnson, "The Black Athlete Revisited—A Lot of Things Seem Better, But . . . ," *Sports Illustrated,* August 5, 1991, p. 49.
32. Almond, "Colleges Play Number Games," p. C7.
33. Howard James Savage, *American College Athletics* (see chap. 2, n. 20), pp. 307–308.
34. Ken Stephens, "College Athletics Interfering With Academics, Survey Says," *The Dallas Morning News,* October 4, 1989, p. B5.
35. Douglas Lederman, "Some College Leaders Are Pushing to Accelerate Pace of Sports Reform," *The Chronicle of Higher Education,* July 26, 1989, p. A30.

36. Dinesh D'Souza, "The Visigoths in Tweed," *Forbes,* April 1, 1991, p. 81.
37. Robert J. Samuelson, "The College Charade," *The Washington Post,* June 3, 1990, p. A23.
38. Ibid.
39. Dennis Kelly, "Top Students Hit Books Just 1 Hour a Day," *USA Today,* October 16, 1991, p. 1D; Robert J. Samuelson, "Why School Reform Fails," *Newsweek,* May 27, 1991, p. 62.
40. Samuelson, "The College Charade," p. A23.
41. Jerry Kirshenbaum, "An American Disgrace," *Sports Illustrated,* February 27, 1989, p. 18.
42. Harry Blauvelt, "Ga. Tech's Ivery Bones Up for Bid at Delayed Degree," *USA Today,* July 3, 1991, p. 9C.
43. "Okla. St. Head Asks Second Chance for Athletes," *The Dallas Morning News,* January 25, 1990, p. B9.
44. "Studies of Intercollegiate Athletics—Report No. 1: Summary Results from the 1987–88 National Study of Intercollegiate Athletics," Center for the Study of Athletics/American Institute for Research, Palo Alto, California, November 1988, pp. 7–8.
45. Murray Sperber, "NCAA Facing Short-Term Gain, Long-Term Pain?" *The NCAA News,* September 30, 1991, p. 4.
46. Austin Murphy, "Goodbye, Columbus," *Sports Illustrated,* September 9, 1991, p. 46.
47. "Ohio State's Smith Says No Way Will He Play," *The Washington Post,* August 31, 1991, p. F2.
48. Valerie Lynn Dorsey, "Analysts: Academic Game Plan Crucial to College Chances," *USA Today,* February 1, 1990, p. 7C.
49. Kevin Blackistone, "Softening No-Pass Law Fails Athletes," *The Dallas Morning News,* May 14, 1991, p. B1.
50. Letter from Franklin Frazier, Director of Education and Employment Issues of the General Accounting Office, to Tom McMillen, August 9, 1990.
51. Valerie Lynn Dorsey, "High School Athletes Scrutinized," *USA Today,* February 1, 1990, p. 7C.
52. Adelman, "Light and Shadows," pp. 8–9.
53. Arthur Ashe, "Why Coddle College Athletes?" *The New York Times,* February 10, 1989, p. A35.
54. "Big-Time Athletes Coming Up Short," *USA Today,* June 19, 1991, p. 8C.
55. Steve Berkowitz, "Far Fewer Blacks Than Whites Get Degrees," *The Washington Post,* July 4, 1991, p. B1.
56. William Oscar Johnson, "The Black Athlete Revisited—How Far Have We Come?" *Sports Illustrated,* August 5, 1991, p. 40.
57. Transcript of the Debate Over Proposition No. 48 at the NCAA Convention in 1983, pp. 115–116.
58. William F. Reed, "A New Proposition," *Sports Illustrated,* January 23, 1989, p. 18.

59. Ibid.
60. Sperber, *College Sports Inc.*, p. 220.
61. "Educating Athletes," *The Washington Post*, June 30, 1991, p. C6.
62. Ralph Wiley, "The Black Athlete Revisited—A Daunting Proposition," *Sports Illustrated*, August 12, 1991, p. 29.
63. In 1988, 85 percent of black freshman athletes in Division I schools satisfied the standards of Proposition 48. Ashe, "Why Coddle College Athletes?" p. A35.

    Moreover, of the roughly eighteen hundred athletes who lost a year's eligibility to Proposition 48 in its first three years on the books, the majority regained their eligibility as sophomores. Reed, "A New Proposition," p. 18.
64. Propositions 42 and 48 face uncertain futures, and their effect was diluted by a later convention. They survived the 1990 NCAA convention but not completely intact. The delegates in 1990 responded to Thompson's protest by opening a new loophole through which partial qualifiers are allowed to receive institutional financial aid as long as it is based on need and not funded by the athletic department.

    The decision not to count such partial qualifiers against a school's limit on athletic scholarships opens the door for renegade schools to "stockpile" more athletes than they could have prior to the passage of Proposition 48. Under the new measure, called Proposition 26, an athlete will be counted against the total number of available scholarships only after he becomes eligible to participate in the sport.
65. Mark Asher, "NCAA to Try Tougher Standards," *The Washington Post*, June 27, 1991, p. A1.
66. Although colleges give special consideration in admissions to certain applicants for a wide variety of reasons (for example, the applicant possesses musical talent, will enrich the campus through ethnic diversity, or was lucky enough to be born to alumni parents), athletic ability is probably the most common reason for a special admission. According to a survey published in *The Chronicle of Higher Education* in 1991, athletes admitted at Division I-A institutions were four times more likely to receive special consideration in admissions than regular students; and football and basketball players were six times as likely to receive special treatment than regular students. William C. Rhoden, "Educators Examine Standards for Athletes," *The New York Times*, May 3, 1991, p. B14.
67. Tom Witosky, "Black Leaders Say U.S. Sports Don't Offer Equal Opportunities," *USA Today*, May 30, 1990, p. 10C.

CHAPTER 4. JACKPOT

1. Dave Klein, "For Crying Out Loud, Colleges: You Have No Right to Complain," *The Star Ledger* (Newark), February 22, 1990, p. 53.
2. Joe Lapointe, "In College Sports, the Real Players Collect Millions From the Networks," *The New York Times*, December 31, 1989, p. E6.

3. "Bowl Results," *The Dallas Morning News,* January 3, 1991, p. C1.
4. Dan Langendorf, "Effects of Irish's TV Deal Still Not Clear," *The Dallas Times Herald,* June 2, 1990, p. C3.
5. Bill Brubaker, "The Shark—He Could Be a Fish Out of Water," *The Washington Post,* May 13, 1990, p. D8.
6. Ibid.
7. Tom Witosky, "Coaches Defend Earnings From Teams' Shoe Suppliers," *The Des Moines Sunday Register,* May 20, 1990, p. D11.
8. John R. Thelin and Lawrence L. Wiseman, "The Old College Try: Balancing Academics and Athletics in Higher Education," ASHE-ERIC Higher Education Report 4, 1989, p. 58; Bill Brubaker, "In Shoe Companies' Competition, the Coaches Are the Key Players," *The Washington Post,* March 11, 1991, p. A6.
9. Witosky, "Coaches Defend Earnings," p. D11.
10. Brubaker, "In Shoe Companies' Competition," p. A6.
11. Thelin and Wiseman, "The Old College Try," p. 59.
12. Ken Denlinger, "For Today's College Coaches, the Shoe Most Certainly Fits," *The Washington Post,* June 24, 1990, p. B10.
13. In 1990 Texas basketball coach Tom Penders was in the first year of a five-year contract, with a total package worth between $200,000 and $300,000 a year, when he led the surprising Longhorns to the Midwest Regional Finals. As the first Longhorns coach in history to take the team to consecutive NCAA tournaments and with an impressive 49–18 record in two years, Penders was approached by Florida about its opening for head coach. Only weeks after the overture from the Gators, UT renegotiated Penders's contract, signing him to a seven-year deal worth from $400,000 to $500,000 a year, depending on bonuses. UT Athletic Director DeLoss Dodds bragged that the new package placed Penders in the top 5 percent of college coaches in salary, even though Penders's base pay still fell a shade below that of the Texas football coach. Steve Richardson, "UT's Penders Gets 7-Year Deal," *The Dallas Morning News,* March 29, 1990, pp. B1, B3.

   Likewise, after Lamar University contacted Texas–El Paso coach Don Haskins, the UTEP boosters club induced their longtime coach to stay in El Paso with a $500,000 retirement annuity. "Boosters Raise $500,000 to Keep Haskins at UTEP," *The Dallas Times Herald,* March 28, 1990, p. C2.
14. Jim Ruppert, "Texas Puts Its Money Where Mackovic Is," *The State Journal-Register,* December 13, 1991, p. 1.
15. Ed Sherman, "U. of I. Pays President Less Than 2 Coaches," *Chicago Tribune,* May 15, 1991, p. C1.
16. Blackie Sherrod, "Ex-Coaches Get Pretty Penny Despite Smudge of Scandal," *The Dallas Morning News,* June 1, 1990, p. B8.
17. C. Rusnock Hoover, "Albino Reveals Coach Contracts," *Daily Camera* (Boulder, Colorado), July 20, 1991, p. A1.
18. Greg Boeck, "Fired Coaches Fire Back at Schools," *USA Today,* March 27, 1991, p. 4C.

19. Ibid.
20. Don Yaeger, *Undue Process* (Champaign, Illinois: Sagamore Publishing Inc., 1991), p. 106.
21. Ken Denlinger, "Dick Schultz, the Great Persuader," *The Washington Post,* December 9, 1990, p. D10.
22. Yaeger, *Undue Process,* pp. 137–138.
23. "Budget's Direct Payments Top $102 Million," *The NCAA News,* September 16, 1991, p. 1.
24. Yaeger, *Undue Process,* p. 138.
25. Ibid., pp. 106–108.
26. George Vecsey, "Who's Hiding the Money," *The New York Times,* April 27, 1988, p. D25.
27. Ira Berkow, "Whose Hand Was That Anyway?" *The New York Times,* November 18, 1989, p. 47.
28. "Ex-Player at Iona Says Valvano Gave Him Money, Paper Reports," *The New York Times,* March 31, 1990, p. 46.
29. "Admission by Shackleford," *The New York Times,* February 26, 1990, p. C6.
30. William F. Reed, "The End May Be Nigh," *Sports Illustrated,* November 11, 1991, p. 89.
31. "Illicit Pay in Wide Use, Study Contends," *The New York Times,* November 17, 1989, p. A33.
32. Steve Wieberg, "Players Admit Greatest Need: $200 a Month," *USA Today,* August 23, 1991, p. 9E.
33. Robert Fachet, "Schultz: Terps Took Penalty Others May Be Evading," *The Washington Post,* December 12, 1990, p. D2.
34. Kent Waldrep, a former Texas Christian University football player who was paralyzed in a 1974 game, has filed a claim for workers compensation, claiming that a college athlete is an employee of his school. Steve Pate, "Case Could Give College Athletes Employee Rights," *The National,* June 4, 1991, p. 5.
35. Sperber, *College Sports Inc.* (see chap. 3, n. 7), p. 68.
36. "Buckeyes Are Billed $300,000 by the IRS," *The NCAA News,* May 22, 1991, p. 20; Gary Miles, "Schools Also Learn Score When Dealing With IRS," *USA Today,* July 10, 1991, p. 6C.
37. *NCAA v. Commissioner of IRS,* 914 F. 2d 1417 (10th Cir. 1990). In that case the Tenth Circuit Court of Appeals held that the NCAA's revenues from selling ads in tournament programs were not taxable. Such revenues are unrelated business income and, hence, taxable only if the following three conditions are met: (1) they are income from a trade or business; (2) such trade or business is regularly carried on by the organization; and (3) the conduct of such trade or business is not substantially related to the performance by the organization of its exempt functions. The Tenth Circuit ruled for the NCAA on the ground that the trade or business of selling ads in programs was not "regularly carried on" by the NCAA.

38. Ivan Maisel, "U.S. House to Consider Bill on Tax Exemption for Bowls," *The Dallas Morning News,* January 9, 1991, p. B12.
39. "Measure Seeks Tax on Revenue From Athletics," *The NCAA News,* March 13, 1991, p. 2.
40. Alfred Dennis Mathewson, "Intercollegiate Athletics and the Assignment of Legal Rights," *St. Louis University Law Journal,* Fall 1990, p. 53.
41. Ibid., p. 42.
42. Ibid., p. 52.
43. Letter from Pete Rozelle to Senator Bennett Johnson, April 20, 1989.
44. "Balancing Act," *USA Today,* July 3, 1990, p. 2C.
45. "NCAA Council Votes to Wait on Draft Rule," *The Washington Post,* August 3, 1991, p. D2.
46. "Schultz: NCAA Can't Be Farm System," *The Sun,* (Baltimore) January 11, 1992, p. C9.
47. "Holtz Proposes System of Pro Sports Schools," *The NCAA News,* May 23, 1990, p. 4.
48. Ben Brown, "Old College Try Not Enough for Some," *USA Today,* July 10, 1991, p. C6.
49. Memo from Charles Neinas to CFA Membership, May 15, 1990.
50. "Most College Sports Lose Money Game," *USA Today,* October 14, 1991, p. 2C.
51. Memo from Charles Neinas.
52. Thelin and Wiseman, "The Old College Try," p. 15.
53. Lapointe, "Real Players Collect Millions," p. E6.
54. "Most College Sports Lose Money Game," p. 1C.
55. Barbara Bergmann, "Do Sports Make Money for the University?" *Footnotes,* Spring 1988, p. 1.
56. Ivan Maisel, "Crunch Time," *The Dallas Morning News,* May 12, 1991, p. J1.
57. E. M. Swift, "Why Johnny Can't Play," *Sports Illustrated,* September 23, 1991, p. 62.
58. Tamara Henry, "Woes of Higher Education Resemble High Finance," *The NCAA News,* August 14, 1991, p. 16. The squeeze on athletics has also hit the nation's high schools, some of which have attempted to compensate for budget cuts with user fees, corporate sponsorships, booster clubs, and other fund-raising activities. Swift, "Why Johnny Can't Play," pp. 66–70.
59. "Terps Freeze Grants in All Sports to Offset Revenue Losses," *The NCAA News,* April 18, 1990, p. 6.
60. "Nebraska Faces Cuts Following $1.8 Million Budget Deficit," *The NCAA News,* April 18, 1990, p. 3.
61. Thelin and Wiseman, "The Old College Try," p. 15.
62. Ibid., p. 30.
63. Leonard Shapiro, "Now, Notre Dame's Golden Season," *The Washington Post,* September 5, 1991, p. B4.

64. Jeff Hardie, "Does College Football Face Realignment?" *The Washington Times,* June 29, 1990, p. D3.
65. William C. Rhoden, "Big College Football Leagues Are Trying to Get Larger Still," *The New York Times,* June 23, 1990, p. 45.
66. Ibid.
67. *NCAA v. Board of Regents of the University of Oklahoma, et al.,* 468 U.S. 85, 135 (1984) (White, J., dissenting).
68. Mark Asher, "FTC Complaint Against CFA Is Dismissed," *The Washington Post,* August 7, 1991, p. C2.
69. Rhoden, "Big College Football Leagues," p. 1.
70. Hardie, "Does College Football Face Realignment?" p. D3.
71. Rhoden, "Big College Football Leagues," p. 45.
72. Hardie, "Does College Football Face Realignment?" p. D3.
73. Ivan Maisel, "NCAA Reformists Finish Cost-Cutting, Miss 'Extra Point,' " *The Dallas Morning News,* January 10, 1991, p. B3.
74. Ibid.
75. "Keeping Faith With the Student-Athlete," Report of the Knight Foundation, March 1991, p. 11.
76. William C. Symonds, " 'March Madness' Is Getting Even Crazier," *Business Week,* April 2, 1990, p. 102.
77. Fachet, "Schultz: Terps Took Penalty," p. D2.
78. Rudy Martzke, "Ratings for Final Slip Without UNLV," *USA Today,* April 3, 1991, p. 3C.
79. Frederick C. Klein, "And Now, Thursday-Night Football," *The Wall Street Journal,* August 9, 1991, p. A7.
80. Tom Witosky, "National Football Playoff Hard to Resist in Crunch," *USA Today,* October 16, 1991, p. 5C.
81. Sperber, *College Sports Inc.* (See chap. 3, n. 7), p. 57.
82. Douglas Lederman, "Plan to Distribute NCAA's TV Bonanza Would Give Big Share to Colleges With Strong Sports Programs," *The Chronicle of Higher Education,* May 30, 1990, p. A33.
83. "NCAA Panel Approves Money Plan," *The New York Times,* July 12, 1990, p. B9.
84. Lederman, "Plan to Distribute NCAA's TV Bonanza," p. A33.
85. Bernie Wilson, "Slicing the Pie," *The NCAA News,* June 19, 1991, p. 4.

CHAPTER 5. MUNICH, 1972

1. Will Grimsley, "Singing Hippies Gulp Beer as Munich Greets Olympians," *The Philadelphia Inquirer,* August 20, 1972, p. D1.
2. Terry O'Neil, *The Game Behind the Game* (New York: St. Martin's Press, 1989), p. 50.
3. The official memorial service was disappointing, but Howard Cosell later established a fitting tribute to the slain athletes. Admitting that he had never felt "more Jewish" than he did at the 1972 Olympics, Cosell inaugurated an annual dinner to honor the slain Israelis by raising funds

to build sports facilities in Israel. This is one of the premier sports dinners in the world, and I have been honored to attend several of them.

In the aftermath of the tragedy, Cosell and I began a long friendship that has blossomed over the years. In 1986, when I was running for my first term in Congress, Cosell recalled the tragic circumstances of our first meeting in one of his newspaper columns:

I've known him for many years, but I first became acquainted with him in Munich, in 1972, at the Olympics. McMillen and I went to the memorial service for the slain Israeli athletes together. McMillen was shaken to the depths of his soul by the massacre and then further shocked by the refusal of the Olympic Committee and the West Germans to cancel the Games.

He was the only athlete I spoke to who no longer cared for his own ambition, his own chance at a medal, his hopes and dreams for the Olympics. He wanted them to cancel the Games. He felt it was only right. I learned all I need to know about his character and his conscience that day.

Howard Cosell, "Tom McMillen's Biggest Triumph," *Daily News* (New York), September 21, 1986, p. 48.

4. Shana Alexander, "Blood on the Playground," *Newsweek,* September 18, 1991, p. 35.
5. William Gildea, "Olympic Group Disallows U.S. Basketball Protest," *The Washington Post,* September 10, 1972, p. D1.
6. "U.S. Five Hit for Actions," *The Sun* (Baltimore), September 10, 1972, p. C4.
7. Ibid.
8. Charles W. Thayer, "A Question of Soul," *Sports Illustrated,* August 15, 1960, p. 73.
9. Lord Killanin, "Eligibility and Amateurism," in *The Olympic Games,* ed. by Lord Killanin and John Rodda (New York: Collier Books, 1979).
10. Bill Parrillo, "Spirit of Olympic Games Lost in Basketball Shuffle," *The Washington Times,* September 29, 1991, p. C4.
11. Robert Z. Lawrence and Jeffrey Pellegrom, "Fool's Gold," *The Brookings Review,* Fall 1989, p. 8.
12. Ibid., p. 9.
13. Chris Spolar and Christine Brennan, "Olympians Caught in Money Crunch," *The Washington Post,* August 28, 1988, p. D6.
14. Ibid.
15. Gene Policinski, "USOC Healing Process Won't Come Easy," *USA Today,* September 20, 1991, p. 1C.
16. Report of the Senate Committee on Commerce on S. 3500, Report no. 93–850, May 15, 1974, p. 16.
17. Policinski, "USOC Healing Process," p. 2C.
18. Lawrence and Pellegrom, "Fool's Gold," pp. 5, 6.

19. Ibid., p. 6.
20. Joanne Lipman, "As Winter Olympic Games Near, CBS Still Has Lots of Ads to Sell," *The Wall Street Journal,* December 2, 1991, p. B1.
21. Lawrence and Pellegrom, "Fool's Gold," p. 7.
22. Bill Saporito, "TV's Toughest Year Is Just a Preview," *Fortune,* November 19, 1990, p. 106. NBC's experiment with pay-per-view for the 1992 Olympics is encountering problems. For example, NBC's three-tiered offer requires three channels, and some cable systems do not have enough available space to carry the entire package. Steve Richardson, "NBC Adds Pay-Per-View for '92 Games," *The Dallas Morning News,* August 22, 1991, p. C6.
23. Leonard Shapiro, "Atlanta Takes Unique Look at Olympic TV Coverage," *The Washington Post,* August 15, 1991, p. B1.
24. Just as my Olympic bill improves the USOC's bargaining position with the IOC, it also puts the European Broadcasting Union (EBU) on notice that it must begin to pay its fair share. Due largely to the proliferation of privately owned networks in Europe and the hard-nosed negotiating of the Atlanta Committee on the Olympic Games (ACOG), the EBU will pay $275 million for the rights to the 1996 Atlanta games—more than a 300 percent increase from its payments for the 1992 competition in Barcelona. Steve Woodward, "1996 European Rights for Games Go for $275 M," *USA Today,* November 21, 1991, p. 3C.

    This represents a marked improvement, and ACOG (and its president and CEO, William Payne) have begun to redress the imbalance. Payne credits my inquiry with helping to pressure the EBU into substantially increasing its bid for the 1996 games. Letter from William Payne to Thomas McMillen, November 18, 1991.

    Because ACOG is targeting $600 million for the U.S. rights, however, there is not likely to be parity between the United States and Europe in broadcasting fees for 1996. Woodward, "1996 European Rights for Games," p. 3C.

Chapter 6. Sound Body

1. Billy Packer and Roland Lazenby, *College Basketball's 25 Greatest Teams* (St. Louis: Sporting News Publishing Co., 1989).
2. Ibid., p. 247.
3. Morin Bishop (Project Director), *100 Years of Hoops* (New York: Sports Illustrated, 1991), p. 182.
4. Bernard Gavzer, "We Can Beat Drugs If . . . ," *Parade Magazine,* July 30, 1989, p. 4; William C. Rhoden, "Survival of the Fittest," *The New York Times,* November 1, 1991, p. B11.
5. Steve Luse, "McMillen Says Sports Fans 'Admiring Wrong People,' " *Cumberland Evening Times,* August 21, 1980, p. 18.
6. Ibid.
7. Arnold Schwarzenegger, "A Secret Tragedy," *Newsweek,* May 21, 1990, p. 9.

242   NOTES

8. Greg Boeck, "Facts About Our Figures," *USA Today,* March 15, 1990, p. 6C.
9. Shari Roan, "Sad Shape," *The Dallas Times-Herald,* May 29, 1990, p. E5.
10. Schwarzenegger, "A Secret Tragedy," p. 9.
11. According to a 1987 study by the Tufts New England Medical Center and the Harvard School of Public Health Research, obesity has increased since the 1960s almost 54 percent among six- to eleven-year-olds and about 39 percent among twelve- to seventeen-year-olds. Roan, "Sad Shape," p. E5.
12. Donna Niewiaroski, "Youth Fitness Shows Shape of Things to Come," *The Washington Post,* May 6, 1990, p. C16.
13. Roan, "Sad Shape," p. E5.
14. Ed Bark, "TV's New Hucksters Litter the Wasteland," *The Dallas Morning News,* June 5, 1991, p. C1.
15. Greg Boeck, "He's Serious About Getting Kids in Shape," *USA Today,* March 15, 1990, p. 6C.
16. "Redefining the Guidelines: Endurance, Flexibility, Strength," *The Dallas Times Herald,* May 29, 1991, p. E1.
17. Boeck, "Facts About Our Figures," p. 6C.
18. "US Reports Rise to $604 Billion in Health Care Spending in 1989," *The New York Times,* December 22, 1990, p. A12.
19. Peter Carlson, "The Thoughts of Chairman Arnold," *The Washington Post Magazine,* June 23, 1991, p. 13.
20. Gabe Mirkin, "Substance Abuse in Athletics: The Realities," ed. by Vanik S. Eaddy, United States Sports Academy Publishing Co., Mobile, Alabama, 1986, p. 1.
21. Kevin Sherrington, "Steroids' Spell," *The Dallas Morning News,* July 9, 1989, p. B18.
22. Brendan Kinney, "The Scars of Playing the Game," *The New York Times,* August 26, 1990, sec. 8, p. 1.
23. Ibid.
24. Sherrington, "Steroids' Spell," p. B18.
25. "Steroid Use by Teen-Agers Cited," *The New York Times,* September 8, 1990, p. A42.
26. Ibid.
27. "Study Shows Steroid Use Higher Than Estimated," *USA Today,* December 11, 1990, p. 11C.
28. Steve Huffman, "I Deserve My Turn," *Sports Illustrated,* August 27, 1990, p. 26.
29. "How Steroids Affect the Body," *USA Today,* August 13, 1991, p. 10C.
30. Robert Lipsyte, "In Track and Field, Time for the Naked Truth," *The New York Times,* June 14, 1991, p. B16.
31. "More Olympic Athletes Used Steroids During Training, Tests Show," *The Sun* (Baltimore), August 26, 1989, p. A1.
32. "Study Shows Steroid Use Higher," p. 11C.

33. Dr. Alan R. Figelman and Patrick Young, *Keeping Young Athletes Healthy* (New York: Fireside, 1991), p. 160.
34. Lyle Alzado, "I'm Sick and I'm Scared," *Sports Illustrated,* July 8, 1991, p. 25.
35. Samantha Stevenson, "Alzado Says Athletes Are Turning Toward Human Growth Hormone," *The New York Times,* July 4, 1991, p. B10.
36. Alzado, "I'm Sick," p. 22.
37. Figelman and Young, *Keeping Young Athletes Healthy,* p. 158.
38. Ibid., p. 209.
39. "Not Above the Law," *Sports Illustrated,* October 8, 1990, p. 21.
40. Jeff Meyers, "Prep Sport—Putting Fun Back," *Los Angeles Times,* February 17, 1990, p. A1; Eric L. Smith, "Little League Coach Says Losers Beat Him Up," *Chicago Tribune,* August 4, 1990, p. 1.
41. Gerald Eskenazi, "Athletic Aggression and Sexual Assault," *The New York Times,* June 3, 1990, sec. 8, p. 1.
42. Sherrington, "Steroids' Spell," p. B18.
43. Tracy Everbach, "Couple to Be Sentenced Today for Selling Steroids," *The Dallas Morning News,* August 22, 1990, p. A8.
44. Mirkin, "Substance Abuse in Athletics," p. 67.
45. Sherrington, "Steroids' Spell," p. B18.
46. Marc Fisher, "E. German Sports: Ruled by Steroids," *The Washington Post,* September 7, 1991, p. A1.
47. George Vecsey, "This Public Servant Isn't Blowing Smoke," *The New York Times,* April 14, 1991, sec. 8, p. 10.
48. Howard Wolinsky, "Tobacco and Sports: An Unhealthy Alliance," *Priorities Magazine,* Spring 1991, p. 9.
49. Ibid.
50. David S. Hilzenrath, "FTC: Tobacco Firm Violated TV Rule," *The Washington Post,* October 30, 1991, p. F1.
51. Joanne Lipman, "Decline of Tobacco Sales in Canada Fuels Ad Debate," *The Wall Street Journal,* June 12, 1990, p. B1.
52. G. Pierre Goad, "Canada's Tobacco-Ad Ban Is Overturned by Judge," *The Wall Street Journal,* July 29, 1991, p. B1.
53. Anthony Ramirez, "Lower Cigarette Sales Linked to Tax Rise," *The New York Times,* June 12, 1990, p. D1.
54. "Baseball Tourneys Focus Attention on NCAA Tobacco Ban," *The NCAA News,* May 29, 1991, p. 5.
55. Wolinsky, "Tobacco and Sports," p. 11.
56. Ron Fimrite, "Puff, You're an Outcast," *Sports Illustrated,* June 3, 1991, p. 94.
57. "Baseball Tourneys Focus Attention," p. 5.

CHAPTER 7. GLOBAL GLADIATORS

1. Roger Vaughan, "Ted Turner's True Talent," *Esquire,* October 10, 1978, p. 38.

2. Ibid., p. 48.
3. David Lieberman, "How Ted Turner Kicked the Cost of NFL Telecasts Through the Roof," *TV Guide,* August 18, 1990, p. 29.
4. Bill Carter, "Brave New TV World: 300 Channels," *The New York Times,* May 13, 1991, p. D1.
5. Ibid.
6. Staff Report to House Subcommittee on Telecommunications and Finance, May 8, 1990, p. 3.
7. Kevin B. Blackistone, "A Losing Proposition," *The Dallas Morning News,* February 13, 1991, p. B6.
8. Staff Report, p. 2.
9. Ibid., p. 3.
10. Ibid., p. 10.
11. William Oscar Johnson, "The Cleanup Hitters," *Sports Illustrated,* June 25, 1990, p. 85.
12. Blackistone, "A Losing Proposition," p. B6.
13. Richard Hoffer, "The Buck Stops Here," *Sports Illustrated,* July 29, 1991, p. 48; Rich Brown, "Baseball Throws CBS a Curve," *Broadcasting,* August 26, 1991, p. 26.
14. Blackistone, "A Losing Proposition," p. B1; Hoffer, "The Buck Stops Here," p. 47; Leonard Shapiro, "Network TV Contracts Going, Going, Gone Too Far," *The Washington Post,* June 12, 1991, p. D5.
15. Keith St. Clair, "Pay-Per-View Sports: It's Closer Than You Might Care to Believe," *The Washington Times,* May 10, 1991, p. D3.
16. Hoffer, "The Buck Stops Here," p. 48.
17. Gerald Eskenazi, "N.F.L. Planning to Add Pay TV to Its Package," *The New York Times,* February 24, 1991, sec. 8, p. 4; Richard Sandomir, "After Mega-Losses, Mega-Alterations," *The New York Times,* November 5, 1991, p. B13.
18. Blackistone, "A Losing Proposition," p. B6. Despite the failure of the Sports News Network, there is a new cable channel for sports news in the wings. Mark Robichaux, "Cable Channel for Sports News Is Coming to Bat," *The Wall Street Journal,* August 28, 1991, p. B1.
19. Thomas Easton, "No Longer Good Sports," *The Sun* (Baltimore), October 6, 1991, p. B1.
20. Bill Saporito, "The Owners' New Game Is Managing," *Fortune,* July 1, 1991, p. 88.
21. Richard Justice, "Gooden Gets $15.45 Million in 3-Year Deal With Mets," *The Washington Post,* April 2, 1991, p. C1.
22. Ronald Blum, "Mets Land Bonilla in Record $29 Million, 5-Year Deal," *The Washington Post,* December 3, 1991, p. E1.
23. Easton, "No Longer Good Sports," p. B1.
24. Leonard Shapiro, "NHL's TV Contract a Slap to Pro Sports," *The Washington Post,* October 6, 1991, p. D1.
25. Ibid., p. D6.
26. Courts have ruled that to some extent the owners' financial muscle vis-à-vis the players from the mid-'80s resulted from collusion and antitrust

violations. Thus, the years from 1985 to 1988 are known as the "collusion era" for Major League Baseball, and the owners have been hit with a damage award to the players of $280 million. John Helyar, "How Peter Ueberroth Led the Major Leagues in the 'Collusion Era,' " *The Wall Street Journal,* May 20, 1991, p. A1.

Similarly, the NFL faces the prospect of a number of antitrust suits challenging its free agency rules. John Helyar, "Recent Rulings Give NFL Players Union Yardage Toward Free-Agency Goals," *The Wall Street Journal,* June 12, 1991, p. B2. With a spate of lawsuits looming ahead, the NFL appears poised to make significant concessions to the players on free agency. Aaron Bernstein, "The NFL Decides It's Finally Time to Punt," *Business Week,* October 7, 1991, p. 40.

27. Saporito, "The Owners' New Game," p. 86.
28. Tony Kornheiser, "Scaling the Mountain: Williams Says He's Hungry for Basketball Now," *The Washington Post,* January 16, 1991, p. D1; "Bullets Suspend Overweight Williams," *The Dallas Morning News,* November 2, 1991, p. B4.
29. E. M. Swift, "From Corned Beef to Caviar," *Sports Illustrated,* June 3, 1991, p. 79.
30. Ibid., p. 80.
31. Ibid., p. 84.
32. Ibid.
33. Christine Brennan, "For U.S. Sports, World Is Steadily Shrinking," *The Washington Post,* May 17, 1989, p. B1.
34. Jack McCallum, "Monsieur Magique," *Sports Illustrated,* October 28, 1991, pp. 38–39.
35. Swift, "From Corned Beef," p. 86.
36. Saporito, "The Owners' New Game," p. 90.
37. Ken Stephens, "The World at Play," *The Dallas Morning News,* October 22, 1989, p. B23.
38. Swift, "From Corned Beef," p. 86.
39. Rich Brown, "First Down and $1 Billion in 4th Quarter," *Broadcasting,* August 12, 1991, p. 40.
40. Stephens, "The World at Play," p. B23.
41. Remarks by Congressman Christopher Shays to House Subcommittee on Telecommunications and Finance, May 9, 1990, p. 3.
42. Martin Tolchin, "Leagues Get Warning on Cable Deals," *The New York Times,* November 15, 1989, p. D20.
43. Gerald Eskenazi, "Pay-Per-View Debate Urged," *The New York Times,* March 3, 1991, sec. 8, p. 7; Brown, "First Down and $1 Billion in 4th Quarter," p. 40.
44. "Mapes Said NBC Is Expecting . . . ," *Communications Daily,* vol. 11, no. 101, May 24, 1991, p. 2; St. Clair, "Pay-Per-View Sports: It's Closer Than You Might Care to Believe," p. D3; Richard Sandomir, "Ebersol Says He's Ready for Pay-Per-View Time," *The New York Times,* May 28, 1991, p. B16.
45. Ibid.

46. Sharon Moshan, "NBC's Pay-Per-View Olympics: Carriage Turmoil," *Broadcasting,* August 19, 1991, p. 21.
47. Sandomir, "Ebersol Says He's Ready," p. B16.
48. Bernie Lincicome, "Three Words That Might Ruin Sports," *The NCAA News,* May 8, 1991, p. 4.
49. Statement of Francis T. Vincent, Jr., before the House Subcommittee on Telecommunications and Finance, May 9, 1990, pp. 5, 7.
50. Statement of Paul Tagliabue before House Subcommittee on Telecommunications and Finance, May 9, 1990, p. 3.
51. Ibid., p. 7.
52. Statement of David J. Stern before House Subcommittee on Telecommunications and Finance, May 9, 1990, p. 4.
53. Ibid., p. 2.
54. Statement of Richard D. Schultz before House Subcommittee on Telecommunications and Finance, May 9, 1990, p. 7.
55. Ibid., p. 3.
56. Ibid., p. 8.
57. "Don't Exempt Baseball, Says Turner," *The Sun* (Baltimore), June 21, 1985, p. C9.
58. Leonard Shapiro, "NFL: Free TV Safe From Pay-Per-View," *The Washington Post,* March 3, 1991, p. D2.
59. "Hitting the Fan," *Sports Illustrated,* March 4, 1991, p. 11.
60. Roger G. Noll, "The Economics of Sports Leagues," in 1991 Sports Law Institute's *Working Materials,* Ed Garvey Sports Seminars and the University of Wisconsin Law School, pp. 116–117. Because of the special status granted pro teams under accounting and tax rules, the "book value" of a team often significantly understates its true value. Thus, a team that appears to be losing money (accompanied by the wailing and gnashing of teeth of the owner) may actually be profitably sheltering income from the owner's other businesses. Dana Wechsler Linden, "Bases Loaded, Nobody Out," *Forbes,* April 1, 1991, p. 44.

    According to Gerald W. Scully, a professor of management at the University of Texas at Dallas, the anomalous IRS rule allowing team owners to amortize their player contracts over several years has no economic justification and creates a tax shelter, which is in effect a taxpayer subsidy to the owners. William Oscar Johnson and Albert Kim, "Wanna Buy a Baseball Team?" *Sports Illustrated,* April 15, 1991, p. 39.
61. Testimony of Howard Cosell before Senate Judiciary Committee, February 6, 1985, Senate Hearing 99–496, pp. 52, 54–55.
62. Keith St. Clair, "Congress Tops List of Toughest and Most Influential Critics," *The Washington Times,* May 10, 1991, p. D3.
63. Tolchin, "Leagues Get Warning on Cable Deals," p. D20.
64. St. Clair, "Congress Tops List," p. D3.
65. "Specter Resolution: Sports Migration to Cable and PPV Escalates Concerns in Congress," *Communications Daily,* August 5, 1991, p. 3.
66. One of the most controversial issues is the provision for "retransmission

consent" in Senate Bill No. 12, which would require cable operators for the first time to pay for the right to retransmit local broadcast signals. Kevin Goldman, "Local TV Stations and Cable Clash in Ads," *The Wall Street Journal,* August 29, 1991, p. B3.

In an effort to spur competition, Congressman Rick Boucher of Virginia has introduced a bill to allow the Bell companies to jump into cable (H.R. 2546).

In addition, Congressman Shays and others have proposed legislation to reregulate the cable industry. Some of the bills are broad in nature, and others directly target sports programming. Among the proposals floating around Congress are the Cable Consumer Protection Act (H.R. 2222), which was introduced by Congressmen Shays and Joseph Lieberman and which returns the right to regulate cable rates to the agencies that granted the franchises. The franchising authorities would have the power to adjust rates in response to programming changes, to exercise greater control over the renewal process, and to require cable systems to carry adequate local broadcast stations.

Senator John Danforth of Missouri and Congressman Jim Cooper of Tennessee introduced the Cable Television Consumer Protection Act (S. 1880/H.R. 3826), which would authorize the local franchising authorities to regulate prices and protect consumers where there was only one cable operator in an area and, hence, no competition. In those few locales with two or more cable operators, the market would determine the rates.

Congressman Charles Schumer of New York sponsored the Baseball Viewers Protection Act of 1989, which requires baseball teams that are entering cable contracts to broadcast at least 50 percent of their games on free TV. Under his bill, which applies only to teams that have traditionally shown 65 percent or more of their games on free TV, the penalty for noncompliance is the loss of the team's antitrust exemption.

67. William Oscar Johnson, "Sports in 2001," *Sports Illustrated,* July 22, 1991, p. 40.
68. Greg Boeck, "Las Vegas: Where Bets Are Business," *USA Today,* March 10, 1990, p. 1C.
69. Elizabeth M. Cosin, "Pro League Officials Support Senate Bills to Ban Sports Lotteries," *The Washington Times,* May 10, 1990, p. B6.
70. Jeffrey L. Katz, "Lottery Fatigue," *Governing,* September 1991, p. 65.
71. Michael Janofsky, "U.S.O.C. Is Cashing In 5 Rings to State Lotteries," *The New York Times,* October 3, 1991, p. B15.
72. Katz, "Lottery Fatigue," p. 63.
73. Eugene M. Christiansen, "U.S. Gaming Handle Up 14% in '90," *Gaming & Wagering Business,* July 15–August 14, 1991, p. 38.
74. Katz, "Lottery Fatigue," p. 63.
75. Christiansen, "U.S. Gaming Handle Up," p. 32.
76. "Experts Peg Gambling the 'Addiction of the 90's,' " *What's Next,* Fall 1991, vol. 13, issue 3, p. 1; Gerry T. Fulcher, "The Dark Side of a Trip to the Track," *Industry Week,* August 5, 1991, p. 15.

77. William Oscar Johnson, "A Sure Bet to Lower Debt," *Sports Illustrated*, September 2, 1991, p. 144.
78. Johnson, "Sports in 2001," p. 45.

CHAPTER 8. LIFE AFTER SPORTS

1. Linda Jean Carpenter and R. Vivian Acosta, "Back to the Future: Reform With a Woman's Voice," *Academe*, Jan./Feb. 1991, p. 23.
2. Ibid. Under its former executive director, Walter Byers, the NCAA's predatory practices were aimed not only at women and the AIAW but also at other amateur athletic associations, such as the Amateur Athletic Union (AAU) and the National Invitational Tournament (NIT). As a result of these predatory practices, the NCAA has assumed a virtual monopoly over college sports.
3. Doug Bedell, "Fight for Gender Equity in Athletics Far From Over," *The Dallas Morning News*, September 4, 1991, p. B10.
4. Doug Bedell, "No Sporting Chance," *The Dallas Morning News*, September 1, 1991, p. B16.
5. Ken Stephens, "Few Called; Fewer Chosen," *The Dallas Morning News*, January 14, 1990, p. B24.
6. Carpenter and Acosta, "Back to the Future," p. 23.
7. Ibid.
8. Donna Lopiano, "Women Need a Level Sports Playing Field," *The Dallas Morning News*, April 28, 1991, p. J3.
9. Ibid.
10. Alison Muscatine, "Women's Sports Making Gains but Still Struggling for Equality," *The Washington Post*, April 1, 1991, p. C8; Donna A. Lopiano, "Fair Play for All (Even Women)," *The New York Times*, April 15, 1990, sec. 8, p. 10.
11. Bedell, "No Sporting Chance," p. B16.
12. Doug Bedell, "Title IX Case Could Set Precedent," *The Dallas Morning News*, September 3, 1991, p. B10.
13. "Keeping Faith With the Student-Athlete," (see chap. 4, n. 75), p. 14.
14. Eric Celeste, "How to Save the Southwest Conference," *D Magazine*, August 1991, p. 77.
15. Don Yaeger, *Undue Process: The NCAA's Injustice for All* (Champaign, Illinois: Sagamore Publishing, 1991), pp. 206–210.
16. Wint Winter, Jr., "NCAA's Actions Affect Too Many to Let It Operate Above the Law," *USA Today*, March 5, 1991, p. 10C.
17. Yaeger, *Undue Process*, pp. 132–133.
18. "Two States Set Limits on NCAA," *The Washington Post*, April 9, 1991, p. E3.
19. Edward Walsh, "Syracuse Escapes Notre Dame, If Not Scrutiny," *The Washington Post*, February 16, 1991, p. D1.
20. Enforcement Program of the NCAA by House Subcommittee on Oversight and Investigations, December 18, 1978, Committee Print 95–69, p. 1.

21. Ibid., p. 58.
22. Scott Woolley, "Panel Urges NCAA to Revise Process of Enforcement," *The Wall Street Journal,* October 29, 1991, p. B10.
23. Michael Janofsky, "N.C.A.A. Panel Recommends New Rules for Investigations," *The New York Times,* October 29, 1991, p. B9.
24. Steve Wieberg, "Legislators to Look at Reforms in College Sports," *USA Today,* June 13, 1991, p. 9C.
25. Statement of Senator Wint Winter, Jr., before the House Subcommittee on Commerce, Consumer Protection, and Competitiveness, June 1991, p. 3; Ivan Maisel, "Schultz Warns State Legislators NCAA Won't Be Intimidated," *The Dallas Morning News,* February 20, 1991, p. B3.
26. Statement of Professor Burton F. Brody before the House Subcommittee on Commerce, Consumer Protection, and Competitiveness, June 1991, pp. 4–5.
27. "Bill Calls for Reforms at NCAA Institutions," *Higher Education and National Affairs,* vol. 40, no. 15, August 12, 1991, p. 4.
28. In contrast to the NCAA, the National Association of Intercollegiate Athletics (NAIA), which has jurisdiction over the sports programs of small colleges, in 1990 installed its Council of Presidents as the ultimate governing body in the organization.
29. Douglas Lederman, "Two Congressmen Lead the Charge Against the NCAA and Big-Time Sports," *The Chronicle of Higher Education,* August 7, 1991, p. A27.
30. D. Stanley Eitzen, " 'Reforms' Don't Fix Commercialization of College Sports," *The Sun* (Baltimore), March 17, 1991, p. N4.
31. William F. Reed, "A Steamroller for Reform," *Sports Illustrated,* January 21, 1991, p. 9.
32. Mark Asher, "Thompson: Reforms Inept," *The Washington Post,* September 28, 1991, p. G1; Michael Janofsky, "Report Applauds Universities," *The New York Times,* September 26, 1991, p. B14; Liz Clarke, " 'Fine-Tuning' May Cut Into NCAA Reforms," *Charlotte Observer,* August 23, 1991, p. C1.
33. Frank Deford, "Blue-Ribbon Panel Can't Cut It, So Feds Must Save College Sports," *The National,* March 15, 1991, p. 28.
34. Bedell, "Fight for Gender Equity," p. B1.
35. Murray Sperber, "NCAA Reforms Barely Eligible," *The New York Times,* January 5, 1991, p. A21.
36. Mark Asher, "Virginia Continues Investigation of Athletic Department," *The Washington Post,* August 14, 1991, p. D1.
37. "Keeping Faith With the Student-Athlete," (see chap. 4, n. 75), p. 14, n. 2.
38. Significantly, an early draft of the Knight Report contained a recommendation that the NCAA be restructured to require control of the NCAA Council by presidents. Unfortunately, that recommendation was deleted from the final report.
39. Tom Witosky, "Athletic Directors Told Changes to Come—Like Them or Not," *The Des Moines Register,* June 11, 1991, p. S4; "Final Revenue

Checks From 1991–1992 Delivered," *The NCAA News,* September 9, 1991, p. 1.

40. The big winners in the NCAA's $1 billion basketball deal in the first year were the ACC (with each team in the conference receiving a total payout of $793,000) and the Big Ten (with each team pocketing $705,000). The ACC and Big Ten fared so well largely because of their historical success in the NCAA tournaments and the size of their sports programs, measured in terms of sports sponsored and scholarships conferred. Steve Wieberg, "ACC Basketball Dribbles to Bank With Top TV Haul," *USA Today,* September 5, 1991, p. C9.

41. Mark Asher, "Gaines: Black Colleges Get 'Crumbs' From Money Pie," *The Washington Post,* September 13, 1991, p. F1.

42. Ibid.

43. Letter from Richard D. Schultz to the Honorable Cardiss Collins, October 9, 1991, pp. 1–2.

44. "1990–91 NCAA Division I Revenue Distribution," *The NCAA News,* September 5, 1991, p. 3.

45. "Keeping Faith With the Student-Athlete" (see chap. 4, n. 75), p. 20.

46. Ibid., p. 20, n. 12.

47. Ibid., p. 30, n. 13.

48. Guerry Clegg, "Crecine: Knight Report May Have 'Minor' Influence," *Columbus Ledger-Enquirer,* May 12, 1991, p. B1.

49. Thomas Boswell, "Collegiate Athletics: Now the Way's Clear," *The Washington Post,* March 20, 1991, p. C5.

50. "Keeping Faith With the Student-Athlete" (see chap. 4, n. 75), p. 7.

51. Ivan Maisel, "Focus Is on Reform at NCAA Convention," *The Dallas Morning News,* January 6, 1991, p. B10.

52. Dinesh D'Souza, "The Visigoths in Tweed" (see chap. 3, n. 36), p. 80.

53. Douglas Lederman, "With Spate of Bills, Congress Turns Up the Heat on NCAA," *The Chronicle of Higher Education,* August 7, 1991, p. A25.

54. Deford, "Blue-Ribbon Panel Can't Cut It," p. 28.

55. Remarks of Louis Harris, Press Conference in Washington, D.C., March 6, 1991.

56. "Academic Sham," *Asbury Park Press,* March 25, 1991, p. A12.

57. Letter from Senator Robert Byrd to Secretary of Defense Dick Cheney, December 3, 1991.

58. Testimony of Charles E. Young before House Subcommittee on Oversight and Investigations of the Committee on Energy and Commerce, Serial No. 98–169, July 31, 1984, p. 90.

59. Mark Asher, "Graduation Rate a Matter of Race," *The Washington Post,* July 26, 1991, p. B7.

60. Elizabeth M. Cosin, "Uniting All in Process Key to Athletic Reform," *The Washington Times,* October 26, 1991, p. C2; Dave Sheinin, "Professors Favor More Reform," *The Washington Post,* October 26, 1991,

p. G2; Elizabeth M. Cosin, "Geiger Calls for End to 'Arms Race,'"
The Washington Times, October 24, 1991, p. D1.

61. William Oscar Johnson, "The Black Athlete Revisited" (see chap. 3, n. 31), p. 52.

62. Rod Groves, "Congress and Sports Reform," *Regency Report,* vol. 10, no. 6, July 1991, p. 2.

ABOUT THE AUTHOR

Tom McMillen grew up in Mansfield, Pennsylvania. One of the most heavily recruited high school basketball players, he attended the University of Maryland, where he starred as an all-American and later became a member of the 1972 Olympic basketball team. After graduation, Tom attended Oxford University as a Rhodes scholar while also playing a season in the Italian professional basketball league. He subsequently played in the NBA for eleven years. He is currently serving his sixth year as a member of Congress from Maryland's Fourth District. Tom has been a leader in sports reform, serving on the Knight Commission on intercollegiate athletics and, in Congress, on the Energy and Commerce Committee, which has jurisdiction over a number of sports issues. He is also a businessman and currently resides in Crofton, Maryland, with his two Labradors, Chocolate and Licorice.

Paul Coggins is a former federal prosecutor and is now a prominent criminal defense attorney. A graduate of Yale University and Harvard Law School, he attended Oxford University as a Rhodes scholar, where he and Tom McMillen became friends.

In 1987 he published a novel, *The Lady Is the Tiger,* and he is currently working on a second novel.

He lives in Dallas, Texas, with his wife, Regina Montoya, and their daughter, Jessica.